Engineering Education

Engineering Education

Accreditation & Graduate Global Mobility

Firoz Alam and Alexandra Kootsookos

CRC Press
Taylor & Francis Group
Boca Raton London New York

CRC Press is an imprint of the
Taylor & Francis Group, an **informa** business

CRC Press/Balkema is an imprint of the Taylor & Francis Group, an informa business

© 2021 Taylor & Francis Group, London, UK

Typeset by codeMantra

Library of Congress Cataloging-in-Publication Data
Names: Alam, Firoz, 1966- author. | Kootsookos, Alexandra, author.
Title: Engineering education : accreditation & graduate global mobility/
by Firoz Alam and Alexandra Kootsookos.
Description: Boca Raton : CRC Press, [2021] |
Includes bibliographical references. Identifiers: LCCN 2020028583
(print) | LCCN 2020028584 (ebook)
Subjects: LCSH: Engineering—Study and teaching (Higher) |
Engineering—Study and teaching (Higher)—Evaluation. |
Competency-based education. | Vocational qualifications. |
Education and globalization. | Transnational education.
Classification: LCC T65.3 .A57 2020 (print) | LCC T65.3 (ebook) |
DDC 620.0071/1—dc23
LC record available at https://lccn.loc.gov/2020028583
LC ebook record available at https://lccn.loc.gov/2020028584

Published by: CRC Press/Balkema
            Schipholweg 107C, 2316 XC Leiden, The Netherlands
            e-mail: Pub.NL@taylorandfrancis.com
            www.crcpress.com – www.taylorandfrancis.com

ISBN: 978-0-8153-9601-7 (hbk)
ISBN: 978-1-351-18200-3 (ebk)

DOI: 10.1201/9781351182003
https://doi.org/10.1201/9781351182003

Contents

Preface

The world we have all experienced is growing smaller, with technology connecting us into a "global village". This is particularly so within the engineering profession and industry, where companies span multiple nations and conduct operations across national boundaries. Engineering professionals of the 21st century are expected to work within and between national and international organisations, which means that engineering qualifications at all levels need to be recognised across and between national jurisdictions.

The aim of this book is to provide an overview of the schemes available for international recognition of engineering degrees, the organisations and processes used to demonstrate equivalence between qualifications, and the implications of global mobility for learning outcomes and curriculum development. As such, this volume will be of interest to professional engineers, higher education institutions, students currently engaged with engineering studies, employers, policymakers, accreditation bodies, and those involved with the delivery of engineering programs and courses within their national boundaries and beyond.

The chapters are arranged in a manner to enable someone unfamiliar with the topic area to gain enough background knowledge to appreciate the complexity and rapid changes which are occurring in the space of multi-jurisdictional accreditation.

Chapter 1 provides information on the transnational nature of tertiary education and tertiary students, as well as the global mobility of academics and other highly trained citizens, and how their distribution across the world may affect national economies. The chapter includes a brief introduction to two main bodies which administer multinational recognition agreements: the International Engineering Alliance (IEA) and the European Network for the Accreditation of Engineering Education (ENAEE). It then discusses what "global competencies" for engineers might look like.

Chapter 2 discusses outcome-based education, what it is and how it relates both to accreditation processes and the development of a program of studies.

Chapter 3 provides detailed information relating to the standards and guidelines for accreditation and accreditation processes used by both the ENAEE and the IEA and compares these two schemes. The chapter concludes with a thorough example of accreditation process requirements via a case study of the accreditation process used by Engineers Australia, the accreditation body for engineering qualifications in Australia.

Chapter 4 examines significant changes which have been made within the IEA regarding the accreditation process required for engineering qualifications delivered "offshore"—so-called "dual accreditation"—and the implications of these changes for higher education institutions, accreditation bodies, quality assurance organisations, industry, government officials and policymakers, and prospective students.

Chapter 5 considers National Qualifications Frameworks and the role they play in maintaining quality and uniformity in the education sector.

Chapter 6 examines the history, criteria and modern-day importance of quality systems used to rank higher education institutions globally.

Chapter 7 highlights the institutional academic program quality assurance processes that higher education institutions widely use.

The authors greatly appreciate the many academics and researchers whose work is cited. References to their work are included at the end. In a work this detailed, it is possible to miss the citation of researchers. We will ensure to include the missing references (if any) in the next edition of the book.

We are profoundly grateful to Mr Alistair Bright from Taylor & Francis for his relentless pursuit to complete the writing and production of this book. If it were not for him, this book would take a long time to see the light. Our heartfelt appreciation goes to him for his encouragement and patience when we were terribly behind the schedule.

Our sincere appreciation is also due to Dr Jeffrey Keddie for his time and patience in going through the manuscript and providing useful comments.

Finally, the authors hope this book will provoke thought and conversations and we look forward to engaging with our readers in further discussion.

Firoz Alam and Alexandra Kootsookos

Chapter 1

Engineering education, economic development and global mobility

1.1 Transnational nature of engineering

The application of the principles of mathematics and science to turn new ideas into solutions for complex problems is called engineering. Using innovation, creativity and knowledge, engineering professionals are making a profound impact on the world. Technically skilled people are driving rapid change in our world, resulting in faster development across all nations. Engineering professionals (graduate engineers, technologists and technicians) are creative, curious and capable of dealing with all aspects of their society and the world. Engineering has no bounds, and those in this profession work tirelessly for the common goal of building a sustainable world. Today, every aspect of engineering is multi-disciplinary in nature. Hence, the amalgamated knowledge from all the engineering disciplines and sub-disciplines, as well as from finance/commerce, the environment and ecology, is required to exploit resources for peaceful, environmentally sustainable and healthy living.

Engineering professionals use the knowledge within a specific industry in order to make things work. In fact, engineering is behind everything: computers, the internet, mobile phones, satellites, make-up, cars, buses, ships, aircraft, spacecraft, trains, shoes, buildings, bridges, roads and tracks, manufacturing and production, destructive equipment and machinery, power generation, transmission and distribution, resources extraction and processing, household appliances, CT scanners, MRI, medical transplants, and much more. The dramatic improvement of healthcare and life expectancy is only possible due to the development of diagnostic equipment, disease cure/management equipment and pharmaceutical products. In our rapidly changing world, new engineering tasks and challenges are constantly emerging alongside new and innovative technologies. Engineering has had, is having and will have a direct and vital impact on the quality of life for all people and our planet. The famous scientist, Albert Einstein, said, "Scientists investigate that which already is; Engineers create that which has never been" [1]. Hence, it is "Science" which discovers the electromagnetic radiation but it is "Engineering" which uses electromagnetic radiation to make a smart TV. All the so-called "wonders of modern Science" are really wonders of modern engineering.

Engineering is one of the most diverse professions in terms of disciplines, types, levels and qualifications [2–4]. An example of engineering degrees offered in various engineering disciplines by the USA higher education institutions in 2018 is shown in Figure 1.1. The nature of engineering employment varies notably both locally and globally. A simple definition of engineering activity is the production and application

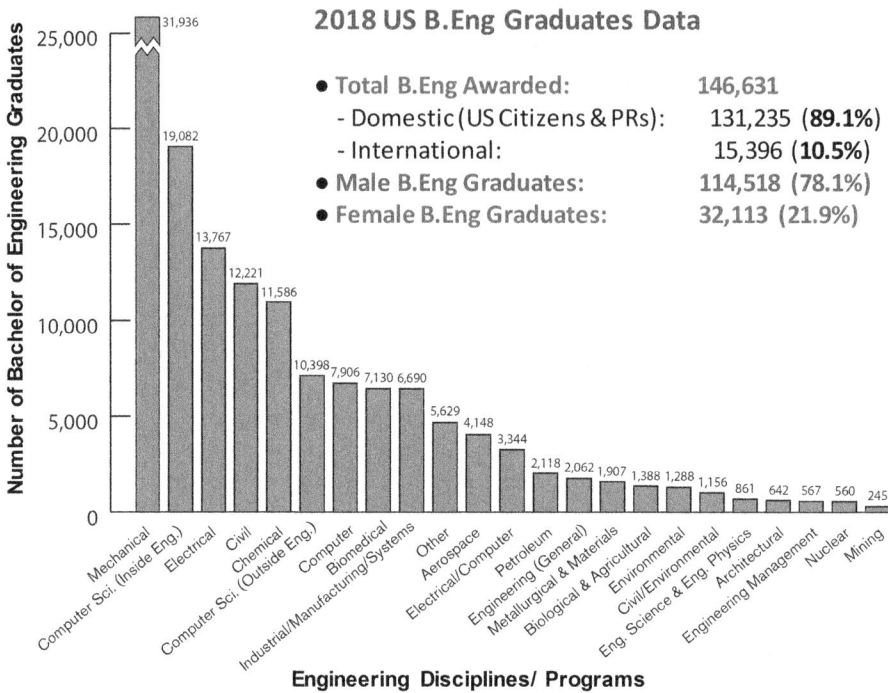

Figure 1.1 Bachelor degrees offered in engineering disciplines in the USA in 2018. (Adapted from Ref. [5].)

of knowledge, patents and technology. Globalisation has been transforming engineering industries by creating international markets for products, raw materials, human resources, ideas and innovations. In addition, new technologies are penetrating the engineering industry and changing modes of practice, habits and education.

1.2 Global movement of engineers

Globalisation is occurring in all engineering activities, from the standardisation of technology across national borders to the development of niche technology, resulting in either the temporary or permanent movement of engineers, technologists and technicians around the world. The increase in technological innovation accelerates the movement of qualified engineers even further.

Dobbs et al. [6] have reported that by 2020, there will be a global shortage of medium- and high-skilled workers and a global surplus of low-skilled workers. The bulk of the required technologically skilled people will be needed in developing countries due to the rapid economic growth, and unless these developing nations invest in appropriate post-secondary education, with an emphasis on engineering and science, and/or encourage their emigrant graduates to return home after an overseas education, the need for skilled human resources will be very difficult to meet. In addition, addressing this shortfall by bringing skilled people from developed nations to developing nations is costly and in most cases unaffordable. This means that by 2030, there will be an acute shortage of technically skilled human resources in populous developing nations such as China, India, Bangladesh, Indonesia, Pakistan, the Philippines, Nigeria, and Brazil.

1.2.1 Global demand for engineering graduates

The engineering profession is well-respected by the global community because the profession's contribution has a significant impact on everyday life, society and the environment. A recent survey for views on a range of engineering issues conducted by Create the Future [7] among 10,000 people across ten countries from Europe, North America, Asia and Africa revealed that engineers are trusted to make the world a better place. The diverse nature of current global challenges means that engineering is now regarded as being more important to the world than ever before.

A report, "Skills Gap Study 2018", by Deloitte and the US Manufacturing Institute revealed that 2.4 million jobs would be unfilled over the next decade in the USA. By 2028, the continued shortage will cause a potential loss of $454 billion in USA's economic output – a massive 17% of the forecasted manufacturing Gross Domestic Product (GDP). The report also stated that there would be another $2.5 trillion economic output loss over the next decade due to engineering skills shortage in the USA [8]. The engineering skills shortage is not just a buzzword. Its impact is both global and local. The need to tackle this challenge is not dependent upon revenue size, organisational demographics or reach of any nation; it will affect the whole world.

In Western nations, there are many issues which have created this skills shortage, and the most significant being a restricted global mobility/labour market, poor investment in science, technology, engineering and mathematics (STEM) education, less interest in STEM careers among young people, birth rate decreases and industrialisation in traditionally populous nations (South Asia, North Asia), an aging population and mass retirement of "baby boomers" in Europe and North America.

Another survey conducted by research firm Gartner in the late 2018 put skills shortages as the main emerging risk faced by businesses worldwide. ManpowerGroup, the international recruiter, puts talent shortage at a 12-year high, citing a strong hiring demand due to global economic growth and changing skills requirements as new technologies and innovations, including artificial intelligence, mechatronics and robotics, continuously emerge [9].

A study undertaken by Korn Ferry Institute [10] reported that the demand for skilled workforce would outstrip supply, resulting in global skills shortages of over 85 million people, by 2030. Among most industries, especially knowledge-intensive engineering and technology companies and manufacturing sectors would be the most affected. The shortage would cause over US$ 8 trillion in unrealised revenue, which is higher than the combined GDP of Germany and Japan. It is emphasised that technology alone cannot deliver the promised productivity gains if there are not enough skilled workers [10]. Figure 1.2 shows the skills shortages in manufacturing industry in the USA between 2018 and 2028. The forecast global skills shortages by 2030 are graphically depicted in Figure 1.3.

Numbers of skilled professionals in the areas of STEM continue to run at a deficit, with industrial demand outpacing supply, as shown in Figures 1.2 and 1.3. The global shortage of STEM-skilled professionals means that nations compete to attract engineering professionals to drive industry, research institutes and universities. For fully developed nations, strategies need to be developed to both recruit and retain national

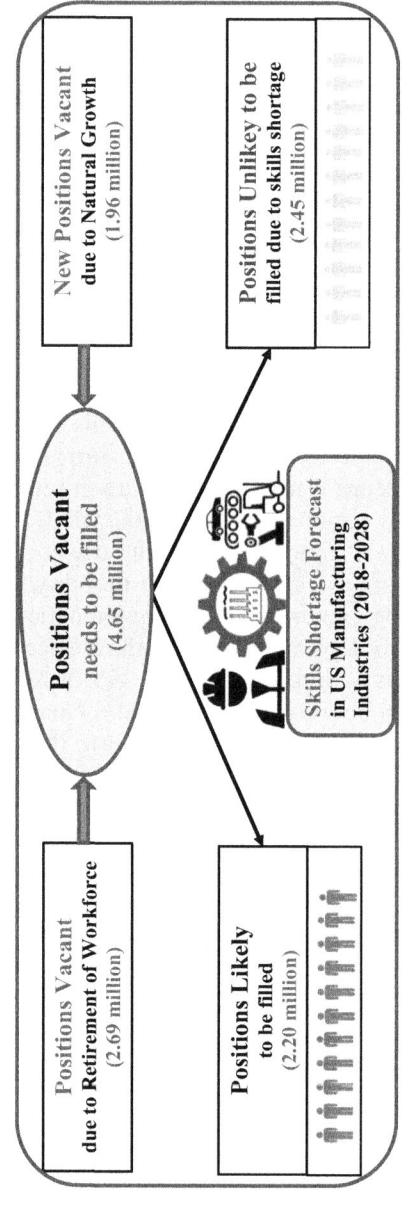

Figure 1.2 Expected skills shortage in US manufacturing industry between 2018 and 2028 (Adapted from Refs. [8,9].)

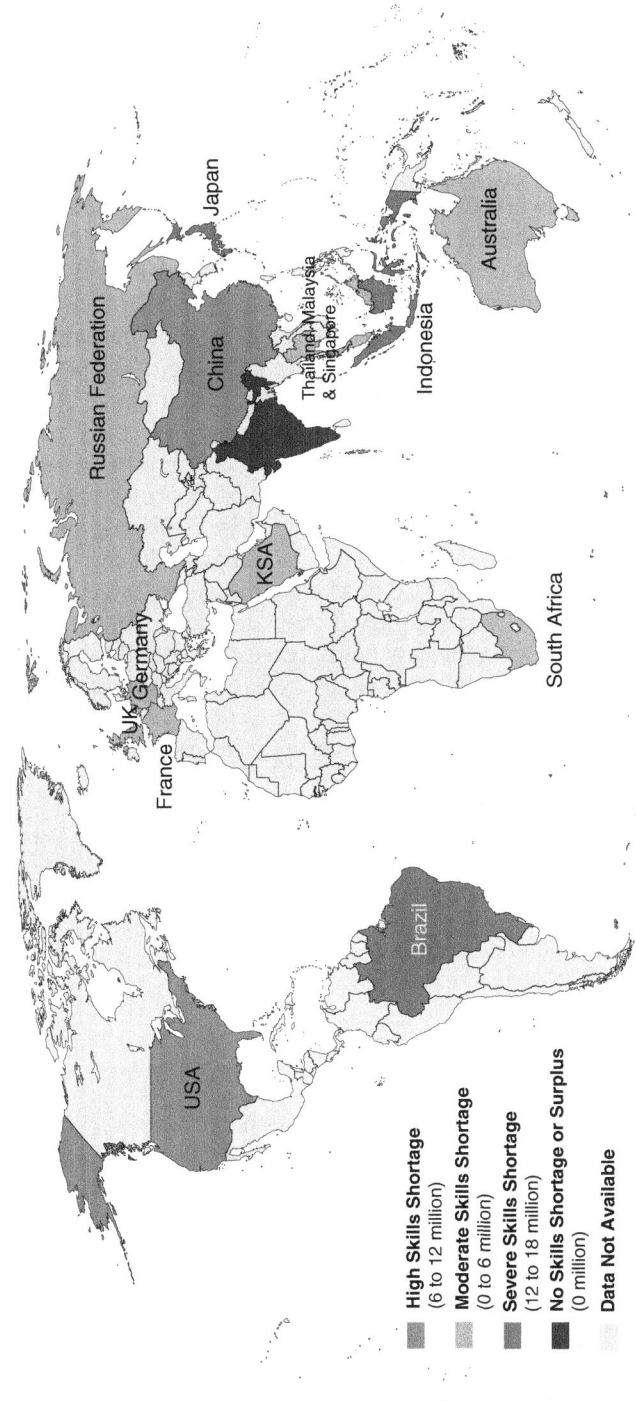

Figure 1.3 Global skills deficit by economy in 2030. (Adapted from Refs. [10,28].)

talent, whereas developing nations have experienced (until recently) an exodus of talent that these countries need to facilitate the process of return migration (see Section 1.4) There have been some success stories in improved return migration, especially in India, South Korea and China [11].

Although there is no exact figure for the total number of higher education institutions, it is believed to be around 22,123, of which over 7,198 are preparing engineering graduates globally. Each year, approximately four million students graduate with an engineering degree worldwide. Considering these numbers and the data in Figure 1.2, this clearly demonstrates the huge demand for engineering graduates. (Four million graduates would only fill the need in the USA alone.) Indeed, a "war" for STEM talent is about to begin, where national prosperity will heavily rely on the successful recruitment of STEM professionals. There needs to be national and international efforts to (i) *Build* by investing in learning and development to grow the talent pipeline and upskill the existing and potential workforce; (ii) *Buy* in a tight labour market, go to the external market to find the best talent that cannot be built in-house in the timeframe required to fill immediate openings; (iii) *Borrow* by cultivating communities of talent inside and outside the organisation, including part-time, freelance, contract and temporary workers to complement the existing workforce; and (iv) *Bridge* by helping people move on and move up to new roles inside or outside any organisation with the engineering skills gaps.

Some countries do invest heavily in STEM education, and Table 1.1 shows the number of engineering students who completed their degree in 2018 from a selection of these nations. Also listed is the professional accreditation body associated with that jurisdiction. Professional accreditation will be examined in Chapter 3.

Table 1.1 Elected countries with yearly engineering graduates in 2018

	Country	Yearly engineering graduates	Professional accreditation jurisdictions
1	India	1,300,000	IEA
2	China	900,000	IEA
3	European Union (excluding UK and Turkey)	516,000	ENAEE
4	Russia	455,000	IEA & ENAEE
5	USA	238,000	IEA
6	Iran	234,000	–
7	Japan	169,000	IEA
8	South Korea	148,000	IEA
9	Indonesia	140,000	–
10	Turkey	115,000	IEA & ENAEE
11	Mexico	114,000	IEA
12	Vietnam	101,000	–
13	UK	69,000	IEA & ENAEE
14	Ukraine	65,000	–
15	Brazil	60,000	–
16	Bangladesh	45,000	–
17	Pakistan	40,000	IEA
18	Canada	21,000	IEA
19	Australia	20,000	IEA

Source: Adapted from Ref. [12].

1.3 Transnational nature of higher education

Developing nations' demand for industrialisation, capacity building and economic progress has driven the worldwide demand for higher education [1,13]. Rapid development of affluent middle classes in the developing world has also increased the demand for higher education [1,13]. In addition, with the progress in communications and transportation (especially air transportation), global travel has become progressively easier, meaning that citizens can pursue an education outside their country of origin. Changes to information and educational technology have also meant that transnational education is available for those who, for whatever reason, are unable to travel [11].

The percentage of cross-border students has remained almost constant over the last 15 years, keeping pace with the growth of the student population, without experiencing a higher growth rate. The stagnated cross-border student growth indicates that many students wishing to pursue higher education are unwilling to leave their home country. This stagnation has presented developed countries' higher education institutions with a new market opportunity to export education (qualifications) directly to students via offshore delivery [15–19].

The direction of travel or flow of students is also changing. In the past, students from developing nations used to migrate to developed nations for education, employment and a better life. More recently, developing economies have been investing in their higher education, making them more attractive destinations for their own students as well as for regional and far-away countries' students at significantly lower cost [15,18,19]. By 2025, major study destinations for foreign students are expected to be China, Singapore, Malaysia and India.

Transnational education can be described as cross-border/offshore or borderless education [14]. Generally, in the transnational education mode, a higher education institution, based in one country (home country), delivers programs/qualifications or even individual courses, modules, units or subjects in another country (host country) [18–21]. How the transnational education is delivered can vary notably and these different transnational education modes are discussed in the following subsection. A formal definition of transnational education is provided by the United Nations Education, Scientific and Cultural Organization (UNESCO), which states that "all types of higher education study programs, or sets of courses of study, or educational services (including those of distance education) in which the learners (students) are located in a country different from the one where the awarding institution is based" [1,13].

In relation to the transnational delivery of education, students must adapt to the instructional design and program delivery practice used by the home country's higher education institution – both of which may be considerably different from that of the student's familiar host country's culture [15,22,23]. Such differences may extend to the perceived quality, relevance and value of the educational program as well as different practices and understanding of appropriate ethical behaviour [15,22,23]. For this reason, there are different ways through which transnational education can be viewed. Each of these views is elaborated in the following section, with the main emphasis being on the perspective of the delivery mode.

1.3.1 Transnational nature of higher education institutions

Three different ways through which the transnational nature of higher education can be viewed are as follows: (i) philosophically, (ii) pedagogically and (iii) focusing on the mode of program delivery and/or course of interest [15,22,23].

i. **Philosophical**

Despite there being a profit-making aspect to transnational education, it has the potential to foster transcultural understanding over time. This aspect of transnational education is often expressed in the knowledge and skills that students are expected to develop through their studies. Students are usually expected to lead local, regional, international or transnational organisations after completion of their degrees and be able to contribute to the solving of problems that might be based at the local, regional, national or transnational levels [19,22,23]. In this way, transnational higher education can establish linkages between nations, regardless of geographic proximity and cultural divide [15,22,23].

ii. **Pedagogical**

From the pedagogical perspective, the academic aspects of transnational education can be emphasised, especially the curriculum used and the teaching approach applied [15,22,23]. The pedagogical view asks the academic staff/faculty members as well as students to focus on different learning styles which may be dominant in different cultures and to include global awareness and knowledge of the world and its interconnectedness into the curriculum. The pedagogical framework fosters transcultural understanding through local, regional or national contexts [15,22,23].

iii. **Program delivery mode**

The program delivery perspective focusses on the situation where the students are physically located in another country, distinct from the home country of the higher education offering institution. In this situation, the delivery of the course/program content can occur via three main mechanisms: (a) distance mode, (b) in-country mode and (c) blended mode. Each of these modes is defined and discussed in turn.

a. **Distance mode**

In the distance mode, the "mobile" component is the program of studies and the curriculum: the providing (home) institution remains in its home country, as does the student and there is no physical contact between the two. There are four main modes used in the distance model of delivery: online learning, instructional audio/visual, correspondence education and massive open online courses (MOOCs).

Online learning

Transnational online learning occurs when the students, situated in their home country, receive a qualification from a higher education institution located in another country. The learning, teaching and assessment processes are mediated by the Internet and tools such as video conferencing, YouTube, Skype, Zoom, Microsoft Teams, Google Classroom, Lectopia, Echo360°, Canvas Studio, Collaborate Ultra and virtual blackboard.

Instructional audio/visual

Under this delivery mode, the main media for transmission of the curriculum is the radio and/or television. The studies can be undertaken via live transmission or re-broadcasting. An example of this is "The School of the Air", which delivers primary and high school education to remote communities in Australia via the radio and video feed. Similar examples can be found in Bangladesh, India and other countries. Although these examples are internal to a nation, the same mode would work for transnational program delivery.

Correspondence education

Correspondence education is the 19th- and 20th-century version of distance education, where the learning instruction and resources materials are provided to the student in printed, audio or video media (pre-recorded).

Massive open online courses

Massive open online courses (MOOC) can be undertaken by an unlimited number of students, via the Internet. It is a continuously evolving mode of delivery for transnational education. MOOC can also include some intensive, face-to-face lectures/workshops that are conducted or delivered or performed at regional support centres.

b.   **In-country delivery mode**

There are four variations of the in-country delivery model: (1) overseas branch campus, (2) franchising, (3) validation and (4) dual/double degree without student mobility. Generally, though, these delivery models occur where a higher education institution has a physical presence in another country, either directly or via a third party (with local partnership).

1. Overseas branch campus

In this mode, the offering institution creates a branch campus in the host country (where the education is being delivered). The curriculum offered may be whole or part of a program of studies. The advantage of this mode for the offering higher education institution is that it provides effectiveness in the delivery of the program or course. However, it is costly and requires serious commitment on the part of the offering institution in terms of resources and staffing. Overseas branch campuses also provide job opportunities and career development for the host country (local) population. Branch campuses are increasingly becoming popular, within the transnational student population in Malaysia, Singapore, China, India, the United Arab Emirates (UAE), Qatar, Bangladesh, Pakistan, Hong Kong, Vietnam, Indonesia and South Africa [16,19,24,25].

2. Franchising

In franchising, the offering higher education institution authorises an educational institution in the host country to provide programs of studies to the host country's population. The completed qualifications, however, come from the providing higher education institution and any testamurs bear the seal and signatures of that institution. The management, business and teaching aspects of these arrangements must be compliant with both countries' government policies and regulations.

3. Validation

Validation occurs when an education institution in the host country develops and teaches a program of studies, while the offering higher education institution examines the curriculum and quality of that program of studies and agrees to award an equivalent qualification. In this instance, the host institution has the responsibility for the delivery and development of the curriculum.

4. Dual/double degree without student mobility

A dual/double degree mode without student mobility occurs when the students situated in the host nation receive face-to-face instruction at the host institution and distance learning (without leaving their home country) from the foreign institution. Upon completion of the program, students are either awarded a dual or joint degree, awarded jointly by both institutions, or a double degree, where one degree is awarded by the host institution and a second degree is awarded by the offering higher education institution.

c. **Blended mode**

Blended mode typically requires either some mobility on the part of the student to attend residential experiences or alternatively some ability of the academic staff/faculty members to provide some instruction in the host country in the face-to-face mode. There are six variants of the blended mode: (I) twinning/articulation, (II) fly-in/fly-out, (III) dual/double degree with student mobility, (IV) joint degree, (V) consecutive degree and (VI) study abroad.

I. Twinning/articulation

Under the twinning mode, students complete courses/subjects/units/ modules of an academic program at their local (host) institution. These completed courses/subjects then allow for credit transfers towards a qualification at the offering higher education institution. Usually, students get only one qualification.

II. Fly-in/fly-out approach

The fly-in/fly-out approach is the most cost-effective mode for transnational education and provides a certain degree of quality [15,16,26]. The fly-in/fly-out mode is where the offering institution flies its faculty members/academic staff to the host institution to provide intensive lectures, tutorials or workshops in specific courses, modules, units or subjects for a short duration (typically 2–3 days for each unit). The remainder of the courses/subjects are taught by the local academic staff/faculty members in consultation with the offering institution's academic staff/faculty members. The quality of program delivery and assessments are monitored and moderated jointly by both institutions from the offering and host countries.

III. Dual/double degree with student mobility

This mode is similar to the dual/double degree without student mobility, the difference being that the student is able to travel and study at both the offering institution and the host institution in the face-to-face mode. This model of delivery is very popular amongst higher education providers in Europe, North America and Australia.

IV. Joint degree

In the joint-degree mode, students study at both the host and the offering institutions in the face-to-face mode and receive one degree with the seal of both institutions.

V. Consecutive degrees

Consecutive degrees are managed by a transnational agreement on the required amount of student mobility. The student receives two nested degrees: one from the host institution and another from the offering institution.

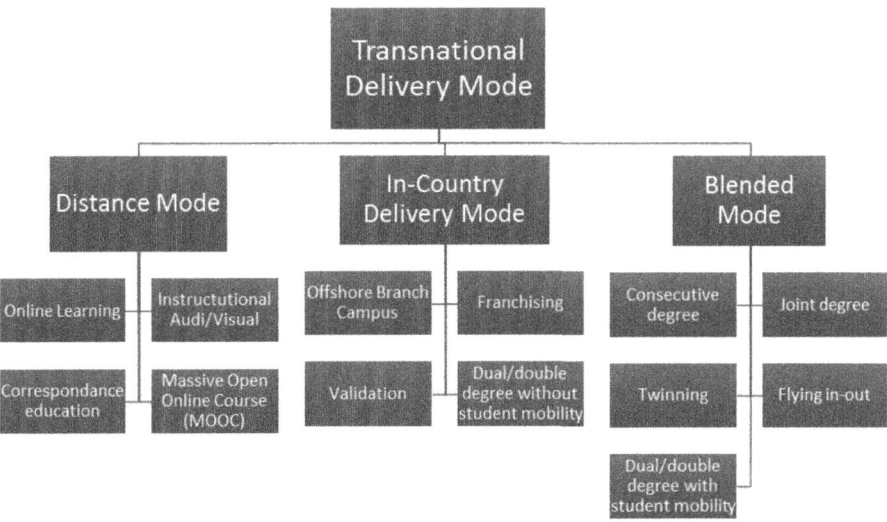

Figure 1.4 Transnational education delivery modes. (Adapted from Refs. [15,27].)

VI. Study abroad

In the study-abroad mode, a student of an institution in one country travels to a different country's institution to undertake study for a set period of time. Upon successful completion of their studies at the host institution, they are granted the relevant credit towards their qualification at their home institution. This type of transnational education is popular among students from developed countries and allows students to experience different cultures, languages, food habit and lifestyles.

The different delivery modes of transnational education are summarised in Figure 1.4.

1.3.1.1 Regional hubs for transnational education

To meet the growing local demand for higher education, and to reduce the individual student education cost, as well as building local academic and research talent, emerging nations are implementing policies which aim to attract reputed foreign universities to offer education programs (qualifications) for local students and, critically, for students from other nations within the same geopolitical region. For example, universities from the UK, the USA, Australia, Canada and France offer their courses and programs in nations such as Singapore, Malaysia, Hong Kong, the United Arab Emirates, Qatar, Vietnam and Indonesia. Tables 1.2 and 1.3 provide further examples. At present, there are over 1,000 programs at either the undergraduate or postgraduate level being offered overseas by developed countries' universities.

China and India, with high local demand for higher education, are increasingly allowing reputable foreign higher education institutions (universities) to open branch campuses within their national boundaries. China, for example, is the leader in North

Table 1.2 Branch campuses of foreign universities in UAE and Qatar

	Institution name	Country of origin	Host country
1	New York University	USA	UAE
2	New York Institute of Technology	USA	UAE
3	Michigan State University	USA	UAE
4	Rochester Institute of Technology	USA	UAE
5	University of Manchester	UK	UAE
6	University of Birmingham	UK	UAE
7	University of Bradford	UK	UAE
8	University of Exeter	UK	UAE
9	Middlesex University	UK	UAE
10	City University of London	UK	UAE
11	University of West London	UK	UAE
12	University of Stirling	UK	UAE
13	University of Bolton	UK	UAE
14	Murdoch University	Australia	UAE
15	University of Wollongong	Australia	UAE
16	Moscow University for Industry and Finance	Russia	UAE
17	Saint-Petersburg State Economic University	Russia	UAE
18	Paris Sorbonne University	France	UAE
19	Amity University	India	UAE
20	Birla Institute of Technology and Science	India	UAE
21	Manipal University	India	UAE
22	Paris-Sorbonne University	France	Qatar
23	Texas A&M University	USA	Qatar
24	Carnegie Mellon University	USA	Qatar
25	Cornell University	USA	Qatar
26	Virginia Commonwealth University	USA	Qatar
27	North-western University	USA	Qatar
28	University of Calgary	Canada	Qatar
29	École Polytechnique Federale of Lausanne	Switzerland	Qatar

Source: Adapted from Refs. [15,27].

Table 1.3 Branch campuses of foreign universities in Southeast and North Asia

	Institution name	Country of origin	Host country
1	École Supérieure des Sciences Economiques et Commerciales	France	Singapore, Morocco
2	DigiPen Institute of Technology	USA	Singapore
3	German Institute of Science and Technology (Technical University of Munich)	Germany	Singapore
4	James Cook University	Australia	Singapore
5	Curtin University of Technology	Australia	Malaysia (1999), Singapore, UAE
6	Swinburne University of Technology	Australia	Malaysia (2004)
7	University of Southampton	UK	Malaysia (2011)
8	Xiamen University	China	Malaysia (2015)
9	Newcastle University Medicine	UK	Malaysia (2007)
10	Heriot-Watt University	UK	Malaysia (2012), UAE
11	University of Reading	UK	Malaysia (2013)
12	University College Dublin	Ireland	Malaysia (2018)

(Continued)

Table 1.3 (Continued) Branch campuses of foreign universities in Southeast and North Asia

	Institution name	Country of origin	Host country
13	Monash University	Australia	Malaysia (1998), China, South Africa
14	Nottingham University	UK	Malaysia (2000), China
15	Liverpool University	UK	China (with Xi'an Jiaotong University)
16	University of Michigan	USA	China (with Shanghai Jiao Tong University)
17	Kean University	USA	China (with Wenzhou University)
18	Duke University	USA	China (with Wuhan University)
19	New York University	USA	China (with East China Normal University)
20	Technion Israel Institute of Technology	Israel	China (with Shantou University)
21	Moscow State University	Russia	China (with Beijing Institute of Technology)
22	RMIT University	Australia	Vietnam

Source: Adapted from Refs. [15,27].

Asia for hosting foreign universities' campuses. In 2017, over 608,000 Chinese citizens travelled overseas for study, and the numbers are expected to increase further [46]. Hence, foreign higher education institutions have been establishing branch campuses in China and exploring opportunities for joint ventures, where the campus is set up with a local higher education institution, in the hope of attracting both outgoing Chinese students as well as those who do not wish to cross the national border for higher education. In addition, educational opportunities for citizens of neighbouring countries can be established. For example, students from India may wish to study at an Australian higher education institution but may be unable to travel to Australia as a "degree-mobile" international student. Such students may be able to travel the shorter distance to either Singapore, Malaysia, Hong Kong, China and still receive an Australian degree at an offshore Australian campus, located at one of the "regional hubs".

The major regional education hubs for foreign higher education institutions are located in Singapore and Malaysia, China and Hong Kong, the United Arab Emirates and Qatar, India, Pakistan and Bangladesh and South Africa. Tables 1.2 and 1.3 provide examples of branch campuses in regional hubs. The physical distribution of these transnational education host nations in geostrategic locations is illustrated in Figure 1.5.

Among these regional foreign higher education institutions' education hubs, the United Arab Emirates and Qatar and Malaysia and Singapore host the highest number of foreign higher education institutions' campuses. By virtue of historic and linguistic links, it is the universities from the UK and Australia that are dominating the Malaysia-Singapore region, whereas North American and European universities are in the UAE and Qatar region. The UAE and Qatar region is particularly interesting because of the investment of the respective governments in establishing special education zones for foreign university campuses (e.g. Dubai International Academic City and Qatar Education City).

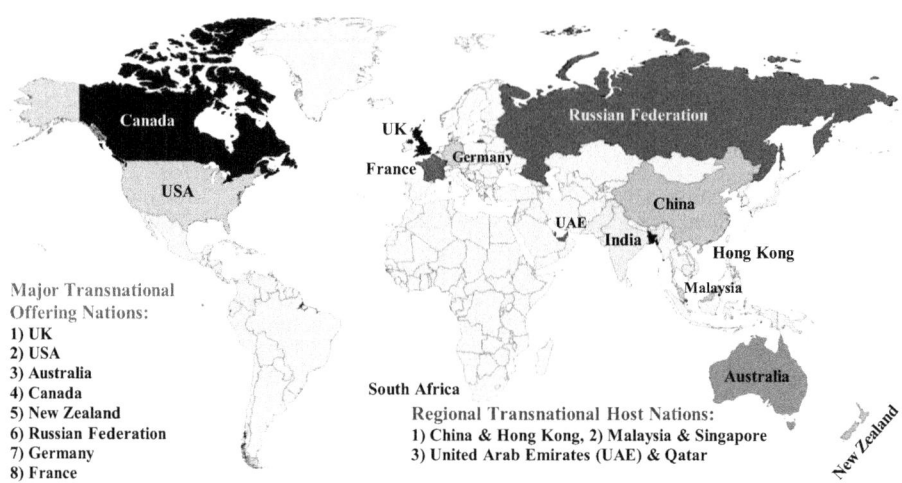

Figure 1.5 Geostrategic locations of regional transnational host nations. (Adapted from Refs. [15,28].)

1.3.2 Transnational nature of higher education students

The number of international students travelling across national boundaries for higher study has quadrupled over the last 12 years, and based on that trend, there will be over eight million international students by 2025 [2,29–31]. The number of students involved in transnational education (which may not require mobility on the part of the student) is also expected to increase [32,33]. Opportunities for study, employment and research are not distributed evenly throughout nations and continents. This means that there is a mass movement of people seeking education [15,34–37]. Furthermore, there is a high proportion of young people in South Asia (led by India) and North Asia (led by China) whose demand for higher education outstrips local capacity. The countries in this situation are constrained by financial resources and cannot invest in their higher education section so as to meet the local demand. The result is that citizens of these countries are forced to consider travelling to another country for education, which is costly to the individual, given the general scarcity of scholarships [39]. Travelling to another country for study also means that the studies must be completed typically in a foreign language and within a new culture. These difficulties combine to create an opportunity for developed countries to offer transnational education in developing countries – the only way to local demand for higher education can be met in an equitable fashion [38,40]. The higher education institutions of developed nations have therefore developed many different modes of transnational education (see Section 1.3.1).

At present, the USA, the UK and Australia attract almost half of the world's total of foreign students, but nations such as China and India (typical host countries for transnational education) are expanding their own education sectors rapidly. Currently, China receives more incoming students than Chinese nationals who go abroad to study [2,18,26,38]. Table 1.4 shows the main destination countries for international students; Table 1.5 indicates the countries of origin for international students.

Table 1.4 Leading host countries for international students in 2018

Ranking	Country	Number of international students	Source countries
1	US	1,094,792	China, India and South Korea
2	UK	506,480	China, USA and Germany
3	China	489,200	South Korea, Thailand, Pakistan
4	Australia	371,885	China, India, Nepal
5	Canada	370,710	China, India, South Korea
6	France	343,386	Morocco, Algeria, China
7	Russia	313,089	Kazakhstan, China, Uzbekistan
8	Germany	265,484	China, India, Russia
9	Japan	188,384	China, Vietnam, Nepal
10	Spain	109,522	Italy, France, USA

Source: Adapted from Refs. [2,31,42].

Table 1.5 Leading source countries of international students in 2018

Rank	Place of origin	No. of students	% of total international mobile students
1	China	363,341	33.2
2	India	196,271	17.9
3	South Korea	54,555	5.0
4	Saudi Arabia	44,432	4.1
5	Canada	25,909	2.4
6	Vietnam	24,325	2.2
7	Taiwan	22,454	2.1
8	Japan	18,753	1.7
9	Mexico	15,468	1.4
10	Brazil	14,620	1.3
11	Nepal	11,607	1.2
	World total	1,094,792	100%

Source: Adapted from Ref. [31].

The data presented in these tables only list those students who are able to study complete programs overseas. These types of students are typically called "internationally mobile students" because they hold a visa for the country they study in and their length of stay in the other country is typically between 1 and 7 years. Sometimes, they are also called "degree-mobile" students, as they receive a degree from a host institution based in a nation where they are non-resident. There is another category of students referred to as "credit mobile students" or "exchange students". No exact figure for this group of students is currently available. The credit mobile students only study abroad for a short time and receive a small number of credits from the host institution. The time period spent abroad by credit mobile students may only be a semester [41], but UNESCO [2] still designates them as "internationally mobile students", not distinguishing them from students who study overseas for a longer period of time.

A more recent development is that many students now wish to obtain foreign qualifications but still remain within their region's geographic boundary by travelling

Table 1.6 Total number of foreign students from all places of origin by the field of study 2015–2016 (USA)

Rank	Field of study	No. of students	% of total
1	Engineering	216,932	20.8
2	Business and Management	200,312	19.2
3	Other/Unspecified Subject Areas	185,107	17.7
4	Mathematics and Computer Sciences	141,651	13.6
5	Social Sciences	81,304	7.8
6	Physical and Life Sciences	75,385	7.2
7	Fine and Applied Arts	59,736	5.7
8	Health Professions	33,947	3.3
9	Education	19,483	1.9
10	Humanities	17,664	1.7
11	Agriculture	12,318	1.2

Source: Adapted from Ref. [11].

not so far from home. For example, between 1999 and 2013, there was an increase of 4% in the number of students from sub-Saharan Africa who travelled within that same region to study. In Central and Eastern Europe over the same time frame, there was an increase of 15% in student numbers, and within Middle East states, the rise was 18% [2]. The change in the flow of students is a result of a variety of factors, such as changes to visa restrictions, increases in tuition fees, post-study work visa permission and immigration opportunities. As mentioned earlier, higher education institutions from the developed nations are investing in infrastructure and quality control processes in their offshore campuses, especially in regional hubs, to attract more international students [11,18].

Table 1.6 shows that students from developing nations are more likely to pursue an education program in the fields of engineering, science and mathematics compared with those of developed nations. Qualifications in STEM will certainly assist their home country in the knowledge economy and in ensuring successful technology transfer from developed nations.

Despite having overwhelming benefits for students from developing countries, transnational education can be perceived as a threat. Some people are concerned that transnational education is increasing the Westernisation of other cultures [43]. Some also fear that overseas universities can be used to stifle innovation and dissent [44]. Therefore, it is important that local higher education institutions should continue collaboration with international higher education institutions while still valuing their local culture, heritage and linguistic identities [43].

1.3.3 Transnational opportunities for academics/faculty members of higher education institutions

The establishment of branch campuses by established foreign universities allows the host country to develop its academics/faculty members' teaching and research capabilities [45,46]. A good example is the foundation of foreign higher education institutions' campuses in China: two of these branch campuses are ranked in the world's top 30 higher education institutions, five are ranked in the top 150, six in the top 500 and three in the top 1,000. This demonstrates that Chinese universities are willing to host foreign universities to improve their own quality ranking, provide research and career development opportunities for their employees and enhance in-house capacity development.

While many higher education institutions emphasise student mobility, there has been less emphasis, so far, on the mobility of academic staff/faculty members. However, the benefits of academic staff mobility can be envisioned in three stages: (a) short term, (b) medium term and (c) long term [47].

In the short term, international visiting academic staff/faculty members motivate students to widen the perspective of their engineering education and develop the use of English for professional communication.

The mid-term benefits include undertaking joint research through academic staff/faculty members of the host institution and the source institutions from where visiting foreign faculty members come. They can also promote interest in international grants and industry linkages.

The long-term benefit is that engineering specialists, both the students and the academic staff/faculty members, are able to compete on the international stage and are capable of attracting foreign investment.

The mobility of academic staff/faculty members can result in more face-to-face contact and cooperation across different institutions, sharing infrastructure and resources. In particular, travelling engineering academic staff/faculty members bring with them the offshore industry contacts that would otherwise be difficult to obtain.

1.4 Social and economic impact of transnational nature of higher education

Transnational education, which is delivered offshore, has several social and economic benefits. For education institutions, it broadens the choice and opportunity of study for students and thereby encourages competition among higher education institutions, improving both teaching and learning quality and research capabilities. Transnational education can also reduce the pressure on the local education system, while still developing the local skill and talent pool. Students can study without leaving their home country or region. For developing countries, it encourages students to remain at home and/or in the region after their graduation, thereby reducing capital outflow and "brain drain".

Transnational education is especially convenient for those students who are working full-time, because it allows them to upskill while still maintaining their employment and standard of living. It is very unlikely that the graduates of this style of transnational education will leave their local area. Such graduates usually fill knowledge and skills shortage gaps. However, if there is no formulated national higher education policy, the social fabric of the community may be distorted with the introduction of a local, highly educated elite. Developing countries' governments should ensure that the transnational educational opportunities are available to as wide a section of the population as possible.

Another advantage of transnational education is that it creates opportunity for highly skilled nationals to return to their country of origin after completing their studies abroad. Such a return provides substantial benefit to their home country by increasing that country's capacity of innovation and productivity, thereby driving the country's economic development.

1.4.1 Student mobility and "brain drain"

"Brain drain" refers to the net movement of highly qualified professionals away from their country of origin. While there are often cultural factors which produce "brain drain" in developed nations (e.g. Australia), more frequently "brain drain" is used within the context of tertiary-qualified nationals of a developing country permanently leaving their country of origin to relocate to a nation of higher socio-economic development. The higher rates of emigration are typically observed in the lower-middle income countries "where people have both the incentives and the means to emigrate" [48]. The highest rates of brain drain occur in the Caribbean, Oceania, Central America and sub-Saharan Africa [49].

Brain drain has huge financial, economic, intellectual and cultural implications for the country of origin. The most apparent cost is that the majority of higher-educated emigrants were educated in government-subsidised higher education institutions.

This loss is further increased due to the loss of earned income and thereby a loss of tax revenues [50,81]. While there is typically some return of personal income to the family in the country of origin, these remittances generally do not compensate for either the lost taxation or investment required in the educational institutions [51]. This is particularly true when the skilled emigrants come from upper middle class or high-income households, where any additional money is spent on higher-end consumption, such as real estate, which does not generally foster the local economy [11]. In contrast, the remittances of skilled emigrants, originating from low-income households, are more beneficial to the country of origin's economy because their money is typically spent on basic needs (such as school fees and small businesses), all of which improve the livelihood and economic development of the local community. Other investments from low socio-economic background-originating emigrants tend to be rural credit or health insurance that is generally absent or scarce in the country of origin.

Apart from the lost revenue, the brain drain can also lead to delayed economic and technological development in the country of origin, because potential innovators leave and do not return. In some cases, this may also slow down societal change. These effects appear to be particularly high where skilled emigration is over 30% [52].

Since the 1960s, developed nations' higher education institutions, especially from the USA, the UK, Canada, Australia and New Zealand, have offered scholarships to developing countries' bright students. The advantage of such schemes is generally couched in the idea that these higher education institutions are skilling people from developing nations so that as graduates they can return to their countries of origin to take part in their national economies. In reality, this approach has mostly the opposite effect. Although the institutions' scholarships to individual students transform the lives of individuals, nearly three quarters of scholarship-holding students do not return to their countries of origin after graduation, thereby making the developing countries no better off.

Many of these scholarship holders are early-career and or mid-level academic staff/ faculty members of the developing countries' higher education institutions who choose to improve their qualifications with a transnational qualification. Because they are often tenured staff, it means that not only do they have a scholarship from the providing higher education institution but that they also draw a salary from their home institution, making their salary an even poorer investment for their home higher education institution. Typically, incentives such as tenure are provided with a hope that after graduation, the graduates will return and take senior roles in the home country's higher education institutions. When these graduates do not return, the home country's institution must sustain an irreparable loss. This accelerated brain drain, through individual scholarships, ends up not only weakening the higher education institutions' capabilities but also forestalls knowledge transfer to students within the home nation and thereby contributes to an acute shortage of skilled human resources that are vital for nation-building activities [53].

It is therefore highly desirable that the developed nations' higher education institutions reimage their current international partnerships practices, so that these do more good than harm to developing countries. If they engage developing countries' higher education institutions through offering dual degrees, split-site scholarships where students can undertake part study in their home country's institutions, and part study at developed nations' institutions, and joint Masters and PhD (doctoral) supervision, instead of offering scholarships to individual students, the brain drain will be minimised and the acute skills shortages will begin to be addressed. Institutional engagement (reimaging) approaches such as these will not only assist the developing countries' skills enhancement and economic development but also build the developed nations' institutions' reputation. These initiatives will also promote joint research outputs, creation and participation in joint research projects, competitive grants and scientific conclaves and conferences.

Currently, a good share of the annual revenue of English-speaking developed nations' higher education institutions comes from the tuition fees of fee-paying international students who are mainly from developing countries. It is true that due to the reduced funding by governments, the developed nations' education institutions increasingly rely on fee-paying international students [54–56]. Thus, the revenue generated by the full-fee paying international students from developing countries in fact subsidises the education cost of students, research activities and research outputs of the developed countries. However, the higher education institutions of the developed nations can make significant impact, with little or no investment in developing countries' institutions, by making partnerships with them, because this kind of partnership will assist in achieving the UN-declared Sustainable Development Goals. In return, the developed nations' higher education institutions will enhance their quality education delivery and global university ranking.

The reverse situation of "brain drain" is "brain gain", when more individuals seek transnational or international education than those who succeed in emigrating, resulting in a net increase in the number of highly educated residents in the country of origin. A study on the impact of brain drain undertaken by Beine et al. [52] in 127 developing nations revealed that the larger developing countries such as China, India, Brazil and Indonesia have had a slight "brain gain". However, smaller nations, such as Pakistan, Bangladesh, Nepal, Nigeria and Ghana, suffered more brain drain, with emigration rates of up to 20%. Across the globe, there is more brain drain (more than 10%) than brain gain (less than 1%) [11,52].

For upper-middle-income countries, an emerging trend of "brain recirculation" has occurred. This is where nationals return to their country of origin after decades abroad, or where transnational knowledge networks and diaspora communities create joint ventures in the country of origin, using capital and state-of-the-art skills gained from organisations, businesses and government departments based in the foreign country. Hong Kong, Taiwan, South Korea and Singapore have all benefitted from the brain recirculation for some time, while, more recently, China and India are also benefitting from the brain recirculation. Evidence of the brain recirculation can be seen in an increase in patenting activity, which can thereby increase foreign investment [11,48]. In brain recirculation, the country of origin and the host country equally benefit, both in terms of the national economy and technological advancement.

More examples of the brain recirculation are available from China, where the government has initiated programs to encourage nationals to return. For example, through the Chinese Academy of Sciences and the National Talent Development Plan research grants, housing allowances and competitive salaries are offered to scientists, incentivising Chinese-born experts to return to China. Other mechanisms have also been used to bring more than 20,000 high-level professionals home [57]. One scheme encourages diaspora-based scientists to participate in the international research activities and another allows Chinese national scientists to have a second research facility in China, allowing them to work between different nations and increase the amount of expertise in China. There are also schemes which enable Chinese scientists to test out the possibility of a return, without having to make a firm commitment. The Chinese government has also developed several "science and technology parks" to attract nationals to return. This strategy has also been successfully used by Taiwan and South Korea [11].

Other good examples of brain recirculation come from India, where fellowship programs have been set up by the Indian Ministry of Science and Technology and the Ministry of Human Resources Development, to attract Indian-born foreign scientists to return to India. Similar programs have also been developed by India's Defence Research and Development organisation. The Indian government has also initiated policies to leverage Indian diaspora talents to accelerate the flow of investment, knowledge sharing, technology transfer and other resources back to India.

Several additional schemes in India focus on the transfer of knowledge and technology back to India. For example, the Visiting Advanced Joint Research Academics (VAJRA) scheme provides opportunities to scientists and academic staff/faculty members who may be non-resident Indians or overseas citizens of India to participate in the collaborative research in high-priority areas. The research is performed at a government-funded higher education institution in India, and there must be at least one or more resident Indian collaborators. The VAJRA academic staff/faculty members need to provide supervision of research students, develop technology and create opportunities for start-up business/entrepreneurship, wherever possible. Another scheme the Indian government has developed is the Global Initiative of Academic Networks (GIAN), which aims at encouraging offshore researchers, scientists and entrepreneurs to engage with Indian higher education institutions to further develop existing academic resources and to accelerate the pace of change in the country's technological capacity. Both schemes (GIAN and VAJRA) are sponsored through the Ministry of Human Resources Development, India.

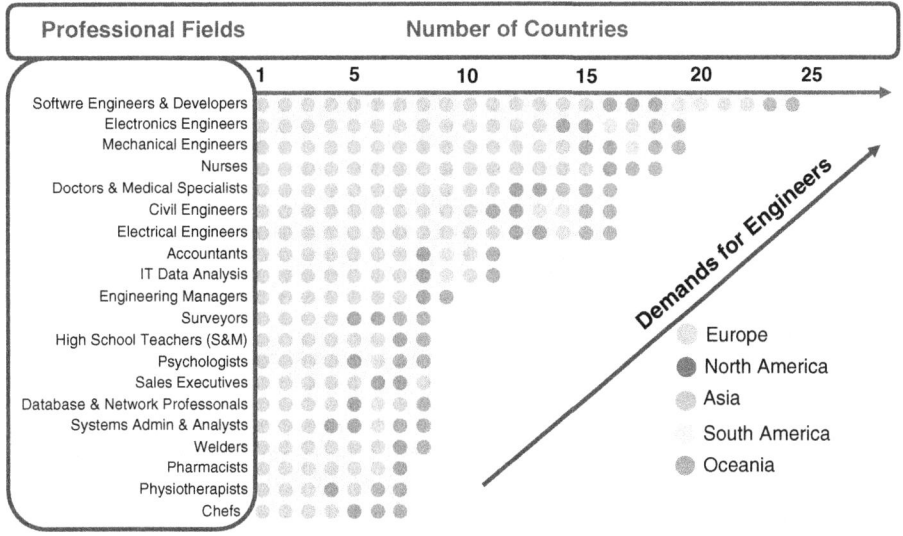

Figure 1.6 Shortages of engineers by specialisation in all continents. (Adapted from Refs. [58,59].)

A newer scheme introduced by the Indian government is the Scheme for Promotion of Academic and Research Collaboration (SPARC). This scheme aims to improve research capabilities of India's higher educational institutions by facilitating academic and research collaborations between Indian institutions and the best institutions from 28 different countries. The SPARC scheme aims to solve problems of national or international relevance.

Despite the fact that brain drain is being mediated by the brain recirculation, on a global scale, the receiving countries are clearly benefitting more, especially in the high-tech corporate sector and the higher education and research sectors [11,60]. Yet, high rates of highly skilled emigration continue to occur from nations with limited higher education and economic opportunities, resulting in delays and impediments to institutional and political reforms in those source countries (countries of origin). Figure 1.6 indicates that the demand for engineers and other professionals within Oceania and Asia is much greater than in other parts of the world, demonstrating that there is still a deficit of engineers in developing nations.

1.5 Need for international recognition of equivalency

The global mobility of students indicates that there is a need for competency frameworks that can be universally applied across national boundaries to ensure that engineering professionals have adequate skills to practise professionally and safely. If an engineering student receives a qualification in one nation, work experience in another and practises in a third nation, then there needs to be a way to highlight common standards and requirements across these different nations. Identification of commonality allows the professional to then concentrate on local variations and conditions, thereby developing technological solutions which fit into the local cultural setting.

As a starting point, there appears to be general consensus, within developed economies, as to the three major types of engineering professionals: (a) "theoretical engineer"; (b) "applied engineer" (in some regions, these professionals are considered as "technologists and/or diploma engineers") and (c) "engineering technician". These three categories generally require different levels of qualification and are associated with different types of work activities. According to the guidelines of the International Engineering Alliance (IEA), the definitions of these three major types of engineering professionals are as follows:

- **Engineering Technicians** (lowest qualification level) use standard techniques to provide solutions to practical engineering problems.
- **Incorporated Engineers** (next level of qualification) apply current and new technology to engineering design and operations. These engineers may also be involved with management and are able to communicate effectively.
- **Chartered Engineers** (highest qualification level) are those practitioners who innovate and create new technologies to provide solutions to engineering problems.

Figure 1.7 illustrates the stages of competencies and career progression of professional engineers.

There are some other practitioners who operate at a lower skill level and are often called "skilled trades" or "engineering operatives" [60]. In terms of qualifications, there are some international agreements which govern the equivalency of different engineering qualifications across nations. These agreements will be examined in Chapter 3, but it is important to note that a qualification often only allows "entry to

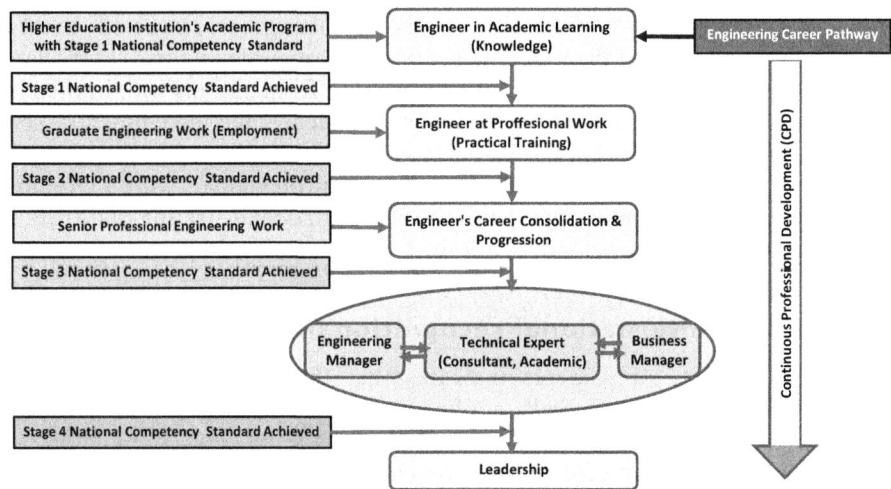

Figure 1.7 Professional pathways of engineers. (Adapted from Ref. [21].)

practice", and further professional development is required on the part of the individual to be licensed or chartered for complex projects. The international agreements (both European and non-European) are based on two-tier recognition models, where the first-tier agreement (recognition) recognises the academic qualification achieved, and the second-tier agreement recognises the skills and experience of the individual engineering practitioner [60].

1.5.1 Avenues for international recognition of equivalency

There are two main multinational agreements that provide a basis for mutual recognition of engineering qualifications and experience. These are administered by the International Engineering Alliance (IEA) for mainly non-European professional organisations (except the UK, Ireland and Turkey) and the European Network for Accreditation of Engineering Education (ENAEE). Each of these will now be briefly examined. A more thorough discussion is provided in Chapter 3. For both agreements, the concept of "substantial equivalence" is important here: it is assumed that differences will not result in limited capabilities of individual engineers and that after several years of professional experience, such differences will not be detectable.

1.5.2 Agreements administered by International Engineering Alliance (IEA)

On 28 September 1989, the Washington Accord was signed by the engineering accreditation organisations of six English-speaking countries: Australia, Canada, the USA, the UK, New Zealand and Ireland [40,60]. The accord is an international agreement which recognises substantial equivalence of bachelor-level qualifications accredited by those member organisations and allows graduates of such accredited qualifications to practise engineering within any of the members' jurisdictions. This alliance has now grown to include 20 accrediting organisations, encompassing more than just bachelor-level qualifications. To aid administration of all agreements across all levels, the International Engineering Alliance (IEA) was established in 2007. It is now the overarching body for the agreements. The two-tier structure of these agreements can be seen as follows.

1.5.2.1 Tier one: agreements covering higher education academic qualifications in engineering

The Washington Accord recognises the substantial equivalence of bachelor-level professional engineering qualifications for a degree. The study duration for such qualifications is typically 4 years.

The Sydney Accord signed in 2001 recognises substantial equivalence between qualifications resulting in the ability to practise as an engineering technologist. The typical study duration in this case is 3 years.

The Dublin Accord signed in 2002 recognises the substantial equivalence of qualifications in the technician domain. The study duration here is typically 2 years.

1.5.2.2 Tier two: agreements covering competence standards for practising engineers

The Asia Pacific Economic Cooperation (APEC) Engineer Agreement started in 1999 is an agreement among APEC member governments. This agreement establishes an international register of engineers administered by APEC members' engineering professional organisations.

The APEC Engineer Agreement applies to individual professional engineers and relates to the extent of that individual's experience. To be listed on the APEC Engineer Register, an individual must demonstrate the following [61]:

- An undergraduate degree accredited or recognised by Engineers Australia must be successfully completed.
- An evaluation by APEC signatories such as Engineers Australia to determine that the individual can practise safely and independently.
- A minimum of 7 years of practical experience after graduation.
- At least 2 years' experience for being responsible for major engineering projects.
- Evidence of continuing professional development at a satisfactory level. It is expected that the professional development is ongoing and will be audited for every 5 years.

Once the individual professional meets these criteria, they are entered on the register and allowed to use the title "APEC Engineer" or "IntPE (Aus)" for Australia and for other APEC agreement signatories IntPE (APEC signatory country code). Similar requirements are implemented by other signatories of the APEC agreement. In addition to APEC, the International Professional Engineers Agreement (IPEA) replaces the Engineers Mobility Forum, which was established in 2001. This agreement broadens the APEC agreement to any engineering organisation of any country [62].

The International Engineering Technologists Agreement (IETA) replaces the Engineering Technologist Mobility Forum which was signed in 2003. This agreement allows for mutual recognition by participating economies/countries of International Engineering Technologists [62].

The International Engineering Technicians Agreement (IETA) was signed off in 2015 by members of the IEA to allow for the mutual recognition of individual engineering technicians.

1.5.3 International agreements for European Countries

The European Union has two overarching organisations which examine the equivalency of engineering qualifications and engineering experience, again reflecting a two-tier model of the engineering professional development.

1.5.3.1 Tier one: agreements covering higher academic qualifications in engineering

The European Network for Accreditation of Engineering Education (ENAEE) was established in 2006 as an outcome of the *European Standing Observatory for the Engineering Profession and Education* (ESOEPE) [63].

The ENAEE oversees the equivalency of engineering bachelor's degrees ("First Cycle" Bologna Stage) and master's degrees ("Second Cycle" Bologna Stage). Like the IEA discussed earlier, the ENAEE has developed criteria for engineering qualifications. Wherever an accrediting body can demonstrate that their accreditation criteria and processes meet or are equivalent to the ENAEE requirements, the accreditation body is then allowed to award the EUR-ACE® label to any accredited degrees.

1.5.3.2 Tier two: agreements covering competence standards for practicing engineers

The European Federation of National Engineering Associations (FEANI) was first established in 1951 to create constructive links in Europe which were vital after the devastation of World War II. Initially, there were seven member associations, and this group has now grown to more than 32 [64]. FEANI is now also a member of the ENAEE [63].

FEANI works to support the mobility of engineering professionals by developing mutual recognition of the different national licensing requirements which professional engineers must demonstrate to practise in Europe [64]. This is the equivalent of the second-tier requirement of the IEA. To do this, FEANI administers the European Engineer (EUR ING) Register. To apply to be on this register, individual professional engineers must submit their credentials to the FEANI European Monitoring Committee. If the credentials, experience and professional development of the individual are sufficient to meet the register requirements, the individual is allowed to use the EUR ING title [65].

The basic requirements for the use of the EUR ING title typically comprise a minimum of 3 years' education in an approved qualification with a minimum 2 years' professional experience. Membership as a EUR ING will generally only be granted with a combination of education and experience of 7 years' duration, so where education and experience fall short of 7 years, the applicant must also demonstrate additional education, experience or training at approved institutions [65].

Unfortunately, within member groups of FEANI, the EUR ING title is not always a guarantee of mobility for the individual professional. As a result, there is also the "Engineering Card" which demonstrates that the engineer is listed on the National Engineering Register and therefore has achieved certain set of competencies [65].

1.6 Challenges to international recognition: are there global competencies for engineers?

1.6.1 Challenges in international recognition

Most challenges to international recognition revolve around the licensing of individuals to practise within set national boundaries; however, occasionally, there can be disagreements even around the basic qualification. An example is the UK engineering education system. In the UK, engineering degrees at the bachelor level consist of 3 years. It took some significant negotiation to include these qualifications within the EUR-ACE label as other European countries typically require more years of study to complete a bachelor degree qualification [64]. Even with international agreements, there can be barriers to the mobility of engineers, particularly due to differences in approach by national regulatory authorities. In particular, some authorities, in reaction to engineering failures, have a very "heavy hand" on regulation, whereas other authorities do not. There can be difficulties for the individual engineer in transferring from those nations with "light touch" regulation to a nation which is more regulated [64].

Furthermore, there are issues which the authorising organisation and the governmental legislation need to deal with. For example, the safety of the general public is less stringent in most developing nations. In contrast, it is vigorously practised and safeguarded in developed countries. The authorising organisations of the developed nations generally do not wish to impede the mobility of an individual engineer; however, the authorising organisations need to ensure the safety of the general public. This is why additional competence is required to be demonstrated by the individual engineer to get engineering professional practice permission in a new jurisdiction [64].

Further complications with legislation can also impede the mobility of engineers, even within the same country. In the USA, for example, there are regional accrediting organisations (at least seven such organisations) which comprise accrediting organisations from different states, in addition to a federal accrediting body (the Accreditation Board for Engineering and Technology or ABET). For individual engineers, then, the ability to practise relies on the state governing organisations, the regional organisations and the federal organisations [64], as well as the specifics of how the legislation is formulated. This situation contrasts with the Australian context, where the Australia Federal Government has vested the power to the Engineers Australia's membership of the IEA to determine any engineer's ability to practise engineering in Australia including immigrants with foreign engineering qualifications from a non-signatory of Washington Accord nation.

1.6.2 Global competencies

One way to address roadblocks to the global mobility of engineers is to develop a set of "global" learning outcomes and graduate attributes. In this context, the work of Warnick [66] provides a good example. Warnick surveyed employers and engineers across the world and, based on their responses, developed eight global competencies. These competencies can be added to or used to refine the competencies used by the two major professional organisations, IEA and ENAEE. Warnick proposed eight competencies and they are as follows:

i.   Cross-cultural Communication
     This competency relates to the ways different cultures communicate, both verbally and non-verbally. Body language varies considerably with culture, and physical posture during discussions can be misinterpreted to the detriment of all. Similarly, colloquial sayings can produce confusion and misunderstandings. In addition, culture also affects how people value time and how people solve problems. An engineer who can communicate cross-culturally is one who is aware of these differences and is able to accommodate and work with them [32,65–69].

ii.   Appreciation and understanding of different cultures

An engineer with an appreciation of different cultures can understand how decisions are made within the local culture and which methods are best for completing tasks. An appreciation of different cultures allows an engineer to see the culture "from the inside" and gives the professional an ability to encounter new environments without causing conflict [66].

iii. Working in international teams

Working in international teams may mean working alongside people of different cultures and languages, either face-to-face or via virtual technology. The basis of engineering practice may then vary according to the team members' understandings of being, thinking and doing [32,66,69–74].

iv.   Exhibition of a global mindset

An engineer with a global mindset has a greater appreciation of diversity and recognises that their own culture is not superior to any others'. This attitude allows the engineer to place relevant technologies within the global environment and to be able to work within multidisciplinary and multicultural problem-solving approaches [66,74–76].

v.   Living and working in a transnational engineering environment

To be able to navigate a transnational environment, the engineer must be able to think critically and solve problems in the context of at least one non-familiar culture or country [65,75–80].

vi.   Demonstration of world and local knowledge

Global and local knowledge allows an engineer to understand the effects of their work and innovations within the broader context of international history, government and economics [66,75–81].

vii. Understanding international business, law and technical elements

Where engineering practice spans multiple nations, it is vital that engineers are aware of national differences in engineering standards, laws and business. Differences in technological elements also need to be appreciated so that technological solutions can be implemented in such a way as to be culturally appropriate and applicable to the level of infrastructure available within that nation [66,72–78].

viii. Speak more than one language including English

English has become the common language for engineering and science throughout the world and is often the only language in common across multiple cultural groups. Proficiency in English is therefore vital to allow an engineer to practise on the world stage. The ability to speak another language provides the professional with experience and a greater understanding of how a different culture behaves [66,68–73].

Further development of the transnational agreements will provide greater explicit coverage of such global attributes. Figure 1.8 shows the interaction needed for transnational engineering quality assurance and professional accreditation organisations to enable the global mobility of engineering professionals.

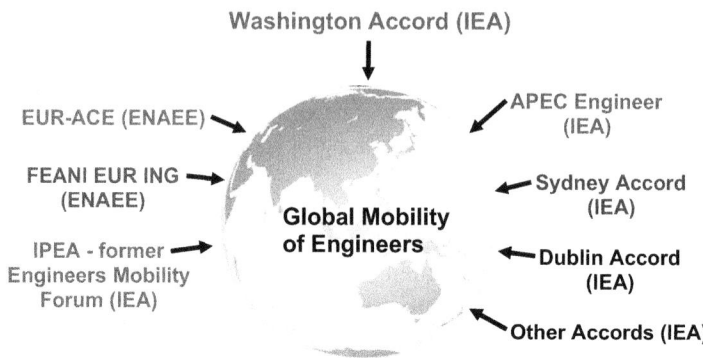

Figure 1.8 Interactions of different engineering professional organisations required global mobility.

Chapter 2

Outcome-based education

2.1 Introduction

An educational structured theory with substantial practices relating each part of an educational system to goals (outcomes) is called outcome-based education (OBE). Through OBE, at the end of an educational experience, each learner (student) should have achieved the set goal or outcome. The OBE has at least three distinctive elements [82]:

- A theory of education
- An educational structure
- A classroom practice (outcome-focused pedagogy).

The OBE originated within the behaviourist theories of learning, where the mind of the learner and the process of learning are deemed to be unseen or within a "black box" [83]. In this instance, appropriate behaviour is produced by the learner through practice and repetition, and learning is deemed to have occurred when expected responses are produced by the learner. One of the classic behaviourist experiments was performed by Pavlov in training dogs to salivate at the sound of a bell [84].

However, as the diversity of the student body in higher education institutions increased, the constructivist approach has been seen to be more useful [82–86]. In constructivism, it is assumed that the learner already possesses some skills and knowledge, and further learning is achieved by doing. Typically, this means that learning is achieved through solving problems, and the method of instruction is less didactic than in the behaviourist-based teaching.

In today's higher education institutions, the constructivist approach is perceived as developing greater student engagement and is therefore more standard across much of the world [87]. In this regard, a "learning outcome" can be defined as a result which academics/faculty members want the students to be able to demonstrate at the end of the learning period and is critically related to how the students can apply their knowledge [88,89]. Learning outcomes are therefore things which can be taught, learnt, practiced and measured [90,91] and are therefore not a psychological state of mind. Learning outcomes do not constitute a particular belief or attitude [89]. When learning outcomes are considered in this light, the OBE is termed student-centred – it is what the student does which is most important, not what the teacher does [88].

OBE in a constructivist setting gives pre-eminence to ends and purposes, rather than focusing on such things as time, procedures and curriculum [89]. In other words, OBE concentrates on what is learned and whether it is learned well. Traditional teaching methods often focus on when a student learns and how they learn it [89]. A simple example of OBE is the attainment of girl guide/scout merit badges, where it does not matter how long it takes for someone to earn the badge: once they have demonstrated the key skills and how they can use their knowledge, the badge is awarded [89]. This focus on what is learned, within a student-centred environment, means that the teaching changes to more of a facilitator, trainer or mentor role, rather than a didactic exponent of the topic area [89]. Therefore, OBE can be used as a framework for learning content [88].

OBE is sometimes used synonymously with competency-based education [86,88]. However, in competency-based (or mastery-based) learning, the content is not critiqued in itself. The key point of difference is that OBE examines why the content is being examined in the first place [86,88]. Sometimes, the distinction is made between an outcome and a capacity. Outcomes comprise capacities and when the capacities are integrated, the outcomes are achieved [86].

OBE is therefore focused on the following:

* What the student can do at the end of a module/unit/subject/course or program
* How the student can apply their knowledge at the end of a module/unit/subject/course or program
* Why subject matter is important.

More specifically, OBE can be seen to be based on four principles [89,92]:

i. **Focus** (learning outcomes are designed by all stakeholders and the learning outcomes' importance is explained to the learners)
ii. **Flexibility**:
   * learning opportunities are varied and multiple (resources are used to support the achievement of learning outcomes, with multiple chances to learners to demonstrate their achievements)
   * assessment is not determined by OBE
iii. **High expectations** (based on the premise that all students can eventually achieve all learning outcomes)
iv. **Design down and Teach up**.

"Designing down" means that the program structure is designed from the final "exit" outcomes (graduate outcomes) working backwards to the entry point. Simultaneously, individual modules/courses/ subjects/ units are then "Taught up" to ensure that the learning outcomes in each course eventually cumulate in the exit learning outcomes [92]. The schematic of OBE closed-loop cycle is shown in Figure 2.1.

In the early 1990s, Australia and South Africa started adopting OBE policies [93,94], with the United States of America (USA) having OBE in place since 1995 [95]. OBE has been developed for different parts of the education system, ranging from higher education in Australia and Hong Kong to Malaysia implementing OBE in their public schools in 2008 [96,97].

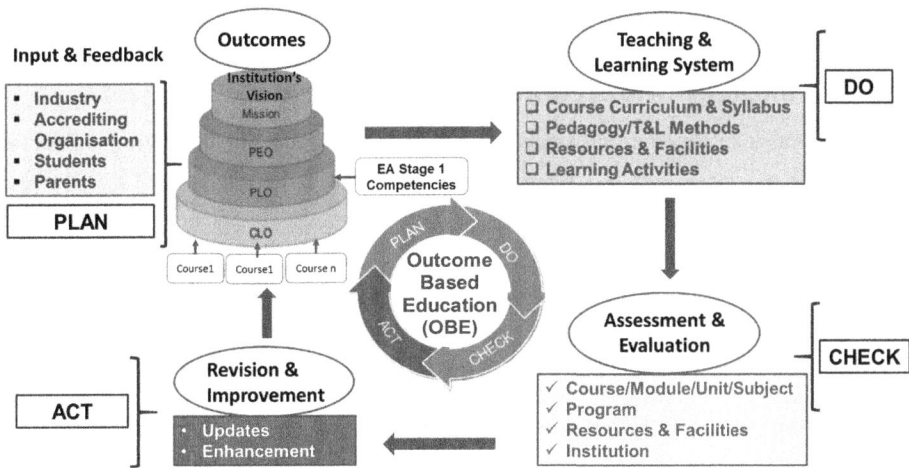

Figure 2.1 OBE life cycle.

In 1989, the Washington Accord was formed as an international agreement between accrediting organisations for mutual recognition of engineering programs. Initially, within Australia, an input-based accreditation model was used, but during the mid-1990s, the accreditation process has been changed to one which is output-based because of the increasing use of OBE [98].

Similarly, the International Engineering Alliance (IEA) which was established in 2007 to oversee the Washington Accord (Bachelor Degree), Dublin Accord (Engineering Technicians), Sydney Accord (Engineering Technologists) and other accords and agreements, expressed accreditation criteria as "graduate attributes": that is, learning outcomes which graduates of particular programs (qualifications) must be able to show upon graduation. These graduate attributes were initially developed in 2001 [82,99]. The original adoption of the graduate attributes occurred in 2007 and between 2009 and 2012. Further improvements were made, with the current version (v3) now in operation [99]. OBE systems are therefore aligned with the current international accreditation criteria of the Washington accord and ENAEE.

OBE was considered a step forward in accreditation because there are three main types [89]:

- Traditional OBE, where the students need to demonstrate mastery of a set curriculum.
- Transitional OBE, where skills such as critical thinking and problem-solving are emphasised, setting up the students to have skills to maintain their ability to learn during their life.
- Transformational OBE, where the students are enabled to complete complex tasks of the "real world".

Using an OBE framework therefore allows higher education institutions to concentrate on developing transitional and transformational OBE, which are easier to map onto an accreditation criteria or quality control requirements, particularly when these are expressed as graduate attributes.

2.2 Advantages of outcome-based education

The OBE has a series of advantages. They are discussed in the following subsections.

2.2.1 The "design down" approach

In OBE, a course, unit, module, subject or program of studies are designed backwards, or reverse-engineered. This means that the initial graduate learning outcomes or graduate attributes are established first, and then, the necessary learning outcomes in the final year of study are derived from the graduate attributes. The penultimate (final) year of study has learning outcomes derived from the final year's learning outcomes, and so on, until the entry requirements are reached. A specific example of this approach is given at the end of this chapter in Section 2.4, but it is important to examine the significant advantages of this approach in general first.

To start with, the learning outcomes upon graduation, program learning outcomes (PLOs) and graduate attributes are established first. In genuine OBE, this means that all the stakeholders must be consulted in establishing the PLOs with particular reference to the national accreditation organisation's competency standard (i.e. graduate attributes) [89,91].

All stakeholders (employers, government, internal and external quality assurance groups/organisations, including accreditation organisations, teaching academics/faculty members, alumni and society, in general) are generally supportive to the higher education institution or changes to the education sector if they are consulted regarding the system of education being used [88,93,100]. As OBE makes it easier to articulate results, society as a whole can be reassured that any government funding provided through taxation is well spent [89]. Consultation with stakeholders also provides a quality assurance loop that education is meeting the needs of the community. The stakeholders' inputs to OBE are shown in Figure 2.2.

Using OBE also makes it easier to produce a national "qualifications framework" which is applicable across multiple disciplines and aids in developing international standards and agreements, as evidenced by the Washington Accord [101–104]. These resulting international agreements then provide mutual recognition of qualifications across national boundaries and allow nations to control the standard of practising professionals who enter and work in their country [104,105]. In these instances, the PLOs (exit outcomes) are the graduate attributes listed in agreements or qualifications frameworks. The design of new programs is then guaranteed to reach the required quality if the exit outcomes are set by standards and agreements.

Once the "design down" process has been completed, the entry requirements to the program of studies are established. The OBE provides advantages here, as the specification of entry learning outcomes ensures that alternative pathways and entry points to a qualification are identified [100]. The focus of the entry point is to specify entry learning outcomes, rather than the completion of a specific certificate or program.

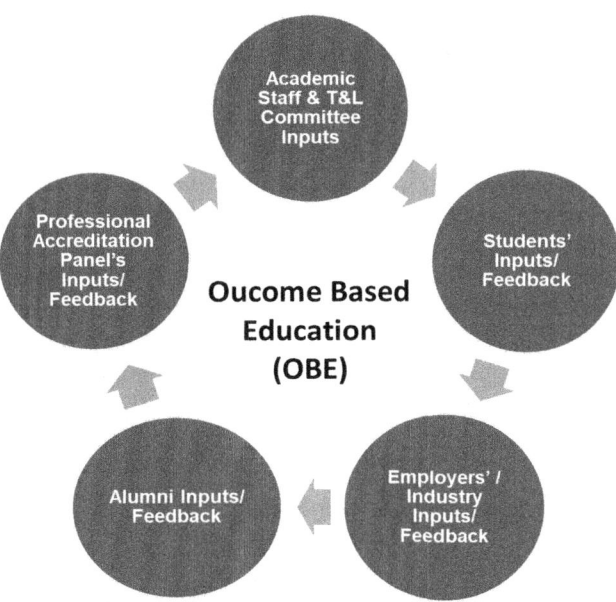

Figure 2.2 Inputs and feedback to OBE.

The "design down" approach is particularly effective as, by focusing on outcomes, the delivery mode of the program is not specified, allowing access to education to more people via online or offshore education [103,104].

In addition, OBE does not specify a particular form or type of assessment, meaning that equivalent assessment can be developed for those with a disability [106]. Indeed, in an ideal situation, OBE can adjust to individual learner needs and provide enough time for every individual to demonstrate the required outcomes [88,93]. Developing learning outcomes sequentially also allows for the development of scaffolding for the students: complex learning outcomes may be the result of summative assessment in later years but only provide formative assessment during the earlier ones [102,107].

OBE also places no restrictions on the design of the program and it does not require specific amounts of time. Once the learning outcomes are achieved, the qualification is awarded [108,109]. Thus, the OBE can provide a system for genuine innovation in program design and delivery [103].

If the national accreditation or governmental organisations use outcomes/graduate attributes to assess the quality of a program of studies, OBE can be used to monitor and continuously improve the program quality.

2.2.2 OBE and accreditation processes

Engineering accreditation criteria require demonstration of a relationship between industry and the higher education institution. In OBE, this is relatively easy to demonstrate, as the development of the learning outcomes needs to occur in consultation with stakeholders, which would include employers and industry groups [100].

The graduate attributes specified within the various agreements are also general enough that they can be contextualised for specific disciplines of engineering – something which would not be possible if the accreditation process focused on specific tasks which engineers need to perform [100,108]. Specifying outcomes enables students to be aware of what needs to be achieved by the end of the program of studies, allowing them to focus on their learning and gives them an understanding of the priorities of the profession they are entering [88].

OBE also enables accreditation to occur more easily as the learning outcomes can be pre-defined by the accrediting organisation [103]. However, the flexibility of OBE in not specifying time periods, forms of assessment or learning activities means that, during accreditation, there must be a significant evidence to show an alignment between the intended outcomes and the curriculum, delivery method and assessments [100].

2.2.3 Structure of learning environment

In a genuine OBE system, time is no longer a rigid schedule. The learners are provided with multiple opportunities to show the learning outcomes. In reality, time cannot be removed from education [89]. However, in OBE, time can be used as a way to organise learning opportunities rather than being a rigid, uncompromising schedule. If students have only one change to learn something due to fixed-time events, then the timetabling is taking precedence over OBE. The advantage here is that repeated opportunities to learn to increase the likelihood that the students (learners) will experience deep learning [89].

2.3 Challenges of outcome-based education

2.3.1 Role of student (learner)

OBE places more responsibility on the student (learner) for learning, and this can be difficult for learners to adjust to if they are more used to mastery-based systems where more responsibilities for learning are placed on academics, faculty members and instructors [92].

In addition, there can be conflicts between the learning outcomes required and the role the student is expected to play [86]: for example, students may be being assessed on an assignment, but the learning outcome may require them to "demonstrate leadership".

2.3.2 Structure of learning environment

OBE can be used to ensure that the maximum number of students reaches the desired outcomes. This means that the students may need multiple attempts to demonstrate the competencies, potentially via a diversity of learning opportunities. This may require instructional or pedagogical change to ensure different learning opportunities are acknowledged and valued. Where instructional or pedagogical change occurs, there may also be needed [86]:

- Reform of the curriculum and its design (including assessment)
- New learning and teaching resources
- Revision of the testing and grading procedures
- What actually constitutes a course or subject

The last two may be particularly controversial. Grading, for example, may change to reflect the number of competencies achieved, rather than the level of achievement in a single competency. In addition, grading processes may need to change from being norm-referenced (where marks are scaled until a normal distribution results) to criteria-referenced (where any student who has demonstrated a particular level of achievement gets awarded that grade, irrespective of the size of the class or the number of other students who have been awarded the same grade).

Currently in most higher education institutions, a course, subject, module or unit are defined by a length of time, credit hours and credit points [86]. If subjects, courses, units or modules become goal-defined, then the role of the academic staff/faculty member will change along with additional planning and resource requirements. In addition, the flow of the students through the education system will also change because their progression relates to the achievement of outcomes rather than being related to the particular age of the student [86].

Reform and redesign of the curriculum can also be difficult because the degree of specificity of the learning outcomes needs to be carefully considered [84,86,88]. In providing multiple ways to demonstrate learning, it can be hard to provide valid evidence that the student (learner) has attained the desired outcomes [93], and broad learning outcomes can mean that the goals of the education are not clear to the students (learners), reducing learning motivation and producing surface learning. On the other hand, if the performance criteria are narrowed, then the student's motivation can also be reduced [86].

Therefore, the learning outcomes need to be clearly defined. Often this is not easy, as there are still some fundamental differences in the way learning outcomes are approached. A learning outcome can be affected by values, attitudes and emotions of students [89,110]. This argument has been extended to mean that transferable skills such as teamwork and communication cannot be taught using OBE [84]. It is also argued that it is the learning and teaching activities which produce these effects [84]. Furthermore, specifying learning outcomes which require transferable skill development can be influenced by the culture and demography of the student cohort [85]. For example, "critical thinking" may look different in different cultures and regions. Other researchers claim the opposite – that OBE requires a multidisciplinary approach which may emphasise attitudes, values and dispositions [93].

Additionally, there has been some confusion around the relationship between the teaching and learning activities, the learning outcomes and the assessment [84,102,107]. In some cases, academics/faculty members reported that, even after they have written the learning outcomes, there was no change in their practice, even if the learning outcomes had been used to alter the assessment. In other words, there is often little change to the approach to learning (pedagogy) when OBE is established [107]. In these instances, the development of the learning outcomes can be considered as an "add-on" which results in more work for the academic staff/faculty members, rather than an opportunity to innovate [107].

Sometimes, the constructive alignment of learning cannot be achieved if the assessment is not aligned and revised. Constructive alignment is where the skills students need to acquire are also the skills needed to successfully complete the assessment. Even with a clear understanding of OBE, the academic staff/faculty members can still find it difficult to identify an appropriate method of assessment [82,84,89,90]. Therefore, there may be a reluctance to abandon the traditional assessment formats such as examinations [89].

Issues around assessment highlight that the deployment of learning outcomes ultimately is the responsibility of the individual academics/faculty members [90]. If learning materials, curriculum and assessment need to be significantly changed, the amount of time and resources spent doing so can be a serious impasse [89]. Some academics/faculty members may perceive the setting of learning outcomes as a threat to their academic autonomy [90]. Finally, measuring the value of different learning activities may mean that academics/faculty members need to consult experts outside of their own field, such as cognitive scientists, taking additional time, resources and support [90].

2.3.3 Origins and standards for learning outcomes

Over the last two decades, the higher education institutions in developed and emerging nations have been increasingly involved in continuous improvement of higher education (program) quality assurance in order to evaluate students' learning outcomes of academic programs that they undertake. In Australia, the introduction of OBE in higher education institutions started with the recommendations of 2008 Bradley Review [111]. Based on OBE frameworks operating overseas, the Australian Universities Quality Assurance Agency (AUQAA) – now TEQSA (Tertiary Education Quality and Standards Agency) – introduced OBE in Australia in 2003. Bradley Review Report [112] advocated for OBE for Australian higher education institutions under which the education programs would be taught to national OBE standards with external evaluation as a dimension of quality assurance. Under the newly introduced OBE, assessments across all levels of teaching would have to be designed, undertaken and marked using a rubric matched to the course learning outcomes (CLOs) and finally some of the PLOs (PLOs). It required academic staff/ faculty members to demonstrate acquisition of the CLOs and PLOs from the pre-outcome-based teaching and assessment practices to comply with the OBE [111]. Hence, there were some objections to OBE as it is a "production-based" discourse [82,84]. The OBE makes easier for quality assurance and accreditation organisations, governments and other stakeholders to measure the outcome of effort, qualitatively and quantitatively, and the outcome of an academic program along with the "return on investment". In summary, the OBE enhances an educational system focusing on accountability and assessment rather than deep learning [84].

Another issue was raised about the standard of outcomes in OBE. As within the accreditation criteria, the graduate attributes listed are the minimum requirements for graduate competency. Similarly, the OBE is considered as setting a minimum standard rather than encouraging excellence [84,105].

2.4 Use of learning outcomes to design program(s)

Here, we will discuss how PLOs as well as CLOs can be used to address the graduate attributes/competencies of professional accreditation organisations. Higher education institutions generally specify "graduate attributes" for all their qualifications. Typically, these are expressed as exit outcomes. They can then be the starting point to develop more contextualised PLOs for individual programs.

The example below lists Graduate Attributes of a typical higher education institution in Australia [113]:

a. Graduate Attribute 1 (GA1): Work ready
b. Graduate Attribute 2 (GA2): Global in outlook and competence
c. Graduate Attribute 3 (GA3): Environmentally aware and responsive
d. Graduate Attribute 4 (GA4): Culturally and socially aware
e. Graduate Attribute 5 (GA5): Active and lifelong learners
f. Graduate Attribute 6 (GA6): Innovative

It is obvious that each graduate attribute is very broad, so that typically "key indicators of attainment", or features, of the program which evidence the attainment of the graduate attributes are needed. Some examples of the indicators of attainment for each graduate attribute listed above are shown in Table 2.1.

When designing an engineering program of studies, the graduate attributes of a higher education institution and accreditation criteria (national competency standards/graduate attributes) and/or governmental requirements must be considered. Multiple outcomes can overburden the program design and result in over-assessing the students, resulting in poorer student achievement and over-burdening of the academic staff/faculty members. To make the program design as efficient as possible, "cross-mapping" is undertaken, where equivalencies between each set of graduate attributes/learning outcomes are developed. One specific set of graduate attributes

Table 2.1 Graduate attributes and example indicators of attainment

Graduate attribute	Example indicators of attainment
GA1: Work ready	Apply sound planning and organisational skills that promote and contribute to the strategic planning of their enterprise or organisation.
	Take responsibility for self-management using skills that contribute to personal and career satisfaction and development.
	Use technology in a manner that contributes to the effective management and execution of a range of tasks.
	Use communication and team working skills to promote productive and cohesive relations among employees and to ensure tasks are accomplished effectively.
	(Continued)

Table 2.1 (Continued) Graduate attributes and example indicators of attainment

Graduate attribute	Example indicators of attainment
GA2: Global in outlook and competence	Analyse, evaluate and articulate the implications of diversity for their interpersonal and work relations. Confidently employ and adapt their professional expertise in different cross-border legal, political, economic, cultural and social environments. Engage with the institution's international education and industry networks which provide a wide range of opportunities for students to enhance their education or research experience. Complete a program of study that is internationally relevant.
GA3: Environmentally aware and responsive	Recognise the interrelationship between environmental, social and economic sustainability. Appraise and critique context-appropriate sustainability measures. Take responsibility for critical decision-making in ensuring sustainable outcomes. Appropriately apply their environmental and sustainability literacy in a highly diverse range of contexts.
GA4: Culturally and socially aware	Recognise and respect the role of cultural difference and diversity in work and social contexts. Practise non-discriminatory attitudes in relation to all kinds of difference and diversity, not simply culturally but also those based on gender, religion, sexual orientation, identity and ability. Appraise and critique the potentially powerful social and economic effects of enterprise and business activities on particular groups and individuals. Show understanding of the social and cultural heritage of Aboriginal and Torres Strait Islander peoples in Australia through active engagement with individuals and communities.
GA5: Active and lifelong learners	Adapt their learning approach to suit different tasks. Appropriately extract and apply knowledge and skills in meaningful and transformative ways. Show a commitment to sustained and ongoing personal and career-related learning. Take a benign attitude to error when being creative and innovative, recognising the usefulness of error in opening the possibility for new directions.
GA6: Innovative	Apply an observant mind to all manners of material and non-material matter. Use imaginative processes to transcend traditional ideas, rules, patterns or relationships. Embrace, investigate and respect the worth of divergent thinking. Apply a sophisticated approach to spatial and aesthetic relationships by exploring the appropriate materials to express and communicate ideas.

Source: Adapted from Ref. [113].

is chosen as a base on which to develop the program-level learning outcomes. Equivalencies to the other set(s) of graduate attributes can then be demonstrated via the cross-map.

For accredited programs, or programs which undergo external review by a peak professional body (such as an accreditation organisation), the graduate attributes required by the accreditation organisation are considered foundational.

An example cross-map is shown in Table 2.2, where the graduate attributes of a higher education institution (listed above) are mapped onto the graduate attributes required by Engineers Australia, the national accrediting organisation for engineering programs delivered by Australian higher education institutions.

The process of cross-mapping can then be applied between multiple systems of graduate attributes. A further discussion of this topic is in Chapter 4. Using the foundational graduate attributes required by Engineers Australia (first column in Table 2.2), CLOs for individual courses can then be developed, using the "design

Table 2.2 EA stage I competency and university graduate attributes

Engineers Australia (EA) Stage I graduate attributes/competencies		University graduate attributes
1.1	Comprehensive, theory-based understanding of the underpinning natural and physical sciences and the engineering fundamentals applicable to the engineering discipline.	GA 1, GA 5
1.2	Conceptual understanding of the mathematics, numerical analysis, statistics and computer and information sciences which underpin the engineering discipline.	GA 1, GA 5
1.3	In-depth understanding of specialist bodies of knowledge within the engineering discipline.	GA 1
1.4	Discernment of knowledge development and research directions within the engineering discipline.	GA 6, GA 5
1.5	Knowledge of contextual factors impacting the engineering discipline.	GA 2, GA 3, GA 4
1.6	Understanding of the scope, principles, norms, accountabilities and bounds of contemporary engineering practice in the specific discipline.	GA 1, GA 2
2.1	Application of established engineering methods to complex engineering problem-solving.	GA 1
2.2	Fluent application of engineering techniques, tools and resources.	GA 1
2.3	Application of systematic engineering synthesis and design processes.	GA 1, GA 6
2.4	Application of systematic approaches to the conduct and management of engineering projects.	GA 1
3.1	Ethical conduct and professional accountability.	GA 1
3.2	Effective oral and written communication in professional and lay domains.	GA 1
3.3	Creative, innovative and pro-active demeanour.	GA 6
3.4	Professional use and management of information.	GA 1
3.5	Orderly management of self and professional conduct.	GA 5, GA 1
3.6	Effective team membership and team leadership.	GA 1

Source: Adapted from Ref. [100].

down" approach. Once the outcomes for each course are determined, the curriculum is then structured from the "bottom up".

The final step is then to ensure "constructive alignment" within each course: that the assessment used in each course can be demonstrably shown to measure the learning outcomes for that course. The next section examines the development of learning outcomes for an individual course, subject, module or unit.

2.4.1 How to construct course learning outcomes

Consider a foundational course/subject/unit/module in Dynamics of Mechanical Systems. In such a course, it would be expected that the following three graduate attributes from Engineers Australia may be covered:

> EA 1.1 Comprehensive, theory based understanding of the underpinning natural and physical sciences and the engineering fundamentals applicable to the engineering discipline
> EA 1.3 In-depth understanding of specialist bodies of knowledge within the engineering discipline
> EA 2.2 Fluent application of engineering techniques, tools and resources. [106]

These attributes need to be contextualised for the discipline in question and resolved into learning outcomes which can be demonstrated by the students. That is, the learning outcomes need to be actions, which can be measured and related to the graduate attributes. More simply, the learning outcomes need to address the graduate attributes by explaining what the student should be able to do after the successful completion of the course. In this case, we might express the outcomes thus:

- Predict the effects of force, motion and their interaction in the design and operational cycles of machines and mechanical components
- Solve, analyse and synthesise a wide variety of practical engineering dynamics problems in a logical and effective manner. [114]

It is important to note that the learning outcomes start with verbs, indicating that they are actionable and measurable. In practice, extensive use of Bloom's Taxonomy [115] aids in expressing the learning outcomes and provides a means for scaffolding cognitive skills throughout the program: that is, it would be expected that lower-order cognitive skills would be learning outcomes in the initial, foundational stages of a program (qualification), with higher-order cognitive skills being demonstrated in learning outcomes in the later years of a program. In the above example, the learning outcomes are mid- to higher-order skills in the application, analysis and synthesis streams [115]. How learning outcomes are developed sequentially through a program of studies is covered in more detail in Chapter 4.

Bloom's taxonomy is a set of three hierarchical models used to classify educational learning objectives into levels of complexity and specificity. The three models cover the learning objectives in: (a) cognitive domain, (b) affective domain and (c) sensory/psychomotor domain. The cognitive objectives have been the primary focus of most traditional education and are frequently used to structure curriculum learning objectives, assessments and activities.

All three models were named after Benjamin Bloom, a Pennsylvania-born American educational psychologist, who made contributions to the classification of educational objectives and to the theory of mastery learning. He chaired the committee of educators that devised the taxonomy. He also edited the first volume of the standard text, Taxonomy of Educational Objectives: The Classification of Educational Goals [116–118].

The cognitive domain (knowledge-based) includes (i) knowledge, (ii) comprehension, (iii) application, (iv) analysis, (v) synthesis and (vi) evaluation.

The affective domain (emotion-based) encompasses (i) receiving, (ii) responding, (iii) valuing, (iv) organising and (v) characterising.

The sensory or psychomotor domain (action-based) deals with (i) perception, (ii) set, (iii) guided response, (iv) mechanism, (v) complex overt response, (vi) adaptation and (vii) origination.

Here we can see that the first two graduate attributes from Engineers Australia are associated with the first CLO, and the last graduate attribute is related to the second CLO. In other words, it can be shown that the CLOs relate to the PLOs (see Table 2.3) and that cross-mapping between the two sets of learning outcomes is possible.

Once the CLOs are established, then the assessment can be designed such that successful completion of the assessment requires the students (learners) to have developed the skill listed by the CLOs (constructive alignment). For example, here we might use the following assessments:

*   Laboratory Work 1: Projectile Motion
*   Laboratory Work 2: Mass Moment of Inertia
    The cognitive domain (knowledge-based) of Bloom's taxonomy is shown in Figure 2.3.

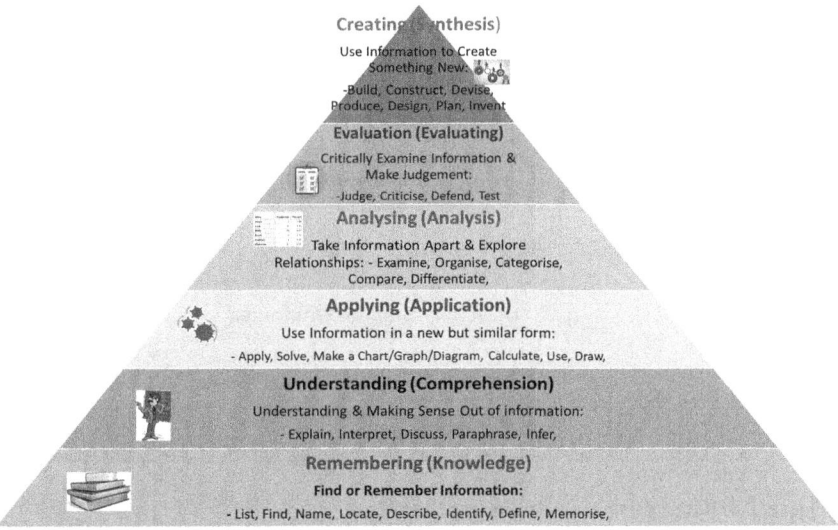

Figure 2.3 Bloom's taxonomy for learning.

These support the development of "EA 2.2 Fluent application of engineering techniques, tools and resources".
- Class tests and examinations

The above assessment tasks support the development of "EA 1.1 Comprehensive, theory based understanding of the underpinning natural and physical sciences and the engineering fundamentals applicable to the engineering discipline" and "EA 1.3 In-depth understanding of specialist bodies of knowledge within the engineering discipline".

Each of these assessments requires the learning outcomes to be taught (T), practised (P) and measured (M), because all three activities (TPM) are covered in the course. It is therefore reasonable to expect that the learning outcomes will be achieved by all successful students.

Finally, a general statement about curriculum can be developed by designing "up" to achieve the learning outcomes by the end of the course:

> In this course you will study the state of rest or motion of bodies under the action of a single force or multiple forces. Therefore, this course deals with Newton's Second Law of Motion which is the foundation for the design and analysis of various structural, mechanical and electrical devices found in a wide range of engineering applications. You will study the kinematics and kinetics of particles and rigid bodies using force and acceleration, work and energy, and impulse and momentum principles [114].

The process of construction of learning outcomes for a specific course, module, unit or subject is thus similar to reverse engineering, where we know what we want the student to achieve and we work backwards from the final result. The diagram in Figure 2.4 clearly shows the fundamental importance of the professional accreditation stage 1

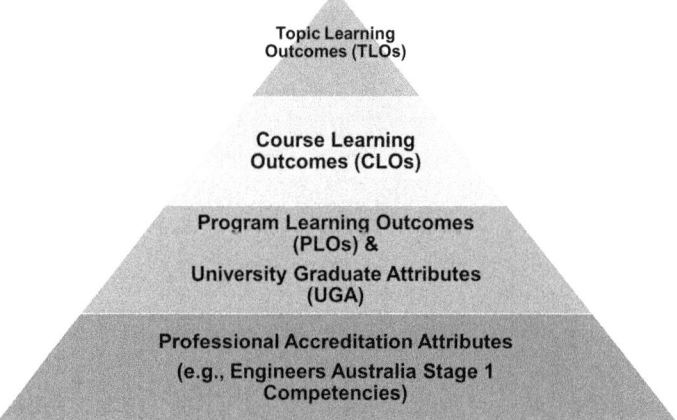

Figure 2.4 The "designing down approach".

competencies as providing a foundation upon which the graduate attributes/PLOs are derived.

It may be noted that the individual higher education institution can develop its own PLOs. However, in this case, the higher education institution must map its PLOs against the accrediting organisation's national competency standards (e.g. stage 1 competencies of Engineers Australia). This is why it is highly recommended to adopt or closely align the higher education institution's individual PLOs to the accrediting organisation's stage 1 competencies. In doing so, additional effort, time and anxiety of the program coordinator/program, director/course, leader/program manager and academic staff/faculty members and students can be reduced. Once the PLOs are established, CLOs, and finally topic learning outcomes, can be developed.

One of the important tasks in outcome-based learning and teaching is the effective design of assessment tasks with appropriate weighting. The assessment tasks need to be designed such that they provide equal opportunities for high achievement by all students starting from slow learners to speed learners. There should not be more than three types of assessment for the CLOs. For example, the aforementioned dynamics course or module or unit or subject has three assessment types (class test, two laboratory practices and the end-of-semester examination). The weightings allocated for these three assessment types are as follows:

Class Test: 20% of the total marks
Laboratory Practices (each 15%): $15 \times 2 = 30\%$ of the total marks
Final Examination: 50% of the total marks

The three assessments add up to 100%, and an overall score of 50% is considered the minimum mark which demonstrates achievement of the CLOs.

It is worth noting that an assessment rubric (assessment marking scheme) must be designed and clearly explained to students so that they understand the academic standards of the course they are undertaking. Students also need to be informed about the CLOs as well as which PLOs are addressed by the course. Examples of an outcome-based Course Guide and Program Guide are included as Appendices to this chapter.

Once all the core courses, with their learning outcomes, have been developed, a check can be made across the whole program to ensure all the required graduate attributes have been covered by the core courses, modules, subjects or units. This process can also be done during a general review cycle to identify any gaps or redundancies in the skill development of the students (learners). An example of a program-wide map for a typical mechanical engineering program is shown in Table 2.3, where the CLOs for individual courses have been related to the graduate attributes required by Engineers Australia. It may be noted that this mechanical engineering program's PLOs are the same as Engineers Australia's stage 1 competencies. Typically, mapping is only required for core or compulsory courses, modules, units or subjects but not for elective courses, because the PLOs/GAs must be demonstrated by all students within a program. If key PLOs are contingent on elective choices, then not all students are given the opportunity to demonstrate complete graduate attribute attainment. The individual courses are listed by shortened course name.

Table 2.3 Mapping of program-level learning outcomes of a 4-year B.Eng. (Mechanical Engineering) program

PLOs	Year 1	Year 2	Year 3	Year 4
Knowledge and skill base				
EA1.1 Comprehensive, theory-based understanding of the underpinning natural and physical sciences and the engineering fundamentals applicable to the engineering discipline.	Mechanics/materials 1 Fluid mechanics	Design and build Mechanics/materials 2 Dynamics 1	Mechanics 3 Mechanical vibrations	
EA1.2 Conceptual understanding of the mathematics, numerical analysis, statistics, and computer and information sciences which underpin the engineering discipline.	Entry maths Further maths Manufacturing	Maths and statistics Design and build	Mechanical vibrations Finite element analysis	
EA1.3 In-depth understanding of specialist bodies of knowledge within the engineering discipline.	Manufacturing	Dynamics 1 Mechanical design	Mechanics 3 Mechanical vibrations Mechanical design 2 Dynamics 2	Renewable energy
EA1.4 Discernment of knowledge development and research directions within the engineering discipline.			Finite element analysis Finite element analysis Research methods	Project 1 Project 2
EA1.5 Knowledge of contextual factors impacting the engineering discipline.	Humanitarian eng. project Thermodynamics Fluid mechanics		Mechanical design 2 Engineering enterprise	Renewable Energy Project 1 Project 2
EA1.6 Understanding of the scope, principles, norms, accountabilities and bounds of contemporary engineering practice in the specific discipline.	Humanitarian eng. project		Mechanical design 2 Engineering enterprise Research methods	Renewable Energy Project 1 Project 2

(Continued)

Table 2.3 (Continued) Mapping of program-level learning outcomes of a 4-year B.Eng. (Mechanical Engineering) program

PLOs	Year 1	Year 2	Year 3	Year 4
EA2.1 Application of established engineering methods to complex engineering problem solving.	Fluid mechanics	Design and build Mechanics/materials 2	Mechanics 3 Mechanical design 2 Dynamics 2 Finite element analysis Engineering enterprise	Control theory Renewable Energy Project 1 Project 2
EA2.2 Fluent application of engineering techniques, tools and resources.	Mechanics/materials 1 Fluid mechanics Thermodynamics	Maths and statistics Dynamics 1 Design and build Mechanics/materials 2 Mechanical design	Mechanical vibrations Mechanical design 2 Dynamics 2 Finite element analysis Computational analysis	Control theory Renewable Energy Project 1 Project 2
EA2.3 Application of systematic engineering synthesis and design processes.	Humanitarian eng. project Computer-aided design	Design and build Mechanical design	Mechanical design 2 dynamics 2 Engineering enterprise	Project 1 Project 2
EA2.4 Application of systematic approaches to the conduct and management of engineering projects.	Humanitarian eng. project	Design and build	Engineering enterprise Research methods	Project 1 Project 2
EA3.1 Ethical conduct and professional accountability	Humanitarian eng. project		Mechanical design 2 Engineering enterprise Research methods	Project 1 Project 2
EA3.2 Effective oral and written communication in professional and lay domains.	Humanitarian eng. project Mechanics/materials 1 Fluid mechanics Thermodynamics	Design and build Mechanics/materials 2	Engineering enterprise Research methods	Project 1 Project 2
EA3.3 Creative, innovative and proactive demeanour.	Humanitarian eng. project	Design and build Mechanical design	Mechanical design 2	Project 1 Project 2
EA3.4 Professional use and management of information.	Humanitarian eng. project	Design and build Mechanics/materials 2	Mechanical design 2 Research methods	Project 1 Project 2
EA3.5 Orderly management of self and professional conduct.	Humanitarian eng. project	Mechanical design	Engineering enterprise	Renewable Energy Project 1 Project 2
EA3.6 Effective team membership and team leadership.	Humanitarian eng. project	Design and build	Engineering enterprise	Project 1 Project 2

From Table 2.3, it can be seen, by examining the rows, whether the graduate attributes are covered within all years (year 1–4). In this instance, there is an obvious gap, where the students do not engage with research in their discipline until third year (fourth row). However, it would be expected that the foundational knowledge was concentrated in the first 2 years, with more advanced and cutting-edge applications examined in the later years.

If a more nuanced view is required, then the "taught-practice-measure" or TPM scale can be used to provide more detailed information. In this process, each learning outcome in each course, subject, module or unit is examined to determine whether the outcome is "taught" (there is content), the outcome is then "practised" (by the students), and finally, whether that same outcome is "measured" (i.e. there is assessment relating to it). This approach highlights where, for example, some learning outcomes in first year may only be taught and practised, but that measurement is performed later on in the program of studies as the students mature. In an ideal situation, a learning outcome is achieved only when it is taught, practised and measured at least once at different levels of complexity. An example of the TPM scheme is shown in Table 2.4.

The PLOs in Table 2.4 have the same numbers as the EA Attributes listed in Table 2.3. In Table 2.4, we can see that for PLOs EA1.1 and EA1.2, which refer to fundamental concepts, the TPM is concentrated in the first 2 years of a program of studies. By third and fourth year, these concepts might be revisited (TP) but not assessed (M).

Other PLOs such as EA1.4, EA1.5, EA1.6 and EA2.2, which relate to the knowledge of current research, contextual factors in engineering design, accountabilities and solving complex problems, are outcomes which require the knowledge of fundamentals with some experience and maturity, and therefore, these PLOs are addressed in the last 2 years of the program, after the student has had some experience. Similarly, PLOs EA2.3 and EA2.4, which relate to design and synthesis, are "higher" learning outcomes using Bloom's taxonomy, and therefore, these would be measured in the later years of study and may not be present until then either.

Some PLOs are relevant across all years (such as EA2.2, which relates to the use of tools and resources), but the complexity of the tools used and the problems solved may increase in complexity as the student continues with their education.

In short, the TPM approach allows academic staff/faculty members to view the PLOs as experienced by the student. It is easy then to see gaps and redundancies: both across the rows to see if any one course, subject, unit or module does too much or not enough assessment and down the columns to see if there are particular PLOs which are not covered sufficiently.

Such mapping allows for constant improvement, quality control and innovation, and is a core advantage for OBE.

The validity of the TPM matrix can be assured by examining the weightings of all assessments and the marking criteria for each assessment. This information then allows a percentage to be put against each PLO, within each piece of assessment. This can be demonstrated in Table 2.5, where the assessment weightings for Year 2 and Year 3 of a B.Eng. (Mechanical Engineering) program (a different plan) have been divided among learning outcomes. (Note: Table 2.5 is an extract from a complete program plan.)

For example, Mechanics of Machines (the first course/subject row) has percentages associated with learning outcomes 1.1, 1.3 and 2.2, and it can be clearly seen that most

Table 2.4 The mapping of TPM across a whole program for students

Subject titles and credit points		1.1	1.2	1.3	1.4	1.5	1.6	2.1	2.2	2.3	2.4	3.1	3.2	3.3	3.4	3.5	3.6
							PLOs that accord with EA stage 1 competencies										
Year 1																	
Humanitarian engineering project	12						TPM	TPM	TP		TPM	TPM	TPM	TPM	TPM	TPM	TPM
Entry mathematics	12	TPM	TPM						TP								
Computer-aided design	12	TPM	TP	TPM					TPM				TPM	TPM		TPM	TPM
Mechanics/materials 1	12	TPM	TP	TPM				TP								TPM	TPM
Thermodynamics	12	TPM	TP	TPM				TP									
Further mathematics	12	TPM	TPM	TPM													
Manufacturing	12	TPM	TP	TPM			TP	TP	TP				TPM		TPM	TPM	
Fluid mechanics	12	TPM	TP	TPM			TP	TP	TPM								
Year 2																	
Math and statistics	12	TPM	TPM	TPM													
Design and build	12	TPM	TPM	TPM			TPM	TPM	TPM	TPM	TP	TPM	TPM	TPM	TP	TP	TP
Mechanics/materials 2	12	TPM	TP	TPM					TPM			TPM	TPM			TP	TP
Dynamics 1	12	TPM	TPM	T		TP		TP	TPM						TP		
Mechanical design	24	TP	TP	TPM		TP		TPM	TPM	TPM	TP	TPM					
Year 3																	
Research methods	12	T	T	TPM	TP	TPM	TPM		TP	TPM	TPM	TPM	TP	TPM	TPM	TP	TPM
Mechanics 3	12	TP	TPM	TPM	TPM	T	TPM		TPM	TP	TPM	TPM	TP			TP	
Mechanical vibrations	12	TP	TPM	TPM	TPM	T			TPM	TP	T	T	TPM	TPM	TPM		
Mechanical design 2	12	TP	T	TPM	TPM	TPM	TP		TPM	TP	TPM	T	TP	TPM	TP	TP	
Finite element analysis	12	TP	TPM	TPM	TPM	T	T		TPM	TP	TP	T	TP	TP	TP	TP	
Engineering enterprise	12	T	T		TPM	TP	TPM		TP	T	TPM	TP	TP	TP	TP		TPM
Year 4																	
Project 1	24	TP	TP	TP	TPM	TPM	TPM	TPM	TPM	TPM	TPM	TP	TPM	TPM	TPM	TPM	TPM
Project 2	24	TP	TP	TP	TPM	TPM	TPM	TPM	TPM	TPM	TPM	TP	TPM	TPM	TPM	TPM	TPM
Renewable energy systems	12	TP	TPM	TP	TPM	TPM	TP	TP	TPM	TP	TP	TP	TP	TP	TP	TP	TP

Table 2.5 Assessment percentages are divided amongst the relevant learning outcomes to check the validity of the relevant TPM table

Course code and titles	Programme outcomes															
	1.1	1.2	1.3	1.4	1.5	1.6	2.1	2.2	2.3	2.4	3.1	3.2	3.3	3.4	3.5	3.6
XXXX Mechanics of machines 1	TPM		TPM	T	T	T	TP	TPM	T			TP				TP
Assignment 1 (10%)	5		5													
Assignment 2 (10%)	5		5													
Class Test (15%)	10		5													
Lab experiment (15%)								15								
Exam (50%)	30		20													
YYYY Mechanics of fluids and solids 2	TPM		TPM	T	T	T	TP	TPM	TP			TPM	T	T		TPM
Assignment 1 (15%)	5		5									5				
Assignment 2 (15%)	5		5									5				
Lab experiment (20%)								10				5				5
Exam (50%)			50													
ZZZZ Further thermofluid mechanics	TPM	TP	TPM	T	T	T	TPM	TPM	T			TP		T		TP
Assignment 1 (10%)	5		5													
Assignment 2 (10%)	5		5													
Presentation (15%)	5		5				5									
Lab experiment (15%)								15								
Exam (50%)	15		20				15									
AAAA Solid mechanics 3	TPM		TPM		T	T	TP	TPM				TP				TP
Weekly exercises (20%)	10							10								
Lab experiment (5%)			5													
Test (25%)	**15**							**10**								
Exam (50%)	**35**							**15**								

(Continued)

Table 2.5 (Continued) Assessment percentages are divided amongst the relevant learning outcomes to check the validity of the relevant TPM table

Course code and titles	Programme outcomes															
	1.1	1.2	1.3	1.4	1.5	1.6	2.1	2.2	2.3	2.4	3.1	3.2	3.3	3.4	3.5	3.6
BBBB Management of mechanical design and research					TPM	TPM	TP	TPM	TPM	TPM	TPM	TP	TPM	TPM	TPM	TPM
Product rev Assig (20%)					5	5								5		5
Product des Assn (40%)						10		10	5				10		5	5
Exam (40%)					5			5	5	10	10					
CCCC Mechanical design 2			TPM		TPM	TPM	TPM	TPM	TP	TP	TPM	TP	TPM	TPM	TP	TP
Project part A (20%)			5		5	10										
Project part B (30%)			5		5	5	10						5			
Exam (50%)			10					20	10	10						
DDDD Dynamics and control	TPM	TPM	TPM				TP	TPM	T			TP				TP
Assignment 1 (15%)	15															
Assignment 2 (15%)		10	5													
Test (20%)		15						5								
Exam (50%)		15	5					10								
EEEE Mechanics of machines 2		TP	TPM		T	T	TP	TPM	TPM	TP	T	TP		T		TP
Assignment (40%)			30						10							
Lab experiment (10%)								10								
Exam (50%)			40					10								
FFFF Finite element analysis	T	TPM	TPM	T			TP	TPM	T			TP		TP		TP
Assignment 1 (15%)																
Assignment 2 (20%)																
Assignment 3 (25%)																
Exam (40%)																
GGGG Renewable energy systems		TPM	TP	TPM	TPM	TP	TPM	TPM	T			TP		TPM		TP

(Continued)

Table 2.5 (Continued) Assessment percentages are divided amongst the relevant learning outcomes to check the validity of the relevant TPM table

Course code and titles	Programme outcomes															
	1.1	1.2	1.3	1.4	1.5	1.6	2.1	2.2	2.3	2.4	3.1	3.2	3.3	3.4	3.5	3.6
Assignment 1 (15%)		5		5			5							5	5	
Assignment 2 (15%)							5	5						5		
Quiz 1 (10%)							5	5								
Quiz 2 (10%)							5									
Exam (50%)			10		10		15	15								
HHHH Advanced engineering control	TP	TPM	TPM	T		T	TP	TPM	TP			TP				TP
Assignment 1 (25%)		10	10					5								
Assignment 2 (25%)		10	10					5								
Exam (50%)		20	20					10								
IIII Applied heat and mass transfer	TP	T	TPM	T		TPM	TPM	TPM	TPM		T	TP		TP		TP
Assignment (20%)			5			5			10							
Experimental analysis (20%)						5	20									
Exam (60%)			35					25								
JJJJ Research project 1		TP	TPM	TPM	TPM	TP	TPM	TPM	TPM	TPM	TP	TPM	TPM	TPM	TPM	TP
Project proposal (20%)				10	10											
Logbook and meeting (15%)			10	10			5									
Written report (40%)								5	5	5		10		5		
Poster (10%)												5	5			
Presentation (15%)										5			5			
KKKK Research project 2	TP	TP	TPM	TPM	TPM	TP	TPM	TPM	TPM	TPM	TP	TPM	TPM	TPM	TPM	TP
Logbook and meeting (15%)		10					5									
Thesis (60%)			10	10	5		5	5	5	5		5	5	5	5	
Research paper (10%)			5									5	5			
Presentation (15%)										5						
	1.1	1.2	1.3	1.4	1.5	1.6	2.1	2.2	2.3	2.4	3.1	3.2	3.3	3.4	3.5	3.6

Note: A different TPM table was used to derive the percentages other than shown in Table 2.4.

of the weighting is for learning outcome 1.1. This is a check as to which learning outcomes are actually being measured.

Going down the rows, it is also possible to derive a total number of percentage points for each learning outcome. Once the total number of percentage points in the whole program is established, then the overall weighting (or relative importance) of each learning outcome can be measured. This allows the academic teaching team to ensure the emphasis is placed in the correct areas and to re-distribute the assessment weightings (or re-design the assessment criteria) if the emphasis is not ideal.

It can be seen therefore that both a holistic (Table 2.3) and detailed (Tabled 2.4) map of PLOs needs to be constructed to create a complete picture of a program of studies.

Chapter 3

International accreditation framework

At present, there are over half a dozen various bilateral, regional and intercontinental agreement schemes for mutual recognition of engineering qualifications across national boundaries. However, there are only two major agreement schemes that are globally dominant. These two major agreement schemes are the EUR-ACE® labelling scheme, which is administered by the European Network for Accreditation of Engineering Education (ENAEE) and the Washington Accord, administered through the International Engineering Alliance (IEA).

This chapter discusses both schemes in detail and concludes with a simple comparison of the requirements of the two schemes.

3.1 European network for accreditation of engineering education

3.1.1 Historical background

In 1998, Germany, France, the UK and Italy signed the Sorbonne Declaration, which expressed the desire to encourage modifications to national higher education systems to allow greater mobility of professionals, which would allow for closer cooperation between nations. Such modifications would allow the formation of the European Area of Higher Education (EAHE) as a means to enable European mobility and employability of graduates through the European Union [119,120].

One year later, in 1999, 29 countries of the European Union signed the Bologna Declaration (Bologna Agreement) to develop a "system of easily readable and comparable degrees" with a view to enabling European citizen graduates to work anywhere within the European Union (EU) [119,120]. The original 29 signatories of the Bologna Declaration are shown in Table 3.1.

The Declaration led to the harmonisation of qualifications, credits and quality assurance processes within higher education systems in the EU. Further agreement was signed to ensure that curriculum, institutional cooperation and mobility schemes for both students and researchers were established and that they retained the necessary European dimensions.

The Bologna Declaration recognises two main cycles (types) of higher education qualifications: (a) "first cycle" comprising a minimum 3-year qualification and (b) "second cycle" leading to a master and/or doctoral qualification.

Table 3.1 Original signatories of Bologna Declaration

The Bologna Declaration signatories

• Austria	• Germany	• Luxembourg	• Slovenia
• Belgium	• Greece	• Malta	• Spain
• Bulgaria	• Hungary	• Netherlands	• Sweden
• Czech Republic	• Iceland	• Norway	• Switzerland
• Denmark	• Ireland	• Poland	• United Kingdom (UK)
• Estonia	• Italy	• Portugal	
• Finland	• Latvia	• Romania	
• France	• Lithuania	• Slovak Republic	

Source: Adapted from Ref. [119].

In 2000, the European Standing Observatory for the Engineering Professional and Education (ESOEPE) was established [120–122]. In 2004, the European Commission initiated, through the EUR-ACE label, the development of accreditation standards for both higher education institutions and engineering programs within European nations. These standards were developed to distinguish between "first cycle" and "second cycle" qualifications [120–122].

The EUR-ACE project ended in 2006, when ESOEPE was transformed into the ENAEE [2–4]. The ENAEE was created to oversee the awarding of the EUR-ACE label (EURopean Accredited Engineer). The ENAEE formally commenced the EUR-ACE system of accreditation in 2007.

At present, only 15 countries' professional engineering organisations (agencies) of the 29 original Bologna Declaration signatories accredit engineering programs within their own country and award the EUR-ACE label. Table 3.2 lists the ENAEE-authorised national accrediting organisations that provide that label. The ENAEE ensures that all 15 national accrediting organisations follow and comply with the EUR-ACE Framework, Standards and Guidelines (EAFSG) when awarding the EUR-ACE label [122]. The national accrediting organisations award the label to specific engineering programs at either the first- or second-cycle level.

3.1.2 EUR-ACE framework, standards and guidelines

The EUR-ACE Framework Standard and Guidelines detail not only the requirements on programs to be EUR-ACE-accredited but also the requirements on accrediting organisations that allow accrediting organisations to award the EUR-ACE label. The process is shown in Figure 3.1.

The following sections elaborate the EUR-ACE framework.

3.1.2.1 Standards and guidelines for accrediting organisations

It is the expectation of ENAEE that accrediting organisations have developed their own quality assurance processes to monitor their internal processes. Nevertheless, there is an expectation that the accrediting organisations should follow standards which are internationally accepted. Each accrediting organisation will have its own

Table 3.2 ENAEE-authorised national accreditation organisations

	Country	Accreditation organisation	Web address
1	Germany	Fachakkreditierungsagentur für Studiengänge der Ingenieurwissenschaften, der Informatik, der Naturwissenschaften, und der Mathematik e.V. (ASIIN)	www.asiin.de
2	France	Commission des Titres d'Ingénieur (CTI)	www.cti-commission.fr
3	UK	Engineering Council (EC)	www.engc.org.uk
4	Ireland	Engineers Ireland (EI)	www.engineersireland.ie
5	Portugal	Ordem dos Engenheiros (ODE)	www.ordemengenheiros.pt
6	Russia	Association for Engineering Education of Russia (AEER)	www.aeer.ru
7	Turkey	Association for Evaluation and Accreditation of Engineering Programs (MÜDEK)	www.mudek.org.tr
8	Romania	The Romanian Agency for Quality Assurance in Higher Education (ARACIS)	www.aracis.ro
9	Italy	Agenzia per la Certificazione di Qualità e l'Accreditamento EUR-ACE dei Corsi di Studio in Ingegneria (QUACING)	www.quacing.it;
10	Poland	Komisja Akredytacyjna Uczelni Technicznych (KAUT)	www.kaut.agh.edu.pl
11	Switzerland	Schweizerische Agentur für Akkreditierung und Qualitätssicherung (AAQ)	www.aaq.ch
12	Spain	National Agency for Quality Assessment and Accreditation of Spain (ANECA), www.aneca.es (in conjunction with IIE – Instituto de la Ingeniería de España)	www.iies.es
13	Finland	Korkeakoulujen arviointineuvosto KKA (FINEEC)	http://karvi.fi/en/
14	Slovakia	Zväz slovenských vedeckotechnických spoločností (ZSVTS)	www.zsvts.sk
15	Kazakhstan	Kazakhstan Society for Engineering Education (KazSEE)	www.kazsee.kz

Source: Adapted from Ref. [120–122].

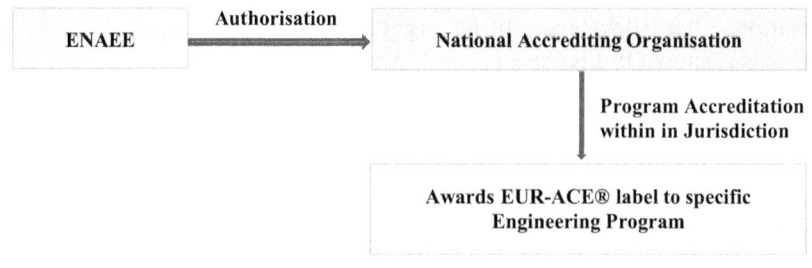

Figure 3.1 EUR-ACE awarding process under ENAEE framework.

history and tradition, and the standards and guidelines are not intended to be prescriptive. However, where there are significant deviations from current, recognised best practice, the accrediting organisation needs to provide significant evidence that its processes are equivalent and of an internationally accepted standard [119–124].

There are seven criteria (also called phases) for EUR-ACE label accreditation competency that each national accrediting organisation must adhere to:

a. Procedures
b. Documentation
c. Accreditation Process
d. Decision-Making
e. Publication
f. Quality Assurance of Accreditation Functions
g. Quality Assurance: Status and Resources.

Each criterion is discussed in turn.

a. **Procedures**
   The most important aspect of an accreditation organisation's procedures is that the organisation needs to demonstrate that the accreditation process occurs with the consultation of all the relevant stakeholders and that the accrediting organisation reviews its methods and standards for accreditation on a regular basis. In particular, the accreditation agency needs to be aware of the continued impact of technology on both the way professional engineers work as well as the way teaching and learning occurs within the higher education environment [121,122].
   Consultation with stakeholders allows the accrediting organisation to remain abreast (up-to-date) with changes in the engineering profession and within higher education institutions. However, it is vital that the higher education institutions should not see innovation as a threat to future accreditation.
   Accreditation organisations can assist higher education institutions in this sense by disseminating good practices in the use of technology in the delivery of curriculum. The member international accrediting organisations on the accreditation board (AB) can provide insight into the future trends in professional practices beyond the national boundary.

b. **Documentation**
   The key requirement with documentation is that all accreditation standards and documents are publicly available (preferably online) and up to date. Where there are online documents, effort must be made to ensure that the documents can easily be located and downloaded. Online documentation must also have an obvious process of version control. Any changes to procedures will require a supporting change to documentation, and these changes must be communicated to all stakeholders [121,122].
   Accreditation standards used by the accrediting organisation should be explicit and comprehensive. In addition, there should be a clear explanation of the accreditation process and the format required for any reports.

c. **Accreditation Process**

The accreditation process must include a self-assessment report from the higher education institution seeking accreditation. In addition, the accrediting organisation should have a site visit to develop a complete picture of the resources available to the students and the learning environment in general. The accrediting organisation should also have the opportunity to meet with the management (various levels) of the higher education institution, the academic staff/faculty members, current students, graduates and employers of the specific program being put up for accreditation [121,122].

During accreditation, the accrediting organisation is represented by an accreditation panel. It is expected that the panel members are trained in the process of accreditation so that they are able to assess evidence which may be presented in a variety of forms: be able to ask clarifying questions and be competent in their judgement of accreditation status. It is recommended that the accreditation panel should comprise at least three people with adequate representation from the relevant engineering disciplines (e.g. a senior academic with a focus on learning and teaching, a practising mid- or higher-level professional engineer and a program-specific senior academic). An observer from the international accrediting organisation can also be included in the panel composition [121,122].

The self-assessment report and the site visit need to demonstrate sufficient information for the accreditation panel to make its decision without making any unnecessary or excessive demands. The accrediting organisation should ensure that it has specified the format, content and detail that are required within the self-assessment report.

The site visit can be of varying length and typically the agenda for the site visit is set by the accrediting agency. During the site visit, the accreditation panel should be able to see the teaching and support facilities.

Usually, the accreditation panel asks for examples of student work, so that the academic rigor of the program of studies can be established. In some instances, the examples of student work are submitted to the accrediting agency before the site visit; in other cases, the examples are examined during the site visit. The order is determined by the accrediting agency.

The self-assessment report and all other relevant documentation are submitted by the higher education institution to the accrediting organisation at least 1 month before the site visit. This must be factored into the overall schedule to ensure that the education institution has sufficient time to gather all the required evidence.

Finally, any template the accrediting organisation uses to confirm accreditation should be publicly available, and the education institution should be cognisant of the basis for the accreditation decision.

d. **Decision-making**

The accreditation panel follows the accreditation process, including site visits, interviews and the interpretation of evidence, and completes a report with recommendations. However, the final determination of the accreditation status is made by the AB, which is separate from the accreditation panel. Before the panel submits its report to the board, the higher education institution is allowed to check the facts of the report. Generally, a member of the accreditation panel presents the accreditation report to the AB for its decision. The AB then makes the decision on whether to give the EUR-ACE label to program completely or partially. It may be noted that any AB usually has a range of accreditation decisions. During this decision-making process, any board member with any past or present connection to the education institution should not be present [121,122].

The process of appointing the AB needs to be well-documented, and the board's rules, procedures and terms of reference also need to be publicly available. It is expected that board membership would represent all sectors of the engineering profession.

The accrediting organisation should also be able to demonstrate that it has procedures for (i) recording decisions, (ii) communicating those decisions to the higher education institutions, (iii) tracking any follow-up actions and (iv) dealing with appeals against an accreditation decision. The process of making a decision in relation to the accreditation outcome needs to be well-documented, and the final accreditation decision needs to be accepted by all the stakeholders [121,122].

e. **Publication**

All accreditation decisions and their currency need to be published. Higher education institutions should be allowed to use accreditation decisions in their institutions' promotional documentation. To foster a common understanding of best practice, accrediting organisations should consider making some parts of the accreditation reports public, as long as this does not breach compliance with confidentiality policies and procedures [121,122].

f. **Quality Assurance of Accreditation Functions**

The organisational structure of the accrediting organisation and all of its processes must be transparent. The procedures and rules of the accrediting organisation should be documented and publicly available. Furthermore, the accrediting organisation should be able to demonstrate that they have quality assurance processes such as a regular review cycle. Review cycle reports of the accrediting organisation's activities are ideally assessed externally. Such reports and reviews should include the opportunity for the accrediting organisation to receive feedback from its external stakeholders [121,122].

g. **Quality Assurance: Status and Resources**

The accrediting organisation must be recognised by the engineering profession within its jurisdiction to have the responsibility for accreditation. Such recognition can be formal and legal, or informal but demonstrable. The standards used by the accrediting organisation need to have been collectively established by the profession. It is important, therefore, that the accrediting organisation receives the support from the profession. However, it is vital that the organisation has financial independence and can demonstrate that there are no conflicts of interest in its operations and funding [121,122].

3.1.2.2 Standards and guidelines for accreditation of engineering programs

The EUR-ACE label was developed during the same time that the European Qualifications Framework (EQF) was established, and therefore, measures were taken to ensure that the EUR-ACE label complies with the EQF, which specifies student loadings for both Bachelor (first cycle) and Master/PhD (second cycle) qualifications. The first-cycle degrees must have 180, 210 or 240 credits of the European Credit Transfer System (ECTS) and the second-cycle degree (Master's/PhD) must have 60, 90 or 120 ECT credits. Note that 1 ECTS constitutes around 25–30 hours of work [123].

The accreditation criteria for programs under the EUR-ACE label therefore specify student loads – a considerable difference from the other international agreement, the Washington Accord, for example, which will be examined in the next chapter.

The accreditation criteria for programs can be categorised as follows [124]:

a.   student workload requirements
b.   program outcomes framework
c.   program management.

Each category is discussed below focussing on the requirements for the first-cycle (Bachelor of Engineering) qualifications.

a.   **Student Workload**
     The sole requirement for bachelor's degree engineering programs is that the program comprises a minimum of 180 ECTS [124].
b.   **Program Outcomes Framework**
     The EUR-ACE standards use the phrase "Learning Outcome" to define **skills, knowledge, understanding** and **abilities** that a student can demonstrate after the successful completion of a module, unit, subject or course. Additionally, the "Program Learning Outcomes" (PLOs) are considered to be the minimum requirement for graduation. The "PLOs" are the knowledge, skill, understanding and ability of students after successful completion of the program (i.e. core courses, units, subjects, courses, modules, etc.) [124,125].

     The standard, however, while prescribing the Learning Outcomes, does not specify how these outcomes are to be achieved, leaving delivery, curriculum development, assessment and learning activities up to the discretion of the higher education institution. Moreover, it is at the discretion of the higher education institution to set appropriate requirements for entry into the program [120,124,125].

     Usually, the PLOs are written such that these guide the process of learning which is assessed, not individual students within the program. Therefore, the accreditation is for the program of studies but not for the individual graduate engineers. For this reason, the standard refers to cycle 1 competencies rather than PLOs [120,124,125].

     Table 3.3 lists the cycle 1 competencies for the Bachelor of Engineering program, in accordance with the EUR-ACE standards. The emphasis in bold is the authors' interpretation of the key phrases and qualifiers within each PLO [124].

     In Table 3.3, the key competencies are listed individually in the top row. Under each competency are the specifics of what successful attainment of that competency might look like. Accrediting organisations typically have their own list of equivalent graduate attributes or competencies. The accrediting organisations then need to examine the PLOs attached to a particular engineering program to see if the PLOs address the competencies they require.

Table 3.3 Descriptors under each PLO

Knowledge and understanding	Engineering analysis	Engineering design	Investigations	Engineering practice	Making judgements	Communication and team working	Lifelong learning
Knowledge and understanding of the **mathematics** and other **basic sciences** underlying their engineering specialisation, at a level necessary to achieve the other program outcomes	Ability to analyse **complex** engineering products, processes and systems in their field of study; to select and **apply relevant methods** from established analytical, computational and experimental methods; to **correctly interpret** the outcomes of such analyses	Ability to develop and design **complex** products (devices, artefacts, etc.), processes and systems in their field of study **to meet the established requirements,** that can include **an awareness of non-technical- societal, health and safety, environmental, economic and industrial- considerations;** to select and apply relevant design and methodologies	Ability to conduct searches of literature, to consult and **to critically use** scientific databases and other appropriate sources of information, **to carry out simulation and analysis** in order **to pursue detailed investigations** and research of technical issues in their field of study	Understanding of **applicable techniques and methods of analysis, design and investigation** and of their **limitations** in their field of study	Ability to **gather and interpret relevant data** and **handle complexity** within their field of study, to inform judgements that include **reflection** on relevant social and ethical issues	Ability to **communicate effectively** information, ideas, problems and solutions **with engineering community and society at large**	Ability to recognise the need for and to **engage in independent lifelong learning**

(Continued)

Table 3.3 (Continued) Descriptors under each PLO

Knowledge and understanding	Engineering analysis	Engineering design	Investigations	Engineering practice	Making judgements	Communication and team working	Lifelong learning
Knowledge and understanding of engineering disciplines underlying their specialisation, at a level necessary to achieve the other program outcomes, including some awareness at their forefront	Ability to identify, formulate and solve engineering problems in their field of study; to select and apply relevant methods from established analytical, computational and experimental methods; to recognise the importance of non-technical-societal, health and safety, environmental, economic and industrial-constraints	Ability to design using some awareness of the forefront of their engineering specialisation	Ability to consult and apply codes of practice and safety regulations in their field of study	Practical skills for solving complex problems, realising complex engineering designs and conducting investigations in their field of study	Ability to manage complex technical or professional activities or projects in their field of study, taking responsibility for decision-making	Ability to function effectively in a national and international context, as an individual and as member of a team and to cooperate effectively with engineers and non-engineers	Ability to follow developments in science and technology

(Continued)

Table 3.3 (Continued) Descriptors under each PLO

Knowledge and understanding	Engineering analysis	Engineering design	Investigations	Engineering practice	Making judgements	Communication and team working	Lifelong learning
Awareness of the wider **multidisciplinary context** of engineering			Laboratory/workshop skills and **ability to design and conduct experimental investigations, interpret data and draw conclusions** in their field of study	Understanding of applicable materials, **equipment and tools, engineering technologies and processes**, and their **limitations** in their field of study Ability to **apply norms** of engineering practice in their field of study			

(Continued)

Table 3.3 (Continued) Descriptors under each PLO

Knowledge and understanding	Engineering analysis	Engineering design	Investigations	Engineering practice	Making judgements	Communication and team working	Lifelong learning
				Awareness of **non-technical-societal, health and safety, environmental, economic and industrial-implications** of engineering practice Awareness of **economic, organisational and managerial issues (such** as project management, risk and change management) in the **industrial and business context**			

Source: Adapted from Refs. [121,122].

Periodically, accrediting organisations must review their own accreditation criteria to ensure that it remains equivalent to that of the EUR-ACE labelling scheme [121,122].

c. **Program Management**

There are five key features of program management which are required to be demonstrated, with solid evidence, for a program to be eligible for accreditation [120,122–124]:

i. Achievement of stated program aims.

ii. Demonstration of teaching and learning processes with the opportunity to develop the PLOs.

iii. Sufficient resources that are required to make the achievement of the PLOs possible

iv. Criteria used to admit/transfer students into the program, and the criteria used for student progression through the program and for graduation need to be specific. All such criteria need to be published, and the decisions resulting from these criteria need to be monitored.

v. The program should be based within quality assurance processes that conform to the higher education institution's internal quality assurance policy (see Chapter 7 for more details) and practices.

These requirements on program management are not designed to be prescriptive, and the above-mentioned five features still allow specific programs to be run within their own local contexts.

Each of these features of program management is elaborated in detail next.

i. **Program aims**

The program aims must be consistent with the aims of the higher education institution in which the program is situated. Generally, the program aims are aligned with the competencies of the national accreditation organisation. If this is not that case, then the higher education institution needs to demonstrate that the PLOs comply with the national competencies. Similarly, every higher education institution can have its own PLOs or attributes differing from the national competency standards. Again, in such cases, the higher education institution needs to demonstrate that these are aligned with the national competency standards.

The needs of students and the needs of employers/ industries should be met by the competencies, taking into account both the breadth of the role of engineering in society and the disruptive aspects of technological development. The career progression of graduates should also feature in the learning outcomes, considering both opportunities for postgraduate study and/or employment [122,123].

ii. **Teaching and learning process**

The program plan should include following details for every unit/course/module/subject in the program guide [120–123]:

- Pre-requisites and co-requisites
- Credit allocation
- Syllabus
- Learning outcomes
- Pedagogy

In summary, the program plan needs to demonstrate that the module, unit, course or subject learning outcomes add up to the PLOs, irrespective of which elective modules the students may take [120–123]. The assessment in each module must be designed to measure the module learning outcomes, and the rigour of the assessment should be demonstrated by moderation and/or second independent marking [120–123].

Any review or moderation process relating to assessment results needs to be well-documented, and the decisions based on assessment need to comply with the appropriate standard [122–125]. Furthermore, students should be given the opportunity to resubmit sub-standard work in such a way that it does not compromise the standard required by the module, subject, course or unit [122–125]. If students are required to study at other institutions, or complete a placement in industry, such activities need demonstrated alignment with the PLOs and should be clearly stated in the program plan [122–125].

iii. **Resources**

There are adequate requirements for resources including adequate academic staff/faculty members, technical and administrative support services staff, and infrastructures/facilities. The required number of academic staff/faculty members with appropriate qualifications and experience is vital for the stable running of the program. Moreover, technical and administrative staff is also required to support the program. Adequate training and professional development opportunities for all staff members must be available. Staff members need to be familiar with the use and application of emerging technologies [120–124].

Facilities or infrastructures such as laboratories, workshop spaces, equipment, computer labs and high-speed internet are required to support program delivery. These facilities are particularly important where the project work is performed by the students. Student access to all these facilities needs to be demonstrably safe and hygienic [121,122]. The higher education institution must also demonstrate that the program is supported by an appropriate budget/funding [120,122–125].

iv. **Admission, transfer and progression criteria**

The admission (entry) requirements for all programs and the criteria needed for progression to completion of the program must be clearly specified [120,122–125].

Special committees, such as a student progress committee/Program Assessment Board, an admissions committee and a program review committee should be set up to oversee student achievement and progression, so that the entry requirements remain relevant and appropriate. All minutes of such committee meetings must be documented, and wherever applicable, the number and reasons for non-completion of the qualification should be recorded. The student performance statistics in each individual module, subject, course or unit should be monitored, analysed and benchmarked, especially where the assessment results differ from the norm [2,122–125].

v. **Quality assurance processes**

There should be a defined and documented process for regular review of the program and individual courses/units. Such a review should include an analysis of the student achievement against the PLOs [122–124].

There should be a closed-loop mechanism in place to receive student feedback on all subjects, modules, courses or units being delivered. Dealing with the day-to-day issues related to the program should be organised such that any urgent and/or important issues can be dealt with adequately and in a timely manner [120–125].

Ultimately, the program must demonstrate quality assurance processes aligned with the education institution that owns the program, and all such quality assurance policies need to be publicly available (preferably online) [120–124]. Furthermore, all program information should also be publicly available [121–124].

3.2 The Washington Accord (International Engineering Alliance)

3.2.1 Historical background

In 1989, six engineering professional bodies agreed to recognise each other's Bachelor of Engineering programs as being equivalent, with equivalent accreditation criteria. To formalise this agreement, the Washington Accord was signed in Washington, DC. The founding signatory professional organisations were (i) Institution of Engineers Australia, (ii) Accreditation Board for Engineering and Technology (ABET) USA, (iii) Engineering Council of the United Kingdom, (iv) Canadian Council of Professional Engineers, (v) Institution of Engineers Ireland and (vi) Institution of Professional Engineers New Zealand [120,126].

The main purpose of the Washington Accord is to ease the mobility of professional engineers. By recognising engineering degrees as equivalent among all signatory countries, it makes it much easier for engineering graduates to gain professional registration in other countries, thereby enhancing employment opportunities and global mobility (circulation and recirculation) of engineering professionals.

At the same time, the Washington Accord upholds the standard of engineering education amongst professional engineering organisations within the signatory nations. In addition, for non-signatory professional engineering organisations, the Accord provides a benchmark against which these organisations can review their own accreditation criteria and accrediting processes.

In order for a country's professional engineering organisation to be part of the Washington Accord, it must ensure that its national higher education institutions develop and deliver the engineering programs according to the Accord requirements. Such requirements relate to curriculum, assessment methodology and program quality assurance mechanisms which should all facilitate the student achievement of the Washington Accord's graduate attributes. The administering body of the Washington Accord, the IEA, also allows accreditation organisations to be "provisional" signatories of the accord. This means they are mentored by a full signatory until their processes fully comply with the accord. In this fashion, the Washington Accord has made a significant impact on engineering education and quality assurance globally. The major benefits of the Washington Accord are pictorially shown in Figure 3.2.

The Washington Accord covers only bachelor-level engineering programs (degrees). As mentioned earlier, this agreement allows engineering graduates of all accredited programs to practise engineering within the jurisdiction of any of the accreditation organisations which have joined the Accord [126–129].

Initially, the accreditation criteria were input-based, but during the late 1990s, with the development of outcome-based learning, the educational standards required by the Washington Accord were rewritten as learning outcomes [126] or "graduate attributes" [130]. Over the same time period, other national engineering accrediting

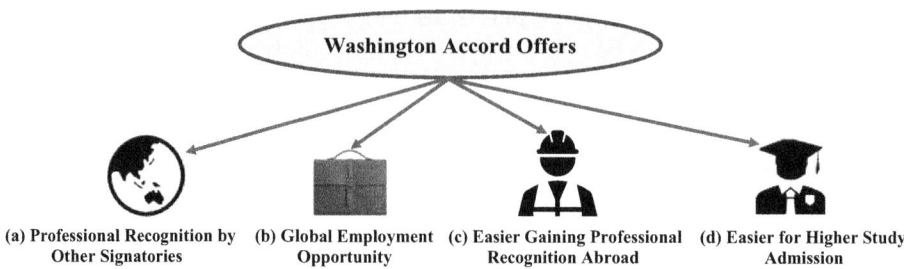

Figure 3.2 Major benefits of Washington Accord.

organisations were interested in becoming signatories or members of the Accord, resulting in the need for a more formal structure with specific rules for membership [126].

In 2003, competency profiles were developed for individual engineers to be listed on the International Register for Professional Engineers, with the Washington Accord forming the educational basis for admission to the register. The profiles were fully adopted by the signatories of the Washington Accord in 2005 [130].

By 2007, it was underscored that the graduate attributes and professional competencies needed improvement, and during 2007 and 2008, a working group formed by the signatories developed new editions of graduate attributes (competencies), which were fully adopted by 2009 [130].

Between 2009 and 2012, further modifications were made and adopted in 2013. These modifications are listed as Version 3 of the Graduate Attributes [126].

Over the period of 2014–2019, the graduate attributes underwent further reviews, focusing on the clarity of the exemplars of the graduate attributes, rather than altering the standard of the learning outcomes required [130].

The Washington Accord covers the graduate attributes required from a bachelor-level qualification. However, engineering can be practised at the professional (bachelor) level, engineering technologist- (3-year qualification) or technician- (2-year qualification) levels, and in the period of 1997–2003, two other agreements were developed which covered the engineering technologist- and engineering technician-levels. These two agreements are known now as the Sydney Accord, signed in 2001, which covers engineering technologist qualifications, and the Dublin Accord, signed in 2002, which covers engineering technical qualifications. Knowledge profiles of the Washington Accord, the Sydney Accord and the Dublin Accord are shown in Table 3.4.

The advantage of expressing the required learning outcomes from each agreement in one table is that the continuous development of engineering skills and abilities can be readily seen. Indeed, the development of an engineering professional is ongoing, and the different accords represent the accomplishment of different stages in progressing from an engineering technician to technologist to professional engineer.

In all cases, it is expected that the engineering practitioners will continue to develop their skills over the course of their career; however, it should be noted that the Washington Accord, which covers bachelor qualifications, considers its graduate attributes to be what are required for entry into the professional level. That is, the Washington Accord forms the educational base for professional engineers, but for further qualification and registration, a significant amount of experience must be demonstrated as well. Typically, this experience is achieved under the mentorship of a senior practising engineer, and the graduate progresses from an assisting role to taking more individual and team responsibility until the individual can apply for registration, chartering or licensing (as appropriate to the jurisdiction). Even after licensing, it is expected that ongoing professional development will occur. Once sufficient experience has been gained, registered engineers (and engineering technologists) can qualify for the international register, allowing these individuals to practise in different national jurisdictions, thereby allowing for global mobility.

In this book, we will not go into the detail of the Sydney Accord and the Dublin Accord; rather, the focus is on the bachelor of engineering graduates (i.e. the Washington Accord and other bachelor-level professional engineering jurisdictions).

While Table 3.4 compares the competencies across agreements, Table 3.5 lists the competencies of the Washington Accord. These include twelve (12) Graduate

Table 3.4 Knowledge profiles of Washington, Sydney and Dublin Accords

Washington Accord program for bachelor engineering knowledge profile provides:	*Sydney Accord program for engineering technologist knowledge profile provides:*	*Dublin Accord program for engineering technician knowledge profile provides:*
WK1: A **systematic**, theory-based understanding of the natural sciences applicable to the discipline.	**SK1:** A **systematic**, theory-based understanding of the natural sciences applicable to the sub-discipline.	**DK1:** A **descriptive**, formula-based understanding of the natural sciences applicable in a sub-discipline.
WK2: Concept-based **mathematics**, numerical analysis, statistics and formal aspects of computer and information science to support analysis and modelling applicable to the discipline.	**SK2:** Concept-based **mathematics**, numerical analysis, statistics and aspects of computer and information science to support analysis and use of models applicable to the sub-discipline.	**DK2:** Procedural **mathematics**, numerical analysis, statistics applicable in a sub-discipline.
WK3: A systematic, theory-based formulation of **engineering fundamentals** required in the engineering discipline.	**SK3:** A systematic, theory-based formulation of **engineering fundamentals** required in an accepted sub-discipline.	**DK3:** A coherent procedural formulation of **engineering fundamentals** required in an accepted sub-discipline.
WK4: Engineering **specialist knowledge** that provides theoretical frameworks and bodies of knowledge for the accepted practice areas in the engineering discipline; much is at the forefront of the discipline.	**SK4:** Engineering **specialist knowledge** that provides theoretical frameworks and bodies of knowledge for an accepted sub-discipline.	**DK4:** Engineering **specialist knowledge** that provides the body of knowledge for an accepted sub-discipline.

(Continued)

Table 3.4 (Continued) Knowledge profiles of Washington, Sydney and Dublin Accords

Washington Accord program for bachelor engineering knowledge profile provides:	*Sydney Accord program for engineering technologist knowledge profile provides:*	*Dublin Accord program for engineering technician knowledge profile provides:*
WK5: Knowledge that supports **engineering design** in a practice area.	**SK5:** Knowledge that supports **engineering design** using the technologies of a practice area.	**DK5:** Knowledge that supports **engineering design** based on the techniques and procedures of a practice area.
WK6: Knowledge of **engineering practice** (technology) in the practice areas in the engineering discipline.	**SK6:** Knowledge of **engineering technologies** applicable in the sub-discipline.	**DK6:** Codified **practical engineering knowledge** in recognised practice area.
WK7: Comprehension of the role of engineering in society and identified issues in engineering practice in the discipline: ethics and the professional responsibility of an engineer to public safety; the impacts of engineering activity: economic, social, cultural, environmental and sustainability.	**SK7: Comprehension** of the role of technology in society and identified issues in applying engineering technology: ethics and impacts: economic, social, environmental and sustainability.	**DK7: Knowledge** of issues and approaches in engineering technician practice: ethics, financial, cultural, environmental and sustainability impacts.
WK8: Engagement with selected knowledge in the **research literature** of the discipline.	**SK8:** Engagement with the **technological literature** of the discipline.	–
A program that builds this type of knowledge and develops the attributes listed below is typically achieved in **4–5 years of study**, depending on the level of students at entry.	A program that builds this type of knowledge and develops the attributes listed below is typically achieved in **3–4 years of study**, depending on the level of students at entry.	A program that builds this type of knowledge and develops the attributes listed below is typically achieved in **2–3 years of study**, depending on the level of students at entry

Source: Adapted from Ref. [130].

Attributes (WA) and eight (8) Knowledge Profiles (WK). The Graduate Attributes form a set of individually assessable outcomes that are the indicative components of an engineering graduate's potential to acquire competence to practise at an appropriate level. The Washington Accord's Graduate Attributes are exemplars of the attributes expected of an engineering graduate from an accredited engineering bachelor program. Graduate attributes are clear, succinct statements of the expected capability of an engineering graduate. The Knowledge Profiles (WK) provide profiles of graduates of higher education engineering programs where engineering graduates can solve complex engineering problems [120,130–132].

Table 3.5 Washington Accord's Graduate Attributes and Professional Competencies

WA	Washington Accord's graduate attributes (WA)	WK	Washington Accord's knowledge profile (WK)
WA1 Engineering knowledge	Apply knowledge of mathematics, natural science, engineering fundamentals and an engineering specialization as specified in WK1 to WK4 respectively to the solution of complex engineering problems.	**WK1**	A systematic, theory-based understanding of the **natural sciences** applicable to the discipline.
WA2 Problem analysis	Identify, formulate, research literature and analyse *complex* engineering problems reaching substantiated conclusions using first principles of mathematics, natural sciences and engineering sciences (WK1–WK 4).	**WK2**	Conceptually-based **mathematics**, numerical analysis, statistics and formal aspects of computer and information science to support analysis and modelling applicable to the discipline.
WA3 Design/ development of solutions	Design solutions for *complex* engineering problems and design systems, components or processes that meet specified needs with appropriate consideration for public health and safety, cultural, societal, and environmental considerations (WK5).	**WK3**	A systematic, theory-based formulation of **engineering fundamentals** required in the engineering discipline
WA4 Investigation	Conduct investigations of *complex* problems using research-based knowledge (WK8) and research methods including design of experiments, analysis and interpretation of data, and synthesis of information to provide valid conclusions	**WK4**	Engineering **specialist knowledge** that provides theoretical frameworks and bodies of knowledge for the accepted practice areas in the engineering discipline; much is at the forefront of the discipline.
WA5 Modern tool usage	Create, select and apply appropriate techniques, resources, and modern engineering and IT tools, including prediction and modelling, to *complex* engineering problems, with an understanding of the limitations (WK6).	**WK5**	Knowledge that supports **engineering design** in a practice area.

(Continued)

Table 3.5 (Continued) Washington Accord's Graduate Attributes and Professional Competencies

WA	Washington Accord's graduate attributes (WA)	WK	Washington Accord's knowledge profile (WK)
WA6 The engineer and society	Apply reasoning informed by contextual knowledge to assess societal, health, safety, legal and cultural issues and the consequent responsibilities relevant to professional engineering practice and solutions to complex engineering problems (WK7).	**WK6**	Knowledge of **engineering practice** (technology) in the practice areas in the engineering discipline.
WA7 Environment and sustainability	Understand and evaluate the sustainability and impact of professional engineering work in the solution of complex engineering problems in societal and environmental contexts (WK7)	**WK7**	**Comprehension** of the role of engineering in society and identified issues in engineering practice in the discipline: ethics and the professional responsibility of an engineer to public safety; the impacts of engineering activity: economic, social, cultural, environmental and sustainability.
WA8 Ethics	Apply ethical principles and commit to professional ethics and responsibilities and norms of engineering practice (WK7).	**WK8**	Engagement with selected knowledge in the **research literature** of the discipline.
WA9 Individual and teamwork	Function effectively as an individual, and as a member or leader in diverse teams and in multi-disciplinary settings.		
WA10 Communication	Communicate effectively on complex engineering activities with the engineering community and with society at large, such as being able to comprehend and write effective reports and design documentation, make effective presentations, and give and receive clear instructions.		

(Continued)

Table 3.5 (Continued) Washington Accord's Graduate Attributes and Professional Competencies

WA	Washington Accord's graduate attributes (WA)	WK	Washington Accord's knowledge profile (WK)
WA11 Project management and finance	Demonstrate knowledge and understanding of engineering management principles and economic decision-making and apply these to one's own work, as a member and leader in a team to manage projects and in multidisciplinary environments.		
WA12 Life-long learning	Recognise the need for and have the preparation and ability to engage in independent and life-long learning in the broadest context of technological change.		

Source: Adapted from Ref. [130].

The Washington Accord's Graduate Attributes aim to assist full signatories and provisional members to develop outcome-based accreditation criteria for use in their respective jurisdictions. Additionally, the Graduate Attributes guide professional engineering-accrediting organisations developing their accreditation systems with a view to seeking signatory status [130–132]. Table 3.5 lists the Washington Accord's Graduate Attributes and Knowledge Profiles.

As of 5 February 2020, there are 20 full members (full signatories) of the Washington Accord. A list of all full members with their joining years is shown in Table 3.6.

Within the Washington Accord, new signatories need to have a period of "provisional status" while they are being mentored by a full signatory [8]. Full signatory and provisional status are reviewed on a 6-year cycle. As of 5 February 2020, there are eight provisional members of the Washington Accord. These provisional members are listed in Table 3.7.

It is worth of note that four full signatories of the current Washington Accord are also full members of the ENAEE. They are the Engineering Council (UK), Engineers Ireland, the Association of Engineering Education (Russia) and MÜDEK (Turkey).

In addition to the Washington Accord, Sydney Accord and Dublin Accord, a series of different agreements were signed by Washington Accord signatories between 1997 and 2019 that relate to different levels of knowledge, skills and organisational management. One of these agreements is the International Professional Engineering Agreement (IPEA) which administers the International Register for Professional Engineers. The educational requirements for listing on this register are still the Washington Accord Graduate Attributes [126,131].

To ensure all agreements were adequately supported, a common secretariat was adopted, and the IEA was formally created by the Washington Accord signatories in 2007 to govern all accords and agreements [131].

Table 3.6 Full signatories of the Washington Accord

	Country	Represented by accreditation organisation	Year	Web address
1	Australia	EA (The Institution of Engineers Australia)	1989	https://www.engineersaustralia.org.au/
2	USA	Accreditation Board for Engineering and Technology (ABET)	1989	https://www.abet.org/
3	UK	Engineering Council United Kingdom (ECUK)	1989	https://www.engc.org.uk/
4	Canada	Engineers Canada (EC) (Canadian Council of Professional Engineers)	1989	http://www.engineerscanada.ca/
5	Ireland	Engineers Ireland (EI) (The Institution of Engineers, Ireland)	1989	http://www.ieagreements.org/www.engineersireland.ie
6	New Zealand	Engineering New Zealand (EngNZ) (Institution of Professional Engineers New Zealand)	1989	https://www.engineeringnz.org/
7	Hong Kong	Hong Kong Institution of Engineers (HKIE)	1995	https://www.hkie.org.hk/en/
8	South Africa	Engineering Council South Africa (ECSA)	1999	https://www.ecsa.co.za/default.aspx
9	Japan	Japan Accreditation Board for Engineering Education (JABEE)	2005	https://jabee.org/en/
10	Singapore	Institution of Engineers Singapore (IES)	2006	https://www.ies.org.sg/Accreditation/EAB10249
11	Chinese Taipei	Institute of Engineering Education Taiwan (IEET)	2007	http://www.ieet.org.tw/en/
12	South Korea	Accreditation Board for Engineering Education of Korea (ABEEK)	2007	http://www.abeek.or.kr/
13	Malaysia	Board of Engineers Malaysia (BEM)	2009	http://www.bem.org.my/
14	Turkey	Association for Evaluation and Accreditation of Engineering Programs (MÜDEK)	2011	http://www.mudek.org.tr/en/hak/kisaca.shtm
15	Russia	Association for Engineering Education of Russia (AEER)	2012	http://www.ac-raee.ru/en/index.htm
16	India	National Board of Accreditation (NBA)	2014	http://www.nbaind.org/
17	Sri Lanka	Institution of Engineers Sri Lanka (IESL)	2014	http://www.iesl.lk/
18	China	China Association for Science and Technology (CAST)	2016	http://english.cast.org.cn/
19	Pakistan	Pakistan Engineering Council (PEC)	2017	https://www.pec.org.pk/
20	Peru	Instituto de Calidad Y Acreditacion de Programas de Computacion, Ingeneria Y Technologia (ICACIT)	2018	http://icacit.org.pe/web/eng/

Source: Adapted from Refs. [120,130,131].

The IEA thus acts to maintain educational and professional practice standards by specifying both the criteria for accredited programs (degrees) via the Washington Accord and by specifying professional experience criteria for individuals to demonstrate so that they can be included on the IPEA register [126]. The IEA also covers

Table 3.7 Organisations with provisional membership of the Washington Accord

	Country	Represented by accreditation organisation	Year	Web address
I	Bangladesh	The Institution of Engineers Bangladesh (IEB)	2016	http://www.baetebangladesh.org/ or www.iebbd.org
2	Costa Rica	Colegio Federado de Ingenieros y de Arquitectos de Costa Rica (CFIA)	2016	http://cfia.or.cr/
3	Mexico	Consejo de Acreditación de la Enseñanza de la Ingeniería (CACEI)	2016	http://cacei.org.mx/
4	Philippines	Philippine Technological Council (PTC)	2016	https://ptc.org.ph/
5	Chile	Agencia Acreditadora Colegio De Ingenieros De Chile S A (ACREDITA CI)	2018	https://acreditaci.cl/en
6	Thailand	Council of Engineers Thailand (COET)	2019	http://www.coe.or.th/http_public/eng/
7	Myanmar (Burma)	Myanmar Engineering Council (MEngC)	2019	http://www.myanmarengc.org/
8	Indonesia	Indonesian Accreditation Board for Engineering Education (IABEE)	2019	https://iabee.or.id/

Source: Adapted from Ref. [130].

the agreement which specifies the criteria that accrediting organisations must demonstrate before they can be included in the Washington Accord [126].

Currently, the IEA comprises engineering organisations from over 30 nations (including five G8 and 11 G20 nations) and is expanding steadily by including the two most populous nations of the world (China and India).

The IEA aims to improve the global quality, productivity and mobility of engineers by being an accepted independent authority on best practice in standards, assessment and monitoring of engineering education and professional competence. The IEA has been working on:

- consistent improvement of standards and mobility
- defining standards of education and professional competence
- assessment of education accreditation and evaluation of competence
- participation in activities that are driven from the engineering profession

The major milestones of Washington Accord since its inception on 28 September 1989 till February 2020 are shown in Figure 3.3.

3.2.2 *Program accreditation outside the jurisdiction of the Washington Accord*

The Washington Accord limits the recognition of programs only to those accredited within the signatories' jurisdictions. However, under the Accord signatories, they can also accredit engineering programs of their home countries' education institutions outside their national boundaries.

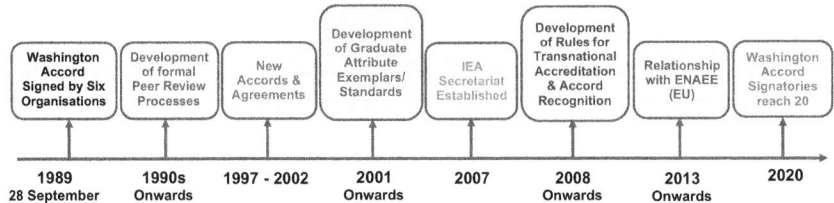

Figure 3.3 Milestones of Washington Accord from 1989 to 2020. (Adapted from Ref. [126].)

For example, where an Australian university offers an engineering program offshore (overseas), that program can be accredited by Engineers Australia (EA), the accrediting organisation within Australia. Where the offshore program is offered in a Washington Accord signatory nation, the offshore program also needs to be accredited by the host country's accreditation organisations. This two-stage accreditation process is called dual accreditation. The dual accreditation processes are discussed in detail in Chapter 4.

It should be noted that before 2007, Washington Accord signatories were allowed to offer accreditation services to foreign higher education institutions. Since 2007 and the formation of the IEA, this is no longer the case.

3.2.3 International professional engineers' agreement

The IPEA is a multi-national agreement between professional engineering organisations which creates the framework of an international standard of competence for professional engineering and then empowers each member organisation to establish a section of the International Professional Engineers' Register. The IPEA recognises the substantial equivalency of the standards used to establish the competency of professional engineers for independent practice. The earlier name of the IPEA was the Engineers' Mobility Forum. As on 5 February 2020, there are 16 full members of IPEA and three provisional members (see Table 3.8).

The IPEA determines that the criteria-accrediting bodies/organisations must meet to be able to have their qualifications compliant with the Washington Accord. The Washington Accord then sets the requirements that the programs must meet to be accredited, and the accrediting organisations therefore need to demonstrate that their local graduate attributes are equivalent to those stated in the Washington Accord [130].

The accreditation process of IPEA is shown in Figure 3.4.

The IPEA lists the criteria which accrediting organisations must be able to demonstrate to be part of the agreement. There are separate criteria for provisional and full members, with the requirement that all provisional criteria must be demonstrated by full members, in conjunction with further criteria required for full membership. These two criteria sets have been amalgamated to make four major categories [123]:

    a.   Status of Accrediting Organisation
    b.   Characteristics of Accreditation System
    c.   Accreditation Criteria
    d.   Management and Sustainability of Accreditation Agency

Table 3.8 Full and provisional signatories of the IPEA

	Country	Full member represented by	Year	Web address
1	Australia	EA (The Institution of Engineers Australia)	1997	https://www.engineersaustralia.org.au/
2	USA	National Council of Examiners for Engineering and Surveying (NCEES)	1997	https://ncees.org/
3	UK	Engineering Council United Kingdom (ECUK)	1997	https://www.engc.org.uk/
4	Canada	Engineers Canada (EC) (Canadian Council of Professional Engineers)	1997	http://www.engineerscanada.ca/
5	Ireland	Engineers Ireland (EI) (The Institution of Engineers, Ireland)	1997	http://www.ieagreements.org/www.engineersireland.ie
6	New Zealand	Engineering New Zealand (EngNZ) (Institution of Professional Engineers New Zealand)	1999	https://www.engineeringnz.org/
7	Hong Kong (China)	Hong Kong Institution of Engineers (HKIE)	1997	https://www.hkie.org.hk/en/
8	South Africa	Engineering Council South Africa (ECSA)	2007	https://www.ecsa.co.za
9	Japan	Institution of Professional Engineers Japan (IPEJ)	1999	https://www.engineer.or.jp/sub09/
10	Singapore	Institution of Engineers Singapore (IES)	2007	https://www.ies.org.sg/
11	Chinese Taipei (Taiwan)	Chinese Institute of Engineers (CIE)	2009	http://www.apec-ipea.org.tw/
12	South Korea	Korean Professional Engineers Association (KPEA)	2000	https://www.kpea.or.kr/kpea/english/main.html
13	Malaysia	Institution of Engineers Malaysia (IEM)	1999	http://www.myiem.org.my/
14	India	Institution of Engineers India (IEI)	2009	https://www.ieindia.org/
15	Sri Lanka	Institution of Engineers Sri Lanka (IESL)	2007	http://www.iesl.lk/
16	Pakistan	Pakistan Engineering Council (PEC)	2018	https://www.pec.org.pk/

Provisional members represented by

1	Bangladesh	The Institution of Engineers Bangladesh (IEB)	–	http://www.iebbd.org/
2	Russia	Association for Engineering Education of Russia (AEER)	–	http://www.ac-raee.ru/en/index.htm
3	Netherlands	Royal Netherlands Society of Engineers (KIVI)	–	https://www.kivi.nl/

Source: Adapted from Ref. [130].

Each of these categories is discussed here in further detail. It is interesting to note that the IPEA includes in the accreditation of agencies an expectation that their accreditation criteria match those of the Washington Accord (item c, above). This is different from the ENAEE, which leaves all program requirements to the EUR-ACE label standards.

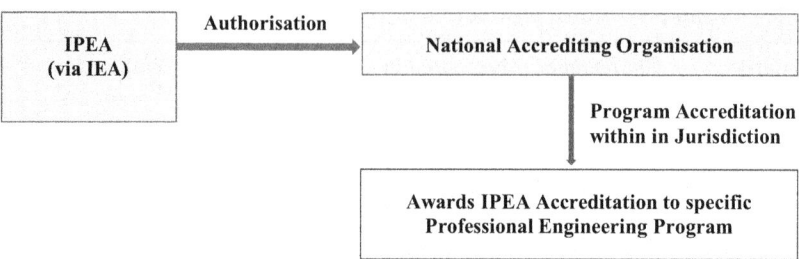

Figure 3.4   The IPEA program accreditation process under Washington Accord framework.

a. **Status of an accrediting agency**

As mentioned earlier, the independence of the accrediting organisation from both the government and any higher education institution within its jurisdiction is vital to ensure the objectivity of any decisions relating to accreditation. In addition, the organisation must be able to make decisions without relying on any other stakeholders. The ability to maintain such independence enables the accrediting organisation to be acknowledged as the only recognised accrediting organisation within its jurisdiction. Typically, accreditation organisations are also legally incorporated [123].

The accrediting organisation must be able to demonstrate that it has policies that support the process of accreditation and that policies are also in place to enact accreditation decisions. It should be in a position to set and approve accreditation criteria [123]. Finally, accreditation should only be available to those higher education institutions that have the legal authority to confer higher education qualifications within the relevant jurisdiction.

b. **Characteristics of an accreditation system**

All procedures and criteria associated with accreditation are documented, publicly available and seen to be applied in accordance with the accrediting organisation's own policies. It is expected that high standards of professionalism, ethics and objectivity will be maintained at all times. The accrediting organisation should also ensure that it publishes a list of accredited programs. Additional documentation is also required to demonstrate that program assessors are trained appropriately [123–125].

Regarding the process of accreditation, the accrediting organisation must be able to accredit individual programs or groups of programs. The accreditation process must include a self-evaluation report which is completed by the higher education institution as well as a site visit to the higher education institution's facilities by the accreditation panel. The accrediting organisation should also ensure that accreditation of programs is reviewed on a regular basis. The accreditation organisation must be in the position to make decisions which benefit the whole community in the longer term: this may mean that, on occasions, difficult decisions need to be made and the response from the affected program is monitored. The accreditation panel should comprise reviewers from industry and from academia. It is expected that these reviewers are of high standards as either educators or as professional engineering practitioners [123–125].

Any decision regarding accreditation is reported, and the accreditation decision which is made needs to be justified and sufficiently detailed to ensure that the higher education institution affected can respond to any requirements. The report should clearly distinguish between recommendations and mandatory requirements. There must also be a process for managing conflicts of interest throughout the accreditation process, and there should be a means for higher education institutions to appeal against any decisions [123–125].

c. **Accreditation criteria**

The PLOs should be consistent with the purpose of the program and should be substantially equivalent to the graduate attribute exemplars listed in the Washington Accord (see Table 3.5). The accrediting organisation needs to ensure that these program outcomes are documented and implemented in practice. The curriculum should be broad to allow engineering graduate practice, and the requirements to enter and progress through the program should be appropriate and clear [123–125].

In terms of the staffing for the program, there needs to be appropriate leadership of the program and suitable practitioners teaching into the program who have appropriate qualifications. In general, the learning environment must be suitable for the program with adequate human, physical and financial resources [123–125].

d. **Management and sustainability of the accreditation organisation**

The viability of the accrediting organisation can be assessed by examining the number of programs and higher education institutions which have sought accreditation and the number of programs which have gone through more than one accreditation cycle [123–125].

The accrediting organisation should also be able to demonstrate the depth of observations made during the site visit and the rigour of any accreditation status decision. The accrediting organisation should also be able to point to the training of its program assessors and show how the training allows assessment to occur at a fine level of detail, for a variety of evidence provided. The accrediting organisation should subject itself to regular review of its policies, criteria and procedures and should be able to demonstrate consistency in its accreditation decisions over time. Active involvement in other Accords may support the accrediting organisation and strengthen its longevity and sustainability [123–125].

3.2.3.1 The Washington Accord: accreditation requirements for programs

The Washington Accord deals explicitly with learning outcomes. Requirements for program design, program resourcing, teaching and learning processes and assessment within the Washington Accord refer back to the rules and procedures listed in IEA website [130,131].

The Washington Accord emphasises that higher education institutions can design programs and pathways which are suitable for them as long as the required graduate attributes are achieved. The Accord does not specify a required delivery mode (face-to-face, distance, supervised, unsupervised, hybrid, full-time or part-time) for any accredited programs. In some instances, accrediting organisations develop performance indicators or indicators of attainment of the Graduate Attributes. This approach is demonstrated in the case study at the end of this Chapter.

The learning requirements for accredited programs are split into a knowledge profile (eight such profiles), which indicates the volume of learning, and a graduate attribute profile (12 such attributes). Within each, certain words and phrases have been explicitly defined [130,131]. The Washington Accord's knowledge profiles and graduate attributes are shown in Table 3.5.

3.2.3.2 Application for membership to the IPEA

The new member admission process is very similar to that required by the Washington Accord, in that applicants must be uncontested agencies that control, or are representative of, the engineering profession and have statutory powers relating to the admission of professionals to the practising engineering community. As such, only organisations can apply for membership, not individuals.

Once membership is sought, the IEA Secretariat is contacted and a preliminary documentation from the applicant is presented to the Executive Committee of the IEA. A part of the application process requires that two authorised members can attest that the applicant organisation meets the requirements for provisional status [130]. In addition, where necessary, the Executive Committee can assign several authorised members to mentor the applicant towards provisional status.

Provisional Membership is achieved by the applicant organisation demonstrating that the registration/licensure schemes for which it has responsibility are similar to those of other Authorised Members of the IPEA Agreement. This demonstration is via both face-to-face presentations and supporting documentation. By conferring Provisional Membership, the Authorised Members have indicated that they consider that the applicant has the potential to be an Authorised Member but this grants the Provisional Member none of the rights of Authorised Members [130,131].

Provisional Membership usually lasts 2–4 years. During this time, the provisional member is guided by at one mentor, and, when the applicant is ready, it may apply for Authorised Member status. At this stage, the Provisional Member's accreditation process, used to assess qualifications, will be witnessed by a verification team who will then submit a report to the other signatories. Once the IEA committee is satisfied by the report and a presentation for the case of full membership has been given to the committee, full membership will be awarded [130,131].

3.2.4 The Asia Pacific Economic Co-operation (APEC) Engineer Agreement

The APEC Engineer Agreement recognises the substantial equivalence of competency standards for professional engineers within the 21 APEC economies. To be a part of the APEC Engineer Agreement, countries need to be both members of APEC and be able to demonstrate that the systems they use to assess the competency of engineers is consistent with the standards set by the APEC Engineer agreement.

The procedures for becoming an APEC Engineer member are exactly the same as for IPEA membership (see Sections 3.2.2 and 3.2.3). There are currently 15 members of the APEC agreement on professional engineering organisations, shown in Table 3.9.

The APEC Engineer agreement allows professional engineers to have their professional standing recognised within the APEC region, via the International Professional

Table 3.9 Signatories of APEC nations

	Country	Member represented by	Year	Web address
1	Australia	EA (The Institution of Engineers Australia)	2000	https://www.engineersaustralia.org.au/
2	Canada	Engineers Canada (EC) (Canadian Council of Professional Engineers)	2000	http://www.engineerscanada.ca/
3	Hong Kong (China)	Hong Kong Institution of Engineers (HKIE)	2000	https://www.hkie.org.hk/en/
4	Japan	Institution of Professional Engineers Japan (IPEJ)	2000	https://www.engineer.or.jp/sub09/
5	Malaysia	Institution of Engineers Malaysia (IEM)	2000	http://www.myiem.org.my/
6	New Zealand	Engineering New Zealand (EngNZ) (Institution of Professional Engineers New Zealand)	2000	https://www.engineeringnz.org/
7	South Korea	Korean Professional Engineers Association (KPEA)	2000	https://www.kpea.or.kr/kpea/english/main.html
8	Indonesia	Persatuan Insinyur Indonesia (PII)	2001	http://pii.or.id/
9	USA	National Council of Examiners for Engineering and Surveying (NCEES)	2001	https://ncees.org/
10	Philippines	Philippine Technological Council (PTC)	2003	https://ptc.org.ph/
11	Thailand	Council of Engineers Thailand (COET)	2003	http://www.coe.or.th/
12	Singapore	Institution of Engineers Singapore (IES)	2005	https://www.ies.org.sg/
13	Chinese Taipei (Taiwan)	Chinese Institute of Engineers (CIE)	2005	http://www.apec-ipea.org.tw/
14	Russia	Association for Engineering Education of Russia (AEER)	2010	http://www.ac-raee.ru/en/index.htm
15	Peru	Peruvian Engineers Association/ Colegio de Ingenieros del Perù (PEA/CIP)	2018	http://apecengineerperu.cip.org.pe/wp/

Source: Adapted from Ref. [126–130].

Engineers' Register, with minimal requirement for assessment by accrediting agencies within the agreement. This enhances the mobility of engineering services and professionals within the APEC region.

As briefly mentioned earlier, the IEA is an umbrella organisation for six multilateral agreements (including the Sydney Accord, Dublin Accord, IPEA agreement and APEC agreement) which establish and enforce amongst their members' internationally benchmarked standards for engineering education for an "entry level" competency to practise engineering.

Figure 3.5 shows all seven agreements of the IEA. The figure also indicates academic qualifications awarded by institutions as foundation stages for entering the second stage of the profession, which is an independent practice competence as a registered/ chartered professional.

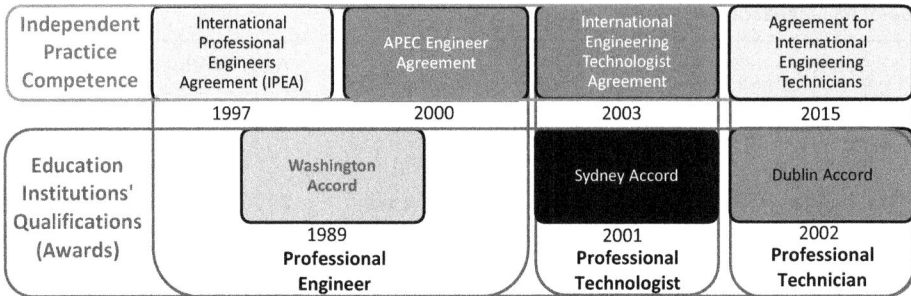

Figure 3.5 Seven agreements of IEA, academic qualifications and independent practice competence. (Adapted from Refs. [120,127,128].)

3.3 The Washington Accord and ENAEE

There are almost identical requirements for accrediting bodies/ organisations of the ENAEE and the Washington Accord Signatories. The Washington Accord recognises that the members of the ENAEE operate similar accreditation processes to similar standards within Europe, and its authorised members provide the EUR-ACE label to accredited programs. As stated previously, four of the Washington Accord's 20 full members (Russia, UK, Ireland and Turkey) are also authorised accreditation members of ENAEE. There is a formal mechanism between the IEA and ENAEE to maximise mutual understanding and potential benefits of these two organisations and their signatories.

The members of Washington Accord can also be the members of other professional organisations, including IPEA, APEC and ENAEE, as shown in Figure 3.6.

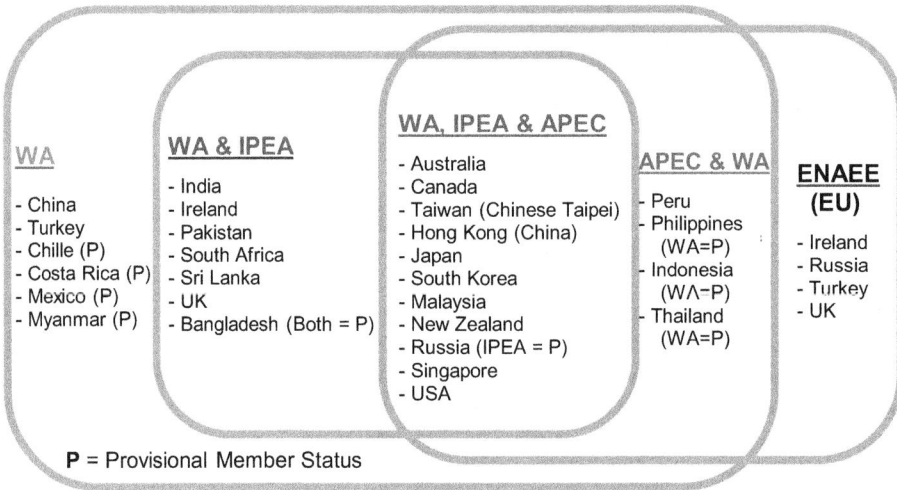

Figure 3.6 Jurisdictions with membership agreements among WA, IPEA, APEC and ENAEE. (Adapted from Refs. [127,128,131].)

Despite the overwhelming similarity between the two major professional accrediting systems, there remain some differences between them. For example, the ENAEE's EUR-ACE system specifies a volume of learning, as indicated by credits, which are defined by a set number of student hours. The Washington Accord is purely outcome-based and therefore has no such loading requirements, although it does specify that the "knowledge profile" should be indicative of the appropriate volume required.

Both systems split the program accreditation criteria into a knowledge base/profile and a list of graduate attributes or skills and attitudes that a graduate needs to be able to demonstrate.

In terms of the knowledge profile, the expectations are similar; however, under the requirements on accrediting organisations, some attributes listed in the knowledge profile of one scheme are listed in the graduate attributes of the other. Again, the division of requirements may be different, but the fine-scale requirements appear to show remarkable similarity. An example of this is that multidisciplinary knowledge and approaches are listed as part of the knowledge profile of the EUR-ACE system but are part of the skills/graduate attributes list for the Washington Accord.

Another example is practical problem-solving skills, which are listed in the skills/graduate attributes of the EUR-ACE system but are listed in the knowledge profile of the Washington Accord. It is also noted that the EUR-ACE system explicitly mentions the use of codes of practice, whereas the Washington Accord refers more broadly to "safety".

In conclusion, there are remarkable consistencies between these two major quality assurance and accrediting benchmark developing systems. However, the organisation of each system clouds the equivalence. As regular dialogues and communications take place between the ENAEE and the IEA, it is certainly hoped that mutual recognition of professional accreditation between these two organisations is only a matter of time.

3.4 Case study of EA Accreditation processes

3.4.1 Stage 1 competency for bachelor of engineering degree

3.4.1.1 Function of accreditations

Accreditation is seen as quality assurance for the education institution and the program or degree being offered. Accreditation can also imply financial security for the higher education institution and reassures current students, employers, government and the general public of the quality of the programs being offered [133]. Through national and international benchmarking, accreditation allows different nations to recognise engineering qualifications of substantial equivalence. This means that graduates of accredited programs have global mobility without the need for reassessment. Thus, a graduate in Australia of a program accredited by EA is able to practise engineering to the same level in all jurisdictions of the signatories of the Washington Accord. While this benchmarking process is the primary function of accreditation, as accredited qualifications are established, the IEA, which administers the Washington Accord, also becomes a forum within which the best practice of engineering education is disseminated. The accreditation process is typically based on an assessment of learning outcomes.

EA not only assists Australian higher education institutions by accrediting and assuring quality of engineering programs designed to prepare graduates for entry to professional practice, it also provides graduates with professional development activities for progression to Registration and Chartered levels. EA also provides similar services to engineering associates and engineering technologists.

3.4.1.2 The basis of the accreditation process

EA's engineering program accreditation is an evidence-based evaluation process to determine if educational programs meet the defined outcomes of its stage 1 competency standards for the bachelor of engineering professional level. The EA stage 1 competency standards (elements) are threshold standards. The accreditation under EA Stage 1Competencies assures that an engineering program is suitably designed and delivered to prepare graduates for entry into professional practice in a specified engineering field. The EA accreditation exercise is undertaken in an international, as well as local, context, upholding the spirit of the Washington Accord and other professional agreements. EA engages directly and consults with all major stakeholders, including the Australian Council of Engineering Deans, Tertiary Education Quality and Standards Agency (TEQSA), IEA, Australian Industry Skills Committee and Australian Skills Quality Authority.

The primary objectives of EA's program accreditation are to [134]

- assess the viability of the applying program to prepare graduates
- assess cohorts of graduates (not individual students)
- ensure the sustainability of the program until the next review period.

EA is the only organisation in Australia which performs engineering program accreditation [120,134]. The sub-units of EA, the Australian Engineering Accreditation Centre, with the associated Accreditation Panels and the Accreditation Board, are the groups that organise and make accreditation decisions [120,134]. The Associate Director (Accreditation) is the main intermediary between the educational institution and the AB [135]. There is typically more than one accreditation manager, and they are directed by the Associate Director (Accreditation) [135]. Individual accreditation managers are typically responsible for an accreditation visit to a particular higher education institution, while the AB is made up of senior, independent experts from the industry and the education sector [120,134]. AB decisions are seen to be independent of EA, operating with reference to EA requirements. The Engineers Australia Accreditation Centre undertakes the following [120,134]:

- formation and briefing evaluation panels
- planning and scheduling visits to higher education institutions who seek accreditation
- organising activities during visits to higher education institutions
- reporting and acting as Secretariat to the AB
- communication of accreditation decisions to education institutions
- maintaining the schedule for general reviews
- interfacing with international education accords on behalf of EA.

The roles, responsibilities and interactions between the Australian Engineering Accreditation Centre (AEAC) and the AB are shown graphically in Figure 3.7.

It needs to be emphasised that the AB accredits program(s) not individuals or higher education institutions, and its outcome relates to the current state of the program, rather than any future developments or previous plans [136]. Sustainability of the program is determined by the criteria associated with the operating environment and the internal quality assurance processes used by the higher education institution [136].

For previously and currently accredited programs, EA sends a reminder when reaccreditation is due, but for new programs, major amendments to existing programs, or new delivery modes, there must be a request from the higher education institution for accreditation [135]. It is worthy of note that accreditation is voluntary. Therefore, it is up to the higher education institution to request accreditation from EA and bear all the associated costs [134]. Accreditation is undertaken on a rolling cycle and takes place every 5 years in Australia for the selected qualifications being accredited [137]. The EA "Accreditation System" is involved in the criteria used for evaluating programs and determines the process by which this evaluation occurs [134]. Typically, higher education institutions have multiple qualifications accredited at the same time, for maximum efficiency of the process [135].

Generally, there are two types of accreditation: (a) provisional (when the program is new and has no current graduates) and (b) full accreditation (when the program has graduated students).

3.4.1.2.1 GENERAL REVIEW PROCESS

Qualifications, which have been previously accredited, are listed in EA's schedule for "General Reviews". The General Review is the standard formulation of the accreditation process. It is the responsibility of the higher education institution to contact the AEAC when provisionally accredited programs have graduates [134,135], and it is the responsibility of the educational institution to notify the AEAC of any changes to a program or its environment which might risk compliance with the accreditation criteria during the standard accreditation cycle [120,134].

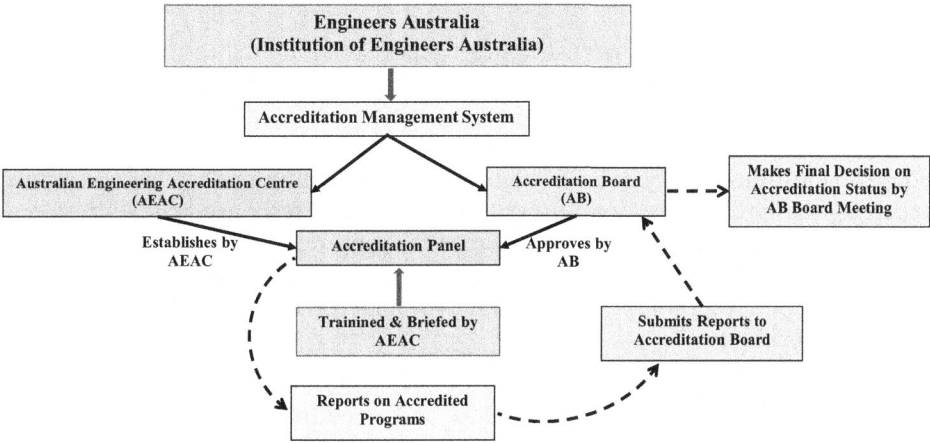

Figure 3.7 Principal structures of EA's program accreditation processes.

After a request or reminder for accreditation has been issued, in the year before accreditation is due, EA and the higher education institution will determine an initial date for the visit and an agreed date by which the initial documents (in the prescribed form) need to be received by EA (typically 8 weeks prior to the scheduled visit). The documents drafted must consist of the main evidence that the accreditation criteria have been met [135]. During this time, the composition of the accreditation panel is established by the AEAC. Once approved by the AB, the panel members are formally notified, the assignment contract is signed and the panel members are trained and briefed by the AEAC.

For accreditation, 3–5 weeks before the visit, there is a meeting of the Accreditation Panel members to review the submission by the higher education institution for accreditation. The Panel members share their initial thoughts after reviewing the documentation and determine the focus of the institutional visit and those issues which need to be clarified. They must also determine if further information is required [135]. A draft schedule will also be discussed at this meeting and sent to the higher education institution, and the education institution must allow access of the Accreditation Panel to staff (academics/faculty members, technical and student services staff), students (selected students from all year levels) and graduates (currently employed), as well as their employers [134,135]. During the institutional visit, the accreditation panel must be given the opportunity to

- examine assessments submitted by current students
- interview groups of recent graduates
- speak with currently enrolled students.

Issues of concern may also be communicated to the relevant engineering program unit at the higher education institution [135]. The final schedule for the visit will be determined by the Associate Director of the AB, in consultation with the higher education institution (generally Deputy Dean for Learning and Teaching) [134,135]. The night before the visit, there is a pre-visit panel meeting which considers any additional information and prepares important qualifying questions [135]. At the end of the visit, the Panel Chair gives initial comments to the higher education institution which reflect the draft report, but which may not accurately anticipate the final decision made by the AB [135].

Within 6–8 weeks after the visit, a draft report is submitted to the AB [135]. This report contains a recommendation to the AB and recommendations (mandatory, M, and advisory, R) for the higher education institution. Once the draft report is discussed at the board meeting and approved by the AB, the report is sent to the higher education institution [135,136]. The higher education institution then has 6 weeks from receiving the report to respond in writing, and such a response may address errors of fact or provide clarification of any issues the higher education institution thought the board had misunderstood [135]. A new report, complete with the higher education institution's response, is sent to the AB for final consideration. The Accreditation decides to [135,136]

- accredit fully for the next 5-year cycle without conditions
- accredit fully for the next 5-year cycle subject to the higher education institution, providing additional information or taking further action within a year; if the

higher education institution response is not adequate, the accreditation status may be changed, and potentially, there will be an additional mid-cycle review (conditional full)

- accredit for less than 5 years followed by an additional submission and optional visit to assess ongoing accreditation
- provisional accreditation until there are graduates of a new or substantially amended qualification
- conditional provisional accreditation: the higher education institution must produce additional evidence or information to reach provisional accreditation; full accreditation can then be sought after there are graduates of the specific program
- suspend accreditation for a specific time interval during which the higher education institution must report on improvements in issues of concern
- Withdraw or not give accreditation: in such situation, accreditation will not be considered for a 2-year period.

Within 2 weeks of receiving the decision, the engineering unit(s) of the higher education institution can appeal against a non-accreditation decision, but it must be on the grounds (typically) of errors of fact or a breach of the EA Accreditation policy, procedure or criteria [134,135]. In the case of an appeal, the management board of EA will appoint a sub-committee to consider the appeal, and as a result, it may be necessary to have another evaluation visit. The sub-committee reports to the management board, and the board's decision is then final [134].

Accreditation reports are confidential and are generally not considered for publication. In the rare instance where they are published, they need to be published in full [135]. Typically, the start date for accreditation is the first year of intake to a new program [134]. There is usually not a termination date published, but it is assumed that accreditation extends to the intake in the year after the next General Review. Where a program is going to be discontinued, an end date will be specified [134].

Conflicts of interest need to be identified during the accreditation process. These may arise within and across the AB, the Accreditation (Evaluation) Panels and advisory and appeal committees [134].

3.4.1.2.2 MEMBERSHIP OF ACCREDITATION (EVALUATION) PANELS

The accreditation panel comprises the Chair, two to six members of a "core" team, typically with one member who has vast academic experience and another who has practising engineering experience and has recently employed graduates [135]. The core team should also have broad experience in contemporary engineering and be able to evaluate program outcomes, pedagogy and quality management systems. The accreditation visit manager is usually a Panel Member, and the visit manager drafts the visit report and finalises it by working with the Chair and other Panel Members [135,136].

The evaluation panel may also contain "non-visiting consultants" who are chosen because of their expertise in the particular discipline being reviewed, and may be appointed to consider situations of multiple offerings (e.g. when both onshore and offshore programs are being offered), or where the standard program has already been reviewed and there must be a confirmation that the same learning outcomes are being achieved via an alternative pathway [135]. This is mandatory for "undifferentiated" offerings. In these situations, the focus is on the local context and the quality management system in the local environment [135]. The "non-visiting" member examines the paperwork only and participates in any pre-visit teleconference so as to be able to provide the Panel with issues and questions which need to be discussed during the visit. The "non-visiting" member also needs to be available to the Panel during the preparation of the visit report, while the Panel is still on its site visit, and the "non-visiting member" also needs to be willing to provide feedback on the draft visit report [135,136].

Observers can observe the Panel process but only with approval from the AB and the higher education institution where accreditation is occurring. Observers can attend all sessions but cannot ask questions or participate in the discussion: if there is a question, request or opinion from the observer which is important, it should be discussed privately with the Panel Chair or the Associate Director of the AB [135].

3.4.1.2.3 ACCREDITATION PROCESSES AND INNOVATION

While innovation is supported by EA, significant deviation from the accepted norms in program structure, delivery, content, resourcing or learning outcomes can indicate a higher level of risk, and in that instance, the higher education institution must show that there is a good reason for the risk or that the risk can be mitigated [134–136]. While accreditation panels seek to be receptive to new approaches, any significant variation is examined diligently in terms of substance and merit [134]. In a broader context, accreditation seeks to balance the need for new specialisations and the formation of new titles which may be short-lived [136]. In addition, the discipline area for any degree needs to be determined with reference to the needs of the community and industry as well as changes in professional practice and national and international trends [136]. Balancing this is the recognition that, over time, the accreditation criteria, competency standards and accreditation policy of EA need to be revised as innovation and development of programs occur [134].

3.4.1.2.4 ACCREDITATION PROCESSES: RISK MANAGEMENT

The use of outcome-based accreditation can be seen to be part of a general risk management strategy [134–136]. There has been some discussion that the risk levels in education may increase over time, with the rapid nature of technological change acting in conjunction with the increasing competitiveness of education at international and national levels [134]. As technology becomes more sophisticated, it may be necessary to move from an outcome-based approach to mitigate any increase in the risk caused by the technological change [134–138].

There are two main types of risk in the accreditation process: (i) a false negative, where the AB fails to accredit an innovative, yet sound, qualification, and (ii) a false positive, where an innovative program is accredited, even though it is not at the required outcome level [134]. The false negative questions the validity of the accreditation process, while the false positive puts all the stakeholders, both internal to the higher education institution and external, at risk. False positives are likely to create more risk for qualifications which provide entry into the professional engineer category, and the experience has shown that innovative programs at this level tend to lack a breadth in the social context [134].

Currently, the AEAC's approach to risk is to remain with outcome-based assessment, ensuring that there is a focus on critical issues during accreditation [134]. Therefore, where there are components of an engineering program that are deemed to be risky, there may be a requirement for more evidence to ensure that the risks are managed satisfactorily. Where the risk is high, a Risk Panel may be convened to further analyse the risk and advice on risk-mitigation strategies. Such strategies may take the form of mandatory reporting or approving accreditation for a shorter cycle than the general review (i.e. fewer than 5 years). The risk-mitigation strategy used is finalised by the AB [134–138].

3.4.1.2.5 OUT-OF-CYCLE ACCREDITATIONS

The AB can also conduct out-of-cycle assessment if it has the reason to believe that the accreditation status of a program should be changed. The AB addresses the issues to the higher education institution which in turn responds. Depending on the response, an evaluation panel may visit the higher education institution to decide on the accreditation status. If there is a decision to revoke accreditation, then that decision can also be appealed, using the earlier-mentioned appeal process [134].

Outside of the general review process, the AB can withdraw accreditation status if it has concerns. The Board can notify the higher education institution of this and ask for a response, and if the response is not sufficient, the Board may organise an evaluation panel to investigate. The panel will provide a rationale if it confirms the decision not to accredit and that decision will be sent to the higher education institute which needs to be responded within 6 weeks [135]. If the higher education institution response is not sufficient, accreditation is revoked. Such a decision may be appealed against under the appeal process [135,136].

3.4.1.3 Accreditation criteria: The Washington Accord

To meet the required standard for the graduate outcomes, each accreditation criterion must be individually achieved [135]. Accreditation criteria are divided as follows:

  i. Academic Program
 ii. Operational Environment
iii. Quality System.

I. ACADEMIC PROGRAM

The accreditation process, as overseen by the Washington Accord, does not seek to prescribe content or pedagogy, but the structure and content of qualifications are considered in terms of the necessary skill development and knowledge acquisition required. This is managed by EA, in Australia, by developing a list of generic attributes it expects from a graduate of a Bachelor of Engineering program to have attained by the time of graduation. The graduate outcomes or attributes are expressed as professional competencies [134]. These attributes are listed in the "stage 1 competency standards", which were developed from input from practising engineers and experienced academics/faculty members and are meant to represent the minimum requirements to enter the engineering profession [136–138].

The Stage One Competences are organised into three different groups: "professional and personal attributes"; "knowledge and skills"; and "the ability to apply knowledge and skills" [136]. It is up to the offering higher education institution to provide sufficient evidence that the qualifications provided give the students sufficient opportunity to develop these competencies by the end of their studies. It is anticipated that the higher education institution can map its own list of PLOs against the competency standards required for accreditation. This mapping process will indicate how the course-learning outcomes (CLOs) accumulate to satisfy both the PLOs and the graduate attributes as listed by EA. Both the specification of learning outcomes and the demonstration of learning opportunities to demonstrate these during the qualification therefore form a major part of the evidence needed to demonstrate accreditation of the academic program.

The stage 1 competency elements was revised in 2011 by EA. The current stage 1 competencies are listed in Table 3.10. Currently, the total number of competency elements is 16, in three broad categories: (a) theoretical knowledge, (b) application of knowledge in engineering practices, and (c) soft skills. Under the theoretical knowledge, there are six elements of competencies. Four are listed under the application of knowledge category. Six are under the soft skills category. Any signatory of the Washington Accord can develop their own sets of competency elements as long as these achieve the objectives of the 12 graduate attributes and eight knowledge profiles of the Washington Accord of IEA. Prior to the competency review in 2011, EA had 17 elements of stage 1 competencies. After the review in 2011, EA consolidated these and made 16 elements of stage 1 competencies that all 4-year full-time engineering programs at the bachelor level must address, in terms of curriculum design, delivery and practices, in order to get accreditation.

To assist individual academic staff/ faculty members, course coordinators, lecturers and higher education institutions in demonstrating learning outcomes and graduate attributes, EA has developed indicators of attainment for all 16 elements (see Table 3.11).

Learning outcomes
EA recognises that there are different drivers of PLOs [138]:

- Institute- and Discipline-expected Learning Outcomes
- National Requirements (Tertiary Education Quality and Standards Agency – TEQSA)
- EA Graduate Capabilities
- Australian Qualifications Framework
- Benchmarking

However, EA expects the higher education institution to be able to demonstrate that the PLOs for any accredited program are consistent with the higher education institution's goals, the likely career paths for graduates, and the needs of external stakeholders [134–138]. In this regard, it is expected that the graduate attributes as listed by EA will be contextualised for the chosen discipline of engineering [136–138]. In addition, EA does consider the suitability of the learning outcomes specified by the teaching institution and whether the design of the program is sufficient to support the desired outcomes.

Table 3.10 EA stage I elements of competencies

1. Knowledge and Skill base (Theoretical Knowledge)

   1.1 Comprehensive, theory-based understanding of the underpinning natural and physical sciences and the engineering fundamentals applicable to the engineering discipline.

   1.2 Conceptual understanding of mathematics, numerical analysis, statistics, and computer and information sciences which underpin the engineering discipline.

   1.3 In-depth understanding of specialist bodies of knowledge within the engineering discipline.

   1.4 Discernment of knowledge development and research directions within the engineering discipline.

   1.5 Knowledge of contextual factors impacting the engineering discipline.

   1.6 Understanding of the scope, principles, norms, accountabilities and bounds of contemporary engineering practice in the specific discipline.

2. Engineering Application Ability (Application of Knowledge in Practice)

   2.1 Application of established engineering methods to complex engineering problem-solving.

   2.2 Fluent application of engineering techniques, tools and resources.

   2.3 Application of systematic engineering synthesis and design processes.

   2.4 Application of systematic approaches to the conduct and management of engineering projects

3. Professional and Personal Attributes (Soft Skills)

   3.1 Ethical conduct and professional accountability.

   3.2 Effective oral and written communication in professional and lay domains.

   3.3 Creative, innovative and proactive demeanour.

   3.4 Professional use and management of information.

   3.5 Orderly management of self- and professional conduct.

   3.6 Effective team membership and team leadership.

Source: Adapted from Refs. [120,130].

It is also expected that there is evidence which demonstrates an alignment and a quality cycle between CLO), course delivery activities and assessment. Assessment in courses can be varied to ensure that adequate opportunities are provided for the students to develop the graduate attributes and achieve all learning outcomes [136]. Assessment also needs to provide students with the opportunity to develop critical review and self-reflection skills, potentially through the use of peer- and self-assessment [136–138]. Assessment needs to be designed such that it is progressive in the degree of difficulty from entry year to exit year, with special emphasis on increasing independent learning skills in the later years of the program [136]. All assessment items need to be mapped against and aligned with the CLOs, PLOs and graduate attributes [136–138]. It is also important that there are clear criteria (rubrics) for grading all assessment

Table 3.11 Elements and indicators for knowledge and skill base

EA	Element of competency	Indicators of attainment
1.1	**Comprehensive, theory-based understanding** of the underpinning natural and physical sciences and the engineering fundamentals applicable to the engineering discipline.	**Engages** with the engineering discipline at a phenomenological level, applying sciences and engineering fundamentals to systematic investigation, interpretation, analysis and innovative solution of complex problems and broader aspects of engineering practice.
1.2	**Conceptual understanding** of mathematics, numerical analysis, statistics and computer and information sciences which underpin the engineering discipline.	**Develops and fluently applies** relevant investigation analysis, interpretation, assessment, characterisation, prediction, evaluation, modelling, decision-making, measurement, evaluation, knowledge management and communication tools and techniques pertinent to the engineering discipline.
1.3	In-depth understanding of specialist bodies of knowledge within the engineering discipline.	**Proficiently applies** advanced technical knowledge and skills in at least one specialist practice domain of the engineering discipline.
1.4	**Discernment** of knowledge development and research directions within the engineering discipline.	**Identifies and critically appraises** current developments, advanced technologies, emerging issues and interdisciplinary linkages in at least one specialist practice domain of the engineering discipline. **Interprets and applies** selected research literature to inform engineering application in at least one specialist domain of the engineering discipline.
1.5	**Knowledge** of contextual factors impacting the engineering discipline.	**Identifies and understands** the interactions between engineering systems and people in the social, cultural, environmental, commercial, legal and political contexts in which they operate, including both the positive role of engineering in sustainable development and the potentially adverse impacts of engineering activity in the engineering discipline. **Is aware of** the founding principles of human factors relevant to the engineering discipline. **Is aware of** the fundamentals of business and enterprise management. **Identifies** the structure, roles and capabilities of the engineering workforce. **Appreciates** the issues associated with international engineering practice and global operating contexts.

(Continued)

Table 3.11 (Continued) Elements and indicators for knowledge and skill base

EA	Element of competency	Indicators of attainment
1.6	**Understanding** of the scope, principles, norms, accountabilities and bounds of contemporary engineering practice in the engineering discipline.	**Applies** systematic principles of engineering design relevant to the engineering discipline. **Appreciates** the basis and relevance of standards and codes of practice as well as legislative and statutory requirements applicable to the engineering discipline. **Appreciates** the principles of safety engineering, risk management and the health and safety responsibilities of the professional engineer, including legislative requirements applicable to the engineering discipline. **Appreciates** the social, environmental and economic principles of sustainable engineering practice. **Understands** the fundamental principles of engineering project management as a basis for planning, organising and managing resources. **Appreciates** the formal structures and methodologies of systems engineering as a holistic basis for managing complexity and sustainability in engineering practice.
2.1	**Application** of established engineering methods to complex engineering problem-solving.	**Identifies, discerns and characterises** salient issues, **determines and analyses** causes and effects, **justifies and applies** appropriate simplifying assumptions, **predicts** performance and behaviour, **synthesises** solution strategies and **develops** substantiated conclusions. **Ensures** that all aspects of an engineering activity are soundly based on fundamental principles – by diagnosing, and taking appropriate action with data, calculations, results, proposals, processes, practices, and documented information that may be ill-founded, illogical, erroneous, unreliable or unrealistic. **Competently addresses** engineering problems involving uncertainty, ambiguity, imprecise information and wide-ranging and sometimes conflicting technical and non-technical factors. **Partitions** problems, processes or systems into manageable elements for the purposes of analysis, modelling or design and then **recombines** to form a whole, with the integrity and performance of the overall system as the paramount consideration. **Conceptualises** alternative engineering approaches and evaluates potential outcomes against appropriate criteria to justify an optimal solution choice. **Critically reviews and applies** relevant standards and codes of practice underpinning the engineering discipline and nominated specialisations.

(Continued)

Table 3.11 (Continued) Elements and indicators for knowledge and skill base

EA	Element of competency	Indicators of attainment
		Identifies, quantifies, mitigates and manages technical, health, environmental, safety and other contextual risks associated with engineering application in the designated engineering discipline.
		Interprets and ensures compliance with relevant legislative and statutory requirements applicable to the engineering discipline.
		Investigates complex problems using research-based knowledge and research methods.
2.2	**Fluent application** of engineering techniques, tools and resources.	**Proficiently identifies, selects and applies** the materials, components, devices, systems, processes, resources, plant and equipment relevant to the engineering discipline.
		Constructs or selects and applies from a qualitative description of a phenomenon, process, system, component or device a mathematical, physical or computational model based on fundamental scientific principles and justifiable simplifying assumptions.
		Determines properties, performance, safe working limits, failure modes and other inherent parameters of materials, components and systems relevant to the engineering discipline.
		Applies a wide range of engineering tools for analysis, simulation, visualisation, synthesis and design, including assessing the accuracy and limitations of such tools, and validation of their results.
		Applies formal systems engineering methods to address the planning and execution of complex, problem-solving and engineering projects.
		Designs and conducts experiments, analyses and interprets result data and formulates reliable conclusions.
		Analyses sources of error in applied models and experiments; eliminates, minimises or compensates for such errors; quantifies significance of errors to any conclusions drawn.
		Safely applies laboratory, test and experimental procedures appropriate to the engineering discipline.
		Understands the need for systematic management of the acquisition, commissioning, operation, upgrade, monitoring and maintenance of engineering plant, facilities, equipment and systems.
		Understands the role of quality management systems, tools and processes within a culture of continuous improvement.

(Continued)

Table 3.11 (Continued) Elements and indicators for knowledge and skill base

EA	Element of competency	Indicators of attainment
2.3	Application of systematic engineering synthesis and design processes.	**Proficiently applies** technical knowledge and open ended problem-solving skills as well as appropriate tools and resources to design components, elements, systems, plant, facilities and/or processes to satisfy user requirements. **Addresses** broad contextual constraints such as social, cultural, environmental, commercial, legal political and human factors, as well as health, safety and sustainability imperatives as an integral part of the design process. **Executes and leads** a whole systems design cycle approach including tasks such as: determining client requirements and identifying the impact of relevant contextual factors, including business planning and costing targets; systematically addressing sustainability criteria; working within projected development, production and implementation constraints; eliciting, scoping and documenting the required outcomes of the design task and defining acceptance criteria; identifying assessing and managing technical, health and safety risks integral to the design process; writing engineering specifications that fully satisfy the formal requirements; ensuring compliance with essential engineering standards and codes of practice; partitioning the design task into appropriate modular, functional elements; that can be separately addressed and subsequently integrated through defined interfaces; identifying and analysing possible design approaches and justifying an optimal approach; developing and completing the design using appropriate engineering principles, tools, and processes; integrating functional elements to form a coherent design solution; quantifying the materials, components, systems, equipment, facilities, engineering resources and operating arrangements needed for implementation of the solution; checking the design solution for each element and the integrated system against the engineering specifications; devising and documenting tests that will verify performance of the elements and the integrated realisation; prototyping/implementing the design solution and verifying performance against specification; documenting, commissioning and reporting the design outcome. **Is aware** of the accountabilities of the professional engineer in relation to the "design authority" role.

(Continued)

Table 3.11 (Continued) Elements and indicators for knowledge and skill base

EA	Element of competency	Indicators of attainment
2.4	**Application of systematic approaches** to the conduct and management of engineering projects.	**Contributes to and/or manages** complex engineering project activity, as a member and/or as leader of an engineering team. **Seeks out** the requirements and associated resources and realistically assesses the scope, dimensions, scale of effort and indicative costs of a complex engineering project. **Accommodates** relevant contextual issues into all phases of engineering project work, including the fundamentals of business planning and financial management **Proficiently applies** basic systems engineering and/or project management tools and processes to the planning and execution of project work, targeting the delivery of a significant outcome to a professional standard. **Is aware** of the need to plan and quantify performance over the full life-cycle of a project, managing engineering performance within the overall implementation context. **Demonstrates** commitment to sustainable engineering practices and the achievement of sustainable outcomes in all facets of engineering project work.

Source: Adapted from Ref. [137].

items, and these criteria should be able to be evidenced. A moderation process for all assessments should be clearly demonstrated [136].

The teaching environment is taken into consideration to ensure that the higher education institution has sufficient resources to effectively deliver the programs to be accredited. It is up to the higher education institution to prove that the curriculum and delivery of the program enable students to attain the required outcomes by the time of graduation [134]. The curriculum must be integrated with multiple courses for developing transferable skills throughout the program [136].

Relationships with external stakeholders   There is a need for a demonstrated relationship with industry and engineering institutions which ensures that the programs are "fit for purpose" with adequate quality [134–136]. It is advisable that the engineering unit, department or school have a program advisory committee (PAC) or industry advisory committee (IAC) for each engineering program. Such a PAC/IAC should have clear terms of reference and needs to consist of senior practising engineers. The PAC/IAC must also be able to demonstrate that it is genuinely engaged in providing feedback [136]. In some instances, the PAC/IAC may consider "big picture" progress, and the sub-committees deal with the fine detail [136–138]. Regular PAC/IAC meetings (at least two such meetings per year) are expected, along with well-documented minutes.

Type of "entry-to-practice" degrees: duration, offerings and alternative pathways For dual-degree programs, where the qualification is a combination of an engineering degree and a non-engineering degree, the accreditation requirement is for the engineering qualification only. Where two engineering degrees form a dual degree, each degree in its own right must meet the accreditation requirements [136–138]. EA also expects each program to relate to a clearly defined engineering discipline and that the graduate attributes for each individual program can be demonstrated, reviewed and revised via formal, documented processes which include all staff who deliver the program as well as feedback from the external stakeholders [136–138]. It is also expected that the program name and final qualification must include the word "engineering" and/or "technology" [136]. If the specification is not in the name of the degree, then it needs to be listed as a major on the academic transcript [136].

Opportunities for accelerated learning are also acceptable as long as there is sufficient time during the program of studies for the student to demonstrate the requisite skill-level achievement [136]. This is particularly important for alternative delivery modes where course and program content must be equivalent to the standard delivery mode [136–138].

All documentations for the accreditation of a program must contain information about offerings that are available at every location, including offshore (if any), and the accreditation panel will visit all offshore locations and interview staff and students at each location [134]. When onshore and offshore graduates receive the same testamur, and the higher education institution claims an undifferentiated offering, accreditation must be achieved at every location, because EA will accredit the program as a single entity [134].

The higher education institution must reimburse EA for any costs incurred for offshore visits, including time in some instances [134–136]. EA generally informs the host nation's accrediting organisation of any requests for accreditation of an offshore program. EA only completes accreditation if this is approved by the local accreditation organisation [134].

Off-campus study mode is considered an alternative pathway. However, the higher education institution must still provide evidence that PLOs have been achieved. For example, distance-learning students should still have the same level of opportunity to interact with other students and academic staff/faculty members, provide feedback to the higher education institution and experience the same quality of experimental and project works as those students experiencing complete face-to-face delivery [134,135].

Alternative pathways, lateral entry and entry points also need to show equivalent learning outcomes. The overall program structure needs to be flexible enough to allow for articulation from other qualifications and provide sufficient support in the initial courses for those students with non-traditional backgrounds [134–138]. To assist students to gain international experience, the program structure needs to be flexible, allowing students to study overseas, and also be attractive to encourage students from abroad to participate in an Australian university exchange experience. Credit transfers, where they exist, should be rigorous and well-documented [136].

Exposure to Professional Practice EA "strongly advocates" a workplace experience of at least 60 days' full-time work, or an equivalent. Ideally, during the senior year levels (Year 3 and Year 4), this work experience in an engineering environment should occur under the supervision of a professional engineer. The exposure to professional practice (engineering work experience) needs to be structured as a learning activity with appropriate and measurable learning outcomes [136–138]. Common assessment items, such as a journal, logbook or portfolio, must be designed such that the students can track their own progress. EA highly recommends that the "Exposure to Professional Practice" is completed before the final study period (graduation) [136].

It is anticipated that during their studies, the students manage at least one project which is complex enough to require them to integrate their knowledge from different technical fields and practise their non-technical skills. It is also anticipated that there will be considerable laboratory and other learning experiences that allow students to have hands-on experience [136–138].

II. OPERATIONAL ENVIRONMENT

Part of the accreditation process is to ensure that the current technical and managerial issues related to the specific discipline area of the program being accredited are addressed within the program structure and that students are given opportunities to cope with such issues. Where mainstream topics are omitted, accreditation may not be granted [136]. In terms of the operational environment, there must be a demonstrated gender balance across all academic/faculty levels as well as an academic workload policy and demonstration of its use. In addition, there must be an organisational unit in charge of engineering education, and there needs to be clear lines of delegation and authority within this unit [136].

The higher education institution also needs to demonstrate that it has a long-term commitment to engineering education, and it must be able to demonstrate a willingness to implement continuous improvement cycles [134–136]. There also needs to be evidence of organisational unit review, program improvement processes and the processes for changing existing programs and developing new ones. There are also staffing requirements with the proviso that no specialisation is reliant on one sole staff/faculty member [136–138]. The academic staff/faculty member profile also needs to show some sensitivity to cultural background, gender and industry and research experience. EA has no objections to the use of practising engineers as casual academic staff/ faculty members as long as there are appropriate induction and support for them, and the recruitment process is clear [136].

The higher education institution needs to demonstrate that there are workload management processes in place to ensure that students are adequately supported [136]. Students also need to be provided with an opportunity to interact with industry (i.e. organisation of regular industry visits, industry evenings, guest lectures by industry practitioners, etc.) [136–138]. Each program needs an academic leader (program coordinator, program director, program manager, course leader, etc.), and the interaction of the whole program team should be obvious to the students [136].

There should be real links between the higher education institution and the research, industry and community groups. Teaching staff/faculty members should also be aware of the current developments in engineering education and pedagogy [136]. Business planning must show sufficient economic support to ensure the viability of the engineering programs, and this will depend in part on demand. The higher education provider needs to demonstrate that consistent and timely demand analysis is being performed. The engineering unit also needs to track enrolment and retention rates as well as be able to monitor the effects of admissions, pathway and mode of study on success, retention and graduation rates. This requires that there are systems in place which allow the tracking of both individuals and cohorts of students. All management systems need to be auditable [136].

Other criteria within the "Operational Environment" may actually be controlled by the overarching administration of the university rather than the engineering department or school *per se*. For example, the criteria require that there should be student counselling, advice and learning support which caters to individual student needs, including those with a disability. All students must be able to access all learning and experimental facilities [134–138]. Other operational factors include providing student learning support, technical and administrative support and the use of best practice in engineering education, as well as progressive pedagogy.

III. QUALITY SYSTEM

The accreditation process assumes that the higher education institution will be able to review the following under its own quality and auditing systems [134]:

- PLOs
- Educational design
- Student assessment
- Program performance

The ability of the higher education institution to continuously monitor and improve quality must be demonstrated. There should also be evidence of the higher education institution receiving and using student feedback in a way which demonstrates to students that their feedback is valued (i.e. a closed-loop mechanism) [134–138]. It is anticipated that review and improvement processes need to focus on the relationship between learning outcomes, learning activities and assessment, and that program and curriculum planning and amendments are made in response to demand trends, quality management processes and external stakeholders [134–138]. Any such changes need to be well-documented. Program guides should refer to stage 1 competencies, and the individual course guides must indicate which competency element is addressed by the course, subject, unit or module. Internal quality assurance processes should encourage benchmarking, which can occur via external assessors or peers, or by an internal moderation process, such as cross-marking of final-year research projects. It is anticipated that such benchmarking may also comprise the sharing of teaching and assessment materials, visits between institutions, and the sharing of data [134–138]. In particular, the award of honours levels should be comparable on a national scale [136]. It may be stressed again that accreditation is a process of review, which is evidence-based, and the evaluation of programs is done against predefined outcomes and quality standards [134–138]. Part of the evidence typically used to demonstrate these competency standards is internal auditing that the higher education institution performs.

The design of the program needs to be undertaken by both a "top-down" approach and a "bottom-up" approach. The "top down" approach uses the PLOs to inform the CLOs, while the "bottom-up" approach starts with the topic learning outcomes and builds these up to the PLOs [136]. These approaches were discussed in more detail in

Chapter 2. Additionally, the evidence for the achievement of PLOs should come from a variety of different sources including a range of assessment items as well as qualitative measures. Program and course curriculum review must incorporate both employers' needs and demands as well as students' feedback [136–138].

An example of a tentative table of contents for a typical accreditation document submission to EA's AB for the accreditation of a Bachelor of Engineering program is listed in Appendix C.

Chapter 4

Cross-border higher education quality assurance and dual accreditation

4.1 Introduction

The cross-border higher education is generally where the academic staff/faculty members, students, courses and programs, higher education institutions and/or course or program materials cross-national jurisdictional borders [139]. Government and private higher education institutions can deliver the cross-border higher education. Modes of delivery of the cross-border higher education range from face-to-face (students travel abroad, overseas branch campuses, study centres and collaborative local partners) to distance learning (using a range of technologies, including e-learning) [139,140].

As observed in Chapter 1, the cross-border (offshore) delivery of higher education started predominantly in the early 1990s with the mobility of students, academic staff/faculty members, courses and programs and higher education institutions (offshore branch campuses, study centres, etc.). With the advancement of information technology and the internet, various innovative modes of education delivery enabled tens of thousands of courses and programs to be delivered in locations far from the mother institution beyond the national boundary or jurisdiction. Although there no exact data on the magnitude of cross-border education, it is believed that more than 34 countries' higher education institutions deliver the cross-border higher education through 250 international branch campuses. Students participating in this education do so in 76 countries. The countries that have most offshore branch campuses are the USA (77), the UK (38), France (28), Russia (21) and Australia (14). The top five countries that host foreign countries' branches of higher education institutions are China (32), the United Arab Emirates (UAE) (32), Singapore (12), Malaysia (12) and Qatar (11) [141–143].

There is no doubt that cross-border (offshore) higher education offers opportunities for improving the skills and competencies of the local population as well as strengthening the quality of national higher education and driving innovation. However, if the offshore education is not of the same standard as that delivered at the home campus, there is a risk that the resulting qualification is of limited value [144]. As offshore delivery of higher education is accelerating, it not only increases the interdependence between countries but also creates pressures for greater consistency between national education systems. Hence, an effective quality assurance and accreditation for the recognition of qualifications from different national jurisdictions are necessary. With increasing numbers of people obtaining foreign qualifications, there is a growing need for safeguards against low-quality cross-border higher education, especially in engineering and other professional qualifications.

Underscoring this urgency, the United Nations Education and Scientific and Cultural Organisation (UNESCO), in close association with the Organisation for Economic Cooperation and Development (OECD), developed guidelines on Quality Provision in the Cross-border Higher Education [139]. The OECD is mainly composed of members from developed nations (listed in Table 4.1).

These guidelines were formally approved by UNESCO's 33rd session of the General Conference in October 2005. Over 90 countries of the United Nations were consulted in the development of the guidelines. The UNESCO-approved guidelines were almost immediately ratified by the OECD Council on 2 December 2005. The guidelines provide an international framework to protect students and other stakeholders from low-quality provision of education and disreputable higher education institutions. The sustainability of the cross-border higher education largely depends on quality delivery that meets the human, social, economic and cultural needs of the host country. The guidelines elaborate the shared responsibilities of governments (offering and host nations), higher education institutions, students, quality assurance and accreditation organisations of the offering country and the host country. The guidelines are framed to preserve the diversity of the offering and the host countries' higher education systems [139,145].

The UNESCO-OECD guidelines 2005 [139,145] recognise four key aspects associated with the cross-border delivery of higher education.

The first is that the cross-border higher education increases higher education access, improves and introduces innovations in the host country's higher education and contributes to the building of international co-operation, which is essential for academic knowledge, and national, social and economic wealth. It also recognises that the cross-border higher education needs to be managed appropriately in order to limit low-quality delivery and identify "rogue" higher education institutions. All stakeholders, including students, need to be better informed about the quality of foreign higher education qualifications and offering institutions.

The second aspect is the need for an international framework to minimise the risk of misleading guidance and information, low-quality education delivery and degree or certificate factories that offer unaccredited qualifications of limited validity, use and value.

Table 4.1 Current OECD nations

Current OECD member nations as of 27 February 2020

• Austria (1961)	• Luxembourg (1961)	• USA (1961)	• Poland (1996)
• Belgium (1961)	• Netherlands (1961)	• Italy (1962)	• Hungary (1996)
• Canada (1961)	• Norway (1961)	• Japan (1964)	• Slovak Republic (2000)
• Denmark (1961)	• Portugal (1961)	• Finland (1969)	• Slovenia (2010)
• France (1961)	• Spain (1961)	• Australia (1971)	• Israel (2010)
• Germany (1961)	• Sweden (1961)	• New Zealand (1973)	• Estonia (2010)
• Greece (1961)	• Switzerland (1961)	• Mexico (1994)	• Chile (2010)
• Iceland (1961)	• Turkey (1961)	• Czech Republic (1995)	• Latvia (2016)
• Ireland (1961)	• UK (1961)	• South Korea (1996)	• Lithuania (2018)

Members on the waiting list for joining OECD

• Columbia   • Costa Rica

Source: Adapted from Ref. [145].

The third aspect is the importance of national sovereignty over higher education and the unevenness and diversity of stages of development of domestic systems to assure the quality of higher education among countries.

The fourth aspect states that some host countries have competent government, and other bodies and relevant frameworks are responsible for quality assurance, accreditation and recognition of qualifications that should take or initiate action in quality assurance of the foreign countries' qualifications offered in their national jurisdictions.

The UNESCO-OECD guidelines recommend that governments, higher education institutions, student organisations and organisations responsible for quality assurance, accreditation and professional recognition take action based on three main principles [145]:

*   Mutual trust and respect among countries and recognition of the importance of international collaboration in higher education.
*   Recognition of the importance of national authority and the diversity of higher education systems.
*   Recognition of the importance of higher education as a means for expressing a country's linguistic and cultural diversity and also for nurturing its economic development and social cohesion.

The UNESCO-OECD guidelines are comprehensive and aimed to assist students (learners) get easy access to reliable information on higher education offered outside their home country and/or by foreign higher education institutions in their home country. The guidelines urge governments, foreign higher education institutions and other stakeholders to make qualifications transparent and to provide greater clarity on the procedures used to establish international recognition of available qualifications. The guidelines contain seven specific recommendations for governments, nine for foreign higher education institutions, three for students and students organisations, seven for academic quality assurance and accreditation organisations, six for academic recognition organisations and four for professional organisations. Some countries have separate organisations to deal with quality assurance and accreditation, academic recognition and professional organisation-related matters. However, others, with smaller populations, tend to have one organisation to deal with such issues. The collaboration of UNESCO and the OECD in developing the guidelines is unique, given that the underlying aims and activities of UNESCO and OECD are notably different. Although these guidelines are not binding, the endorsement by two reputable international organisations comprising more than 190 countries provides a formidable and significant force for implementation [139,145–147].

Traditionally, responsibility for the quality assurance for higher education lies with both sovereign governments and immobility of higher education institutions. Today, however, higher education institutions are increasingly mobile, especially in developed nations, and are becoming multinational in delivering their education programs and courses [142, 143]. The higher education institutions from the developed nations, especially from the English-speaking world, have been delivering courses and programs offshore using various modes (fly-in-fly-out, branch campus, franchising, dual degree, joint degree, online, etc.). The internationalisation of higher education through cross-border delivery of courses and programs in the era of globalisation and the information technology revolution creates a formidable challenge to accountability and quality assurance efforts. It also creates concerns for sovereignty, legal jurisdiction and economic and geopolitical dynamics that cannot necessarily be addressed by using traditional accountability frameworks of the offering and host countries [141–143].

With the rapid expansion of offshore higher education delivery, the quality assurance and accreditation organisations face challenges in developing effective evaluation process for the cross-border higher education acceptable under both host and offering countries' rules and regulations. The foreign higher education institutions need to comply with both countries' rules and regulations [146]. As the delivery methods and modes of offshore education are generally not the same as those used onshore, the "undifferentiated" course and program learning outcomes (PLOs) become the primary focus used to ensure quality. This creates a challenge for the offering institution as well as for quality assurance and accreditation organisations, because the established threshold of quality is difficult to apply and the measurement of equivalent course or PLOs is open to interpretation.

The processes become further complicated due to the fact that the offshore delivery of higher education is market-driven, and the profitability of offshore education can be the primary focus of the offering institution. Stiff market competition and a profit-making desire can drive foreign higher education institutions to compromise the quality of the course or program delivery, and it is within this context that the host country's quality assurance and accreditation organisations must operate and take part in quality assurance processes.

In addition, sustainable delivery of education in the host country is often seen as a quality indicator. The result is that foreign higher education institutions are required to have multiple quality assurance exercises to comply with both the home and host countries' quality assurance and accreditation organisations. Such multiple accreditations create additional financial burdens, because the offering foreign institution needs to bear the cost of all such exercises. Furthermore, the cycle duration for reaccreditation and quality assurance exercises is generally much shorter than that required at the home campus courses or programs. Therefore, the frequent and short cycles for such exercises make offshore delivery not only financially challenging but also resource-intensive.

Such periodic reviews are typical for engineering programs and qualifications, because these professionals make decisions that can affect the safety of citizens, and hence, external accreditation of quality is necessary. The higher education institutions in developed nations mostly offer engineering programs and qualifications that are accredited by the professional accreditation organisations within the national jurisdictions. As discussed in Chapters 1 and 3, two major organisations (International Engineering Alliance, or IEA, and European Network for Accreditation of Engineering Education, or ENAEE), through their full signatories, undertake professional accreditation of engineering programs within each signatory's jurisdiction. Frequently, offshore engineering programs need accreditations by professional accreditation organisations of the home country as well as of the host country. This double accreditation is called dual accreditation.

4.2 Dual accreditation and its importance

Dual accreditation is the process by which a higher education institution needs a particular engineering program (qualification) accredited by more than one accreditation organisation. That is to say, the process described in Chapter 3 must have been undergone multiple times to satisfy each accrediting body/organisation. This current chapter focuses on the requirements of dual accreditation as determined by the IEA. Some examples of multiple accreditations are also discussed.

As mentioned briefly in Chapter 3, the Washington Accord limits recognition of programs to those accredited within the signatories' jurisdiction. However, under the Accord signatories, there is a need to accredit undifferentiated engineering programs of their home countries' education institutions if the programs are also offered outside their national boundaries. As an example, if an engineering program of an Australian university is offered in Australia (onshore) and offshore, and both offerings are substantially equivalent, or 'undifferentiated", then both offerings need to be accredited by Engineers Australia. In that case, too, if the offshore program is offered in a Washington Accord signatory nation, then the offshore program needs to be accredited by both countries' accreditation organisations (i.e. Engineers Australia and the host country's accreditation organisation). When there are two Washington Accord signatories' accreditations, these are called dual accreditation.

Dual accreditation is seen to be significant because it is the only process by which offshore-offered programs can be assessed in terms of quality and professional standard. Quality of qualifications reassures the general public and employers that engineers are being trained adequately [148–150]. In addition, as the program is offered outside the mother campus of the higher education institution, the host country's government and professional organisations, and the general public, need to be reassured about the quality and undifferentiated learning outcomes of the program. Second, the students and parents wish to see that their money and effort are well spent on the foreign qualification [148–150].

More broadly, a larger proportion of the population is seeking higher education than ever before, so that it is incumbent on accrediting and government bodies to ensure that there is a suitable regulatory framework in place [151]. This is particularly important now that many higher education institutions are offering qualifications across national boundaries [151].

4.3 Stakeholders of dual accreditation

Accreditation is generally important to higher education institutions, the general public, students in accredited programs, and companies, industries and employers that employ graduates of accredited programs. Dual accreditation has the same stakeholders, with the added provision that the general public and employers may be offshore and face specific, local conditions. In addition, the learning environment for students

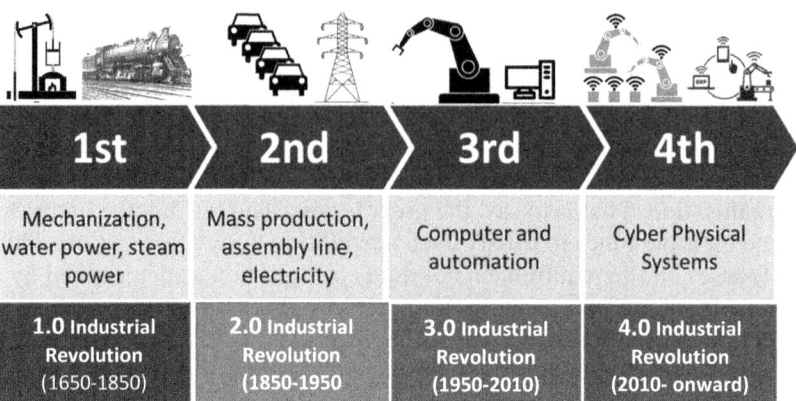

Figure 4.1 Industrial revolutions and continuous changing technological demands. (Adapted from Ref. [152].)

may be considerably different, depending on the place of delivery and, indeed, the delivery mode of the program of studies. Dual accreditation seeks to ensure that, irrespective of the location and delivery mode, the education is of the standard claimed and that the final qualification will be recognised in multiple nations.

Dual accreditation is of increasing importance within the practice of engineering because of the globalised nature of the engineering industry and the multi-national companies which operate within the sector. In addition, with the use of internet technology and the arrival of "Industrial Revolution 4.0" (as shown in Figure 4.1), engineers operating within their home nation may still be implementing technology overseas so that mutual recognition of engineering qualifications within this context is therefore key.

4.4 Examples of multiple accreditations: Australia and the USA

While not specifically understood as "dual accreditation", there are several instances where either programs or higher education institutions need to go through an accreditation process. It is relevant to discuss these here to endeavour to identify any common patterns or themes between these situations and the specific case of "Dual Accreditation" as determined by the Washington Accord.

The most obvious example of multiple accreditations occurs within the United States of America, where accreditation is performed as a quality assurance process for both/either higher education institution and/or a particular qualification [148,150]. Higher education institutions can be accredited by a regional or state-based accreditor (who accredits higher education institutions within a specific region or state), a faith-based accreditor (who accredits higher education institutions affiliated with a specific religious doctrine), a career-related accreditor (who accredits for-profit and career-based institutions) or a program accreditor (who accredits particular programs within a specific discipline).

In the USA, therefore, engineering degrees need to be accredited by the Accreditation Board for Engineering and Technology (ABET), a program accreditor, i.e. the accreditation organisation which is a signatory of the Washington Accord within that jurisdiction, and the relevant regional organisation which accredits higher education institutions. There are five regional accreditors, where each services a particular geographic region of the US. Typically, these two accreditation procedures are conducted independently, with an increased financial burden placed on the higher education institution [148,150].

Accreditation generally ensures that students receive a good quality, industry-relevant education and value-for-money education. As the regional accreditors accredit across disciplines and types of qualifications, there are some reservations about the measures used for such a breadth of higher education institutions and qualifications [148,150]. Another issue associated with the accreditation within the US is the lack of transparency in the decision-making process. In addition, the process does not keep pace with changes in society and technology. The quality assurance and quality improvement aspects of accreditation are performed separately in two different processes. The regional and state accreditors are also required to enforce compliance with federal legislation, making the process more of a quality assurance exercise than a chance to improve quality of the program or qualification [148–150].

Despite numerous attempts to establish one overarching organisation, recognising different accrediting organisations (five regional organisations) within the US, a consensus on mutual agreements between regional and state accreditation organisations is yet to be reached. This is believed to be due to complicated relationships between regional and state accrediting organisations, state and federal legislation and financial interests [153]. To achieve the true spirit of the Washington Accord, IPEA, APEC and other international agreements and true global mobility of graduate professional engineers, technologists and technicians, it would be very good if the regional quality assurance and accreditation organisations of the US could mutually agree to form an organisation that would work as an umbrella organisation for all regional accreditation organisations.

Within Australia, the situation is completely different. The Australian federal government, in consultation with all states and territory governments, has established the Tertiary Education Quality and Standards Agency (TEQSA), which ensures that higher education institutions deliver a minimum level of quality education. More specifically, TEQSA provides registration and renewals of higher education institutions, course and program accreditation and renewals, and CRICOS registration or renewal. It also deals with domestic students' complaints, international students' complaints and other stakeholders' complaints. The CRICOS (Commonwealth Register of Institutions and Courses for Overseas Students) is mandatory for any course or program that is open to international students in Australia on student visas.

In addition to TEQSA, there is the Australian Qualifications Framework (AQF), which describes the learning outcomes required to achieve different levels of qualifications and programs [149]. However, program-specific professional accreditation is left to individual professional accreditation organisations. For example, the professional accreditation for engineering programs is vested in Engineers Australia in all states and territories. As all programs and qualifications offered by Australian institutions are compliant with AQF descriptors since 2015, Engineers Australia has developed equivalencies between the AQF and its own professional categories (Washington Accord, Sydney Accord and Dublin Accord). This equivalency reduces the burden on higher education institutions within the national context, but it does not aid in the accreditation of offshore programs (see Chapter 5).

4.5 Example of dual accreditation: the Washington Accord

4.5.1 What's changed

Within the context of the Washington Accord, dual accreditation refers to the situation where a qualification is offered in a country (or "jurisdiction") other than the jurisdiction in which the higher education institution is located. The most common example of this type of education model is that of "offshore education", where a higher education institution delivers qualifications outside its home nation.

In recent times, within the IEA, the process of dual accreditation has been significantly altered. Previously, if an engineering program or qualification was offered offshore, then accreditation by the professional organisation which manages the home jurisdiction of the higher education institution was all that is necessary to accredit the offshore degree. This is now no longer the case. Currently, if the host nation's engineering accreditation organisation is a signatory to the Washington Accord, all offshore qualifications must be accredited by the accrediting organisation of the offering institution's jurisdiction *and* by the accrediting organisation of the jurisdiction within which the qualification is being offered.

This is a significant shift in process and is still being examined in terms of the long-term implications for higher education institutions and accreditation organisations [154]. One of the more significant aspects of dual accreditation is the role and use of evidence in showing that the program or qualification being offered covers the graduate attributes required by each accrediting organisation. Moreover, a separate accreditation exercise is required for the program or qualification to be compliant with the host country's national qualifications framework.

4.5.2 Process and interpretation of cross-mapping

As accreditation is outcome-based, the evidence used to demonstrate the attainment of these outcomes is critical. In addition, there needs to be some consideration that an appropriate standard for achieving the learning outcomes has been employed [151].

The evidence must demonstrate that there is alignment between the intended learning outcomes and the educational process and that the curriculum is aligned with the delivery method [155]. The program-level learning outcomes also need to relate to the graduate attributes of the Washington Accord, contextualised for the specific discipline of engineering being studied. It is generally understood that the evidence for demonstrating achievement of the PLOs should come from a range of different sources and may include assessment items as well as qualitative measures [155].

Cross-mapping is the process used to show that the PLOs map onto the graduate attributes required by the accrediting organisation and that multiple PLOs may be necessary to demonstrate coverage of one graduate attribute [155]. Table 4.2

Table 4.2 Course-level learning outcomes contributing to developing a program-level
          learning outcome

Program-level learning outcome: mechanical engineering	CLO first year course	Course-level learning outcome second year course	Course-level learning outcome third year course	Course-level learning outcome fourth year course
"Comprehensive, theory-based understanding of the underpinning natural and physical sciences and the engineering fundamentals applicable to the engineering discipline" [157]	"Determine internal forces, stress and strain in simple pin-jointed trusses, beams and frames including normal force, bending moment and shearing force diagrams" [158]	"Calculate the shear, torsional, axial, and bending stresses which occur at a point or which act on a section, and express this state of stress either algebraically or graphically using Mohr's Circle for Stress" [157]	"Solve advanced practical engineering problems in the field of non-linear stress analysis" [159]	"Simulate engineering applications using non-linear modeling and simulation of engineering applications" [160]

Source: Adapted from Refs. [149–151,156].

illustrates how individual course learning outcomes (CLOs) contribute to the development of a PLO.

In Table 4.2, it can be seen that the program-level learning outcome is mapped across the different course-level learning outcomes, where each course-level learning outcome is contextualised by the year-level expectations. In this way, we can see

Table 4.3 Program-level learning outcome with related graduate attribute of Engineers
          Australia

Program-level learning outcome: mechanical engineering	Graduate attribute from Engineers' Australia	Equivalent graduate attribute from the Washington Accord
"Comprehensive, theory-based understanding of the underpinning natural and physical sciences and the engineering fundamentals applicable to the engineering discipline" [157]	"Comprehensive, theory-based understanding of the underpinning natural and physical sciences and the engineering fundamentals applicable to the engineering discipline" [155]	"Apply knowledge of mathematics, natural science, engineering fundamentals and an engineering specialisation as specified in WK1 to WK4 respectively to the solution of complex engineering problems" [161]

that the CLOs should "add up" as evidence to prove that the program-level learning outcomes have been achieved.

In the process of single accreditation, the next step is to map the program-level learning outcomes onto the graduate attributes described by the accrediting organisation, as shown in Table 4.3.

Table 4.3 shows that the program-level learning outcome has been associated with a particular graduate attribute from Engineers Australia. The graduate attribute from Engineers Australia has been associated with an equivalent learning outcome from the Washington Accord. In this way, the alignment of the program's learning outcomes with EA's graduate attributes can be demonstrated, and therefore, because EA's graduate attributes are aligned with the Washington Accord, the program is also aligned with the Washington Accord, and graduates are therefore able to practise across different geographical jurisdictions.

In dual accreditation, there is an additional cross-check which needs to occur. There must be cross-mapping between the graduate attributes required by one accrediting organisation to the graduate attributes required by the other accrediting organisation.

This is demonstrated in Table 4.4, where a program-level learning outcome is mapped to both Engineers Australia and Hong Kong Institution of Engineers (HKIE) graduate attributes. For completeness, the relevant graduate attribute from the Washington Accord is also provided.

The cross-mapping process in dual accreditation can therefore become quite complex, and there are two obvious ways to achieve it:

a.   Keep the accreditation processes separate and map the PLOs to the graduate attributes of each single accrediting body individually,
     or

Table 4.4 Comparison between graduate attributes

The Washington Accord	Graduate attribute from Engineers Australia	Equivalent graduate attribute from the HKIE	Program-level learning outcome
"Communicate effectively on complex engineering activities with the engineering community and with society at large, such as being able to comprehend and write effective reports and design documentation, make effective presentations, and give and receive clear instructions" [161]	"Effective oral and written communication in professional and lay domains" [155]	"an ability to communicate effectively" [162]	"Comprehensive, theory-based understanding of the underpinning natural and physical sciences and the engineering fundamentals applicable to the engineering discipline" [157]

b. Develop an agreed cross-mapping table between the graduate attributes of each accrediting body, and the same table can then be used for each separate accreditation process.

In case of (b), the cross-mapping exercise needs only to be performed once, saving time and reducing the administrative burden on higher education institutions: something which multiple accreditations have tended to produce in the past. The difficulty is that there are often very different interpretations of what the graduate attributes actually mean and which ones are equivalent.

If one were to try to derive such a cross-mapping table, the simplest way to start may be to look at the cross-mapping of each accrediting body's graduate attributes to those of the Washington Accord. Unfortunately, while accrediting bodies clearly publish their own required graduate attributes, they rarely explain how their graduate

Table 4.5 A cross-map between the graduate attributes of Washington Accord [161] and Hong Kong Institute of Engineers (HKIE) [162]

Washington Accord (IEA)			HKIE
Knowledge profiles	**WK 1**	A systematic, theory-based understanding of the **natural sciences** applicable to the discipline.	**(a)** An ability to apply knowledge of mathematics, science, and engineering appropriate to the degree discipline.
	WK 2	Concept-based **mathematics**, numerical analysis, statistics and formal aspect of computer and information science to support analysis and modelling applicable to the discipline.	- -
	WK 3	A systematic, theory-based formulation of **engineering fundamentals** required in the engineering discipline.	**(a)** An ability to apply knowledge of mathematics, science, and engineering appropriate to the degree discipline.
	WK 4	Engineering **specialist knowledge** that provides theoretical frameworks and bodies of knowledge for the accepted practice areas in the engineering discipline; much is at the forefront of the discipline.	- -
	WK 5	Knowledge that supports **engineering design** in a practice area.	

(Continued)

Table 4.5 (Continued)   A cross-map between the graduate attributes of Washington
                        Accord [161] and Hong Kong Institute of Engineers (HKIE) [162]

Washington Accord (IEA)		HKIE	
	WK 6 Knowledge of **engineering practice** (technology) in the practice areas in the engineering discipline.	(1)	An ability to use the computer/IT tools relevant to the discipline along with an understanding of their processes and limitations.
	WK 7 **Comprehension** of the role of engineering in society and identified issues in engineering practice in the discipline: ethics and the professional responsibility of an engineer to public safety; the impacts of engineering activity: economic, social, cultural, environmental and sustainability.	-	-
	WK 8 Engagement with selected knowledge in the research literature of the discipline.	-	-
Graduate Attributes	WA 1 Apply knowledge of mathematics, natural science, engineering fundamentals and an engineering specialization as specified in WK1 to WK4 respectively to the solution of complex engineering problems.	-	-
	WA 2 Identify, formulate, research literature and analyse *complex* engineering problems reaching substantiated conclusions using first principles of mathematics, natural sciences and engineering sciences (WK1 to WK 4).	(e)	An ability to identify, formulate and solve engineering problems.

(Continued)

Table 4.5 (Continued) A cross-map between the graduate attributes of Washington
              Accord [161] and Hong Kong Institute of Engineers (HKIE) [162]

Washington Accord (IEA)		HKIE
WA 3	Design solutions for *complex* engineering problems and design systems, components or processes that meet specified needs with appropriate consideration for public health and safety, cultural, societal, and environmental considerations (WK5).	**(c)** An ability to design a system, component or process to meet desired needs within realistic constraints, such as economic, environmental, social, political, ethical, health and safety, manufacturability and sustainability.
WA 4	Conduct investigations of *complex* problems using research-based knowledge (WK8) and research methods including design of experiments, analysis and interpretation of data, and synthesis of information to provide valid conclusions.	**(b)** An ability to design and conduct experiments, as well as to analyse and interpret data.
WA 5	Create, select and apply appropriate techniques, resources, and modern engineering and IT tools, including prediction and modelling, to *complex* engineering problems, with an understanding of the limitations (WK6).	**(k)** An ability to use the techniques, skills, and modern engineering tools necessary for engineering practice appropriate to the degree discipline.
WA 6	Apply reasoning informed by contextual knowledge to assess societal, health, safety, legal and cultural issues and the consequent responsibilities relevant to professional engineering practice and solutions to complex engineering problems (WK7).	**(h)** An ability to understand the impact of engineering solutions in a global and societal context, especially the important of health, safety and environmental considerations to both workers and the general public.

(Continued)

Table 4.5 (Continued) A cross-map between the graduate attributes of Washington Accord [161] and Hong Kong Institute of Engineers (HKIE) [162]

Washington Accord (IEA)		HKIE
WA 7	Understand and evaluate the sustainability and impact of professional engineering work in the solution of complex engineering problems in societal and environmental contexts (WK7).	- -
WA 8	Apply ethical principles and commit to professional ethics and responsibilities and norms of engineering practice (WK7).	**(f)** An ability to understand professional and ethical responsibility.
WA 9	Function effectively as an individual and as a member or leader in diverse teams and in multi-disciplinary settings.	**(d)** An ability to function on multi-disciplinary teams.
WA 10	Communicate effectively on *complex* engineering activities with the engineering community and with society at large, such as being able to comprehend and write effective reports and design documentation, make effective presentations, and give and receive clear instructions.	**(g)** An ability to communicate effectively.
WA 11	Demonstrate knowledge and understanding of engineering management principles and economic decision-making and apply these to one's own work, as a member and leader in a team, to manage projects and in multidisciplinary environments.	- -
WA 12	Recognise the need for and have the preparation and ability to engage in independent and life-long learning in the broadest context of technological change.	**(i)** An ability to stay abreast of contemporary issues. **&** **(j)** An ability to recognise the need for and to engage in life-long learning.

Table 4.6 A cross-map between graduate attributes of Washington Accord [161] and stage 1 competencies of Engineers Australia (EA) [155]

Washington Accord (IEA)			Engineers Australia (EA) stage 1 competencies	
Knowledge profile	**WK 1**	A systematic, theory-based understanding of the **natural sciences** applicable to the discipline.	**1. Knowledge and skills base**	**1.1 Comprehensive, theory-based understanding** of the underpinning natural and physical sciences and the engineering fundamentals applicable to the engineering discipline.
	WK 2	Concept-based **mathematics**, numerical analysis, statistics and formal aspect of computer and information science to support analysis and modelling applicable to the discipline.		**1.2 Conceptual understanding** of the mathematics, numerical analysis, statistics, and computer and information sciences which underpin the engineering discipline.
	WK 3	A systematic, theory-based formulation of **engineering fundamentals** required in the engineering discipline.		**1.1 Comprehensive, theory-based understanding** of the underpinning natural and physical sciences and the engineering fundamentals applicable to the engineering discipline.
	WK 4	Engineering **specialist knowledge** that provides theoretical frameworks and bodies of knowledge for the accepted practice areas in the engineering discipline; much is at the forefront of the discipline.		**1.3 In-depth** **&** **understanding** of specialist bodies of knowledge within the engineering discipline. **1.4 Discernment** of knowledge development and research directions within the engineering discipline.

(Continued)

Table 4.6 (Continued) A cross-map between graduate attributes of Washington Accord
                        [161] and stage 1 competencies of Engineers Australia (EA) [155]

Washington Accord (IEA)	Engineers Australia (EA) stage 1 competencies
WK 5 Knowledge that supports **engineering design** in a practice area.	**1.5 Knowledge** of engineering design practice and contextual factors impacting the engineering discipline.
WK 6 Knowledge of **engineering practice** (technology) in the practice areas in the engineering discipline.	**1.2 Conceptual understanding** of the mathematics, numerical analysis, statistics, and computer and information sciences which underpin the engineering discipline.
WK 7 Comprehension of the role of engineering in society and identified issues in engineering practice in the discipline: ethics and the professional responsibility of an engineer to public safety; the impacts of engineering activity: economic, social, cultural, environmental and sustainability.	**1.6 Understanding** of the scope, principles, norms, accountabilities and bounds of sustainable engineering practice in the specific discipline.
WK 8 Engagement with selected knowledge in the research literature of the discipline.	**1.4 Discernment** of knowledge development and research directions within the engineering discipline.

	Washington Accord (IEA)		Engineers Australia (EA) stage 1 competencies
Graduate attributes	**WA 1** Apply knowledge of mathematics, natural science, engineering fundamentals and an engineering specialization as specified in WK1 to WK4 respectively to the solution of complex engineering problems.	**2. Application ability** **3. Professional and personal attributes**	**2.1 Application** of established engineering methods to complex engineering problem solving.

(Continued)

Table 4.6 (Continued) A cross-map between graduate attributes of Washington Accord [161] and stage 1 competencies of Engineers Australia (EA) [155]

Washington Accord (IEA)	*Engineers Australia (EA) stage 1 competencies*
WA 2 Identify, formulate, research literature and analyse *complex* engineering problems reaching substantiated conclusions using first principles of mathematics, natural sciences and engineering sciences (WK1 to WK 4).	- -
WA 3 Design solutions for *complex* engineering problems and design systems, components or processes that meet specified needs with appropriate consideration for public health and safety, cultural, societal, and environmental considerations (WK5).	**2.3 Application** of systematic engineering synthesis and design processes.
WA 4 Conduct investigations of *complex* problems using research-based knowledge (WK8) and research methods including design of experiments, analysis and interpretation of data, and synthesis of information to provide valid conclusions.	- -

(Continued)

Table 4.6 (Continued) A cross-map between graduate attributes of Washington Accord [161] and stage I competencies of Engineers Australia (EA) [155]

Washington Accord (IEA)	*Engineers Australia (EA) stage I competencies*
WA 5 Create, select and apply appropriate techniques, resources, and modern engineering and IT tools, including prediction and modelling, to *complex* engineering problems, with an understanding of the limitations (WK6).	**2.2 Fluent application** of engineering techniques, tools and resources
WA 6 Apply reasoning informed by contextual knowledge to assess societal, health, safety, legal and cultural issues and the consequent responsibilities relevant to professional engineering practice and solutions to complex engineering problems (WK7).	- -
WA 7 Understand and evaluate the sustainability and impact of professional engineering work in the solution of complex engineering problems in societal and environmental contexts (WK7).	- -
WA 8 Apply ethical principles and commit to professional ethics and responsibilities and norms of engineering practice (WK7).	**3.1 Ethical** conduct and professional accountability.

(Continued)

Table 4.6 (Continued) A cross-map between graduate attributes of Washington Accord [161] and stage 1 competencies of Engineers Australia (EA) [155]

Washington Accord (IEA)	*Engineers Australia (EA) stage 1 competencies*
WA 9 Function effectively as an individual and as a member or leader in diverse teams and in multi-disciplinary settings.	**3.6 Effective** team membership and team leadership.
WA 10 Communicate effectively on *complex* engineering activities with the engineering community and with society at large, such as being able to comprehend and write effective reports and design documentation, make effective presentations, and give and receive clear instructions.	**3.2 Effective** oral and written communication in professional and lay domains.
WA 11 Demonstrate knowledge and understanding of engineering management principles and economic decision-making and apply these to one's own work, as a member and leader in a team, to manage projects and in multi-disciplinary environments.	**2.4 Application** of systematic approaches to the conduct and management of engineering projects.
WA 12 Recognise the need for and have the preparation and ability to engage in independent and life-long learning in the broadest context of technological change.	- -

(Continued)

Table 4.6 (Continued) A cross-map between graduate attributes of Washington Accord
[161] and stage I competencies of Engineers Australia (EA) [155]

Washington Accord (IEA)	Engineers Australia (EA) stage I competencies	
	3. EA's additional graduate attributes	**3.3** Creative, innovative and proactive demeanour **3.4** Professional use and management of information **3.5** Orderly management of self and professional conduct

Note: Engineers Australia (The Institution of Engineers Australia) has 16 stage I
competencies.

attributes map onto those of the Washington Accord. Tables 4.5 and 4.6 therefore show
the cross-mapping the authors have completed of the HKIE attributes with the Washington Accord and the EA graduate attributes with the Washington Accord. (These tables were developed by the authors and do not represent the understanding of equivalent
graduate attributes which may be generated by the accrediting organisations.)

The next step would be to use the Washington Accord graduate attributes as the
common factor and thereby develop a cross-map between the two different accrediting
bodies' graduate attributes. Before completing this next cross-mapping exercise, there
are some observations which can be drawn from Tables 4.5 to 4.6.

First, while both Engineers Australia and the HKIE are signatories to the Washington Accord, there are gaps between their graduate attributes and those listed by
the Accord. For example, the HKIE lists "an ability to identify, formulate and solve
engineering problems" as a graduate attribute. In Table 4.4, this has been cross-
mapped against WA2, "Identify, formulate, research literature and analyse *complex* engineering problems reaching substantiated conclusions using first principles
of mathematics, natural sciences and engineering sciences (WK1–WK4)", leaving
WA1, "Apply knowledge of mathematics, natural science, engineering fundamentals and an engineering specialization as specified in WK1–WK4 respectively to
the solution of complex engineering problems", as unmapped. It could be argued,
however, that the HKIE graduate attribute can be used to cross-map against both
WA1 and WA2. Hence, the cross-mapping exercise is very open to interpretation.

If we examine the graduate attributes specified by Engineers Australia, we can see
that EA specifies "3.4 Professional use and management of information" which does
not really map across to any Washington Accord attribute but which might be part
of "WK8 Engagement with selected knowledge in the research literature of the discipline" or contained within "WA4: conduct investigations of complex problems using research-based knowledge (WK8) and research method including design of experiments,
analysis and interpretation of data, and synthesis of information to provide valid conclusions". It seems, then, that in the context of engineering in Australia, the use of information is significant enough in it to be drawn out as a separate graduate attribute, and
ideally, these local variations need to be preserved through the cross-mapping process.

Once the cross-maps between HKIE and the Washington Accord and between EA and the Washington Accord are established, cross-mapping between HKIE and EA can be directly derived from the common WA graduate attributes. A cross-mapping of EA stage 1 competencies and HKIE graduate attributes is shown in Tables 4.7 and 4.8.

Two issues thus confront us with cross-mapping: the preservation of local variations and the degree of subjectivity in the cross-mapping process itself. Yet, if dual accreditation is possible, there must be equivalency across different accrediting bodies who are signatories to the same agreement. How can this equivalency be captured if the process of cross-mapping is so subjective? Does this not mean that the process will change over time and potentially depend on who performs the accreditation? There may also be drifts in the graduate attributes according to the demands of the local engineering industry. How are these addressed? These are questions which must be considered as the process of dual accreditation becomes more prevalent and necessary in the now globalised world of education.

Meanings and equivalences of graduate attributes will also need to be negotiated. For example, Table 4.8 is also a cross-map of the EA and HKIE graduate attributes, but here the graduate attributes have been written out in full to consider some fine details.

For example, Engineers Australia specifies "Creative, innovative and pro-active demeanour", which the HKIE does not on its face have an equivalent for, and yet it could be argued that this EA graduate attribute is a sub-attribute of the HKIE attribute "e an ability to identify, formulate and solve engineering problems". Such interpretations, again, may need specific negotiation: it will depend of the perspective of the accrediting panel. One accrediting body may, for example, use the cross-mapping holistically, whereas another may take a more granular approach.

Table 4.7 Cross-mapping of graduate attributes of HKIE and EA

HKIE Graduate attributes	Engineers Australia stage I competencies															
	1.1	1.2	1.3	1.4	1.5	1.6	2.1	2.2	2.3	2.4	3.1	3.2	3.3	3.4	3.5	3.6
a.	X	X	X	X			X	X								
b.		X	X				X									
c.		X	X	X	X	X	X	X	X							
d.												X			X	X
e.		X	X		X	X			X							
f.				X							X				X	X
g.												X			X	X
h.				X	X											
i.				X	X											
j.													X			
k.							X	X	X	X						
l.		X												X		

Note: "X" mark is placed to the appropriate boxes in the matrix to indicate relationships between EA stage I competencies (16 Graduate Attributes) and HKIE graduate attributes (12).

Table 4.8 A cross-map between EA [16] and HKIE [162] graduate attributes

Engineers Australia graduates attributes	*HKIE graduate attributes*	
1.1 **Comprehensive, theory-based understanding** of the underpinning natural and physical sciences and the engineering fundamentals applicable to the engineering discipline.	(a)	An ability to apply knowledge of mathematics, science and engineering appropriate to the degree discipline.
1.2 **Conceptual understanding** of the mathematics, numerical analysis, statistics, and computer and information sciences which underpin the engineering discipline.	(l)	An ability to use the computer/IT tools relevant to the discipline along with an understanding of their processes and limitations.
1.3 **In-depth understanding** of specialist bodies of knowledge within the engineering discipline.	(e)	An ability to identify, formulate and solve engineering problems.
1.4 **Discernment** of knowledge development and research directions within the engineering discipline.	(e)	An ability to identify, formulate and solve engineering problems.
1.5 **Knowledge** of engineering design practice and contextual factors impacting the engineering discipline.	(h)	An ability to understand the impact of engineering solutions in a global and societal context, especially the importance of health, safety and environmental considerations to both workers and the general public.
	(i)	An ability to stay abreast of contemporary issues.
1.6 **Understanding** of the scope, principles, norms, accountabilities and bounds of sustainable engineering practice in the specific discipline.	(h)	An ability to understand the impact of engineering solutions in a global and societal context, especially the importance of health, safety and environmental considerations to both workers and the general public.
	(i)	An ability to stay abreast of contemporary issues.
2.1 **Application** of established engineering methods to complex engineering problem solving.	(e)	An ability to identify, formulate and solve engineering problems.
2.2 **Fluent application** of engineering techniques, tools and resources.	(k)	An ability to use the techniques, skills and modern engineering tools necessary for engineering practice appropriate to the degree discipline.
	(b)	An ability to design and conduct experiments as well as to analyse and interpret data

(Continued)

Table 4.8 (Continued) A cross-map between EA [16] and HKIE [162] graduate attributes

Engineers Australia graduates attributes	HKIE graduate attributes
2.3 Application of systematic engineering synthesis and design processes.	**(c)** An ability to design a system, component or process to meet desired needs within realistic constraints, such as economic, environmental, social political, ethical, health and safety, and sustainability.
2.4 Application of systematic approaches to the conduct and management of engineering projects.	**(e)** An ability to identify, formulate and solve engineering problems.
3.1 Ethical conduct and professional accountability	**(f)** An ability to understand professional and ethical responsibility.
3.2 Effective oral and written communication in professional and lay domains	**(g)** An ability to communicate effectively.
3.3 Creative, innovative and pro-active demeanour.	**(j)** An ability to recognise the need for, and to engage in life-long learning.
3.4 Professional use and management of information.	- -
3.5 Orderly management of self and professional conduct	**(d)** An ability to function on multi-disciplinary teams.
3.6 Effective team membership and team leadership	**(d)** An ability to function on multi-disciplinary teams.

4.5.3 Learning environment and a higher education institution's support services and infrastructure

The accreditation process, while assessing the attainment of graduate attributes, also assesses the learning environment. Here, too, there may be local differences and contexts which can lead to difficulties when a higher education institution is seeking dual accreditation. The means by which the learning environment is described also varies between different accrediting organisations. Engineers Australia, for example, groups these factors into one umbrella term "operational environment", while other groups distinguish between the administrative services within the higher education institution and the business and finance resources [149,155].

All accreditation organisations also require or expect an academic staff/faculty member profile which is consistent with the programs being delivered at each institution [149,155,161]. In addition, there may be requirements for the staffing to cover diversity measures across all academic levels [149,155,161]. In this instance, in particular, sensitivity to local conditions is important, because it may be that availability of higher-level academics is limited within some jurisdictions.

Similar comments are also relevant for the accreditation requirements relating to equipment, computer facilities, information services and libraries. There may be some locations where these services are limited or relatively expensive.

4.6 The way forward

4.6.1 For higher education institutions

The need for basing curriculum on outcome-based education will continue with the potentially ever-increasing demands for accreditation [163]. The administrative load on higher education institutions in the short term will increase, with, at this stage, little prospect of rationalisation of parallel and similar processes. To maintain competitive advantage, however, higher education institutions are required to continue to be current with all accreditation requirements. This is one instance where change may be driven by the higher education institutions, rather than by industry, due to the sheer workload required to meet dual and multiple accreditations. Governmental and accrediting organisations need to begin a conversation with higher education institutions to determine which processes may overburden staff by (potentially) over-assessing programs or qualifications.

Within the Australian context, the requirement for work experience has now changed, such that Engineers Australia requires students to be exposed to professional practice via experiential learning and (it is strongly suggested) some work experience [155]. As opportunities for this work experience broadens to include other countries and study abroad, higher education institutions may find it advantageous to encourage students to work and study in jurisdictions covered by the same accrediting organisations as their home degree. In this case, alliances of accreditation organisations will allow higher education institutions some flexibility where the student works and studies, and students can more easily access a truly globalised education.

Increasingly, higher education institutions are also under scrutiny to ensure that they comply with the relevant national quality standards for education. It is significant to remember that accreditation is typically viewed as the minimum standard which must be met, and therefore, there may be significant differences in approaching accreditation compared to ensuring educational standards [164].

4.6.2 For accreditation organisations

Dual accreditation has highlighted the flexibility in the accreditation process by concentrating on learning outcomes rather than pedagogy. However, as experience with accreditation generally accumulates, there may arise a need to demonstrate how the learning outcomes are related to pedagogy, as part of the evidence needed for accreditation. This may be necessary because, while higher education institutions can show alignment between assessments and learning outcomes, the relationship between learning outcome attainment and pedagogy, or, indeed, pedagogy and assessment, is less clear [165]. There is currently no way to see if learning outcomes require a change in the pedagogy and whether that change is actually implemented [165].

Furthermore, the focus on outcome-based education also raises issues in dual accreditation. The attainment of learning outcomes does not necessarily mean that the program gives students experience in integrating their knowledge and skills. This may be an area where different accrediting organisations have substantially different requirements and where there may be significant variations of requirements within the local context [166].

Each accreditation organisation must decide how much local (host-country) variation is allowable [148]. Sensitivity to local culture is also important, as non-local accrediting organisations can appear to be a new form of neo-colonialism, which may, in turn, suppress local innovation [148,167]. The host country's government can be instrumental here by ensuring that education is delivered to an appropriate standard, while also still supporting academic autonomy [151]. Different host countries' conditions may mean different mixtures of top-down/bottom-up approaches to accreditation to ensure the offered programs are sensitive and responsive to the host country's conditions and culture [151]. For example, prior to 2007, ABET used to accredit programs in 29 countries (outside of its national jurisdiction), using the same criteria as those which were used for programs based within the US. However, for non-US accreditation, ABET tried to include evaluators (assessors) from the region in question to ensure there was an understanding of the local culture and local engineering practices [164,168]. It may be noted that, since 2007, no signatory to the Washington Accord has been allowed to accredit engineering program(s) of foreign higher education institutions that are offered outside of its member's national jurisdiction.

4.6.3 For accreditation organisations (IEA and ENAEE)

As experience with dual accreditation accumulates, there is the possibility of using this experience to develop single accreditation framework across alliances of accreditation organisations: for example, between the IEA and the ENAEE [169].

Although the accreditation frameworks use the same language, there is no clarity as to the definitions of the words being used. Thus "design" is a commonly used engineering term, yet it can mean different activities within different contexts [169]. Despite some linguistic differences, the Washington Accord and ENAEE's competencies and accreditation principles and procedures are very similar. Some signatories to the Washington Accord are also authorised accreditation organisations of the ENAEE. Therefore, mutual recognition between the Washington Accord and the ENAEE will further pave the way to greater mobility of engineers, technologists and technicians.

Resistance to alliances across accreditation organisations may occur from higher education institutions, because they may be concerned that accreditation will devolve into a ranking system without taking into account the context and culture [156]. With increasing emphasis on transferable skills within engineering accreditation criteria, this is important, because something like "critical thinking" may look different in Asia and Africa compared to the US and Europe [156]. As the learning outcomes are assessed at the end of the learning process, the higher education institutions with a more diverse student cohort may be unfairly penalised, because there is greater work required in bringing all students up to the same standard [156].

4.6.4 For industry

The challenge for the industry remains being able to guide higher education institutions in establishing a minimum or threshold standard [170], as the general understanding of the graduate attributes required by accreditation organisations guarantees a minimum only, without being overly prescriptive [171]. To do so across multiple local contexts could thus become a significant problem.

Outcome-based education makes accreditation a measurable and auditable process. However, integration of the knowledge and skills cannot be completely achieved at a higher education institution. It is therefore incumbent on the industry to always be responsive to the need for co-ops, industry placements and internships, which will help students to synthesise knowledge and also help develop the skills needed to work in a team environment [151]. Here "co-op" means cooperative education – a structured method of combining classroom-based education with practical work experience. A cooperative education experience allows academic credit for the structured job experience.

4.6.5 For students (learners)

Students need to have an awareness of where their qualification allows them to practise. The choice of institution, academic program or qualification and offering institution's home country should be based on the professional recognition of programs, especially by the Washington Accord signatories or ENAEE signatories. Undertaking a program not accredited by a signatory to the Accord or ENAEE means that on graduation the individual will not be able to get mutual recognition of academic qualification equivalency in most developed and middle-income developing nations.

Students undertaking programs through transnational education need to be more careful. Students need to know if any engineering programs offered by a foreign higher education institution in transnational education hubs or in other countries are accredited by a signatory to the Washington Accord or ENAEE. If the host country is also signatory to the Accord, the program needs to be accredited by both signatories (home and host country) of the Accord. At present, only some higher education institutions of developed countries have offshore degrees which are accredited by both host and home country signatories to the Accord.

It is worth mentioning that getting accepted for Master's and PhD programs at Washington Accord and ENAEE signatory nations' higher education institutions from a non-accredited qualification or program does not give professional recognition. Graduates of non-accredited qualifications still need to apply for individual qualification assessment to the signatory to the Accord and/or ENAEE to attain professional recognition. Such individual quality assessment is time-consuming and expensive. Most importantly, there is no guarantee that the qualification will meet the Washington Accord or ENAEE standard.

Chapter 5

Education qualifications frameworks

5.1 Background

The aftermath of World War II and the collapse of colonialism ushered in a new era of establishing education institutions in newly independent nations. Colonial countries have also established more education institutions for their own populations as well as attracting talent from developing nations. This growth of education institutions and population is seen and is being experienced in many nations across the globe, from Australia to India, China, the European Union and the United States of America. For countries with already skilled and semi-skilled workforces, education now contributes significantly to the gross domestic product, and for those countries rapidly improving the skills of their population, education is a key to the future prosperity and economic development [172–174].

The result is that education can be considered an earning industry or human resources development factory, and it therefore must be regulated by government. This is particularly the case where institutions offer qualifications in different disciplines, ranging from the humanities, business and finance, and law to the sciences, engineering, medicine, hospitality and tourism, and film and art. Private education institutions are now allowed to deliver education alongside government or public education institutions in almost every country in the world. There must be a tangible evidence that the qualifications being issued are of the standard claimed and that graduates of such qualifications are able to safely practise their skills and get due recognition [175].

In many countries, therefore, there is a "Qualifications Framework" which seeks to standardise different qualification levels and state what skills can be expected from a graduate at any particular level [176,177].

Qualifications frameworks stand apart from the process of accreditation, yet to be able to deliver education, education institutions must comply with the qualifications framework of their country of operation [178]. This means that education institutions need to be aware of both accreditation and qualification framework criteria and have evidence to demonstrate that both are being complied with. Similarly, employers need to be conversant with the levels of attainment required by the qualification frameworks in their regions of operation and students need to be reassured that the time, effort and money they invest in their education will result in a recognised qualification.

It is therefore beneficial to consider what a qualifications framework is, what its goals, aims and objectives are, and how these may or may not be covered by the accreditation criteria of various engineering accreditation bodies. Within this chapter, the National Qualification Frameworks (NQF) of Australia, India, Hong Kong, South Africa, the European Union (EU) and Malaysia are discussed to demonstrate key concepts relating to qualifications frameworks.

5.2 Qualification framework: definition, operating environment and advantages

5.2.1 Definition

A qualifications framework is a formalised structure in which learning outcomes (LOs) are used to classify different qualifications according to (a) skills, (b) knowledge and (c) competencies required at each level. This allows for the ability to develop, assess and improve quality education in a number of contexts, from secondary school education through to doctoral (PhD) studies.

The qualifications framework allows students (learners), training providers (universities, institutions, polytechnics, Technical and Further Education (TAFEs), technikums, colleges, schools, etc.), employers, governments and the general public to gain information about the broad equivalence of qualifications. Qualification frameworks are typically of national standing and are administered by an authority within the national or federal or state government. Over 100 countries, including Australia, Malaysia, South Africa and Sri Lanka, have already developed their own national qualifications frameworks, and the European Union has also developed a framework which applies to that region and other adjacent countries.

5.2.2 Operating environment

Qualifications frameworks are typically national or federal because of the need to standardise qualifications across a large region. To have a working qualifications framework which is effective across a wide range of education institutions typically requires the following to be already established [179]:

- A National Skills Authority
- Sector Education and Training Authorities
- Skills Development Planning Unit
- An institutional framework to devise and implement National Skills Development Policies and Strategies to develop and improve the skills of the nation's workforce
- Integration of the National Skills Development Policies and Strategies within the NQF
- Provision of work experience that leads to recognised Occupational Qualifications
- Motivation for workers to participate in work experience or other training programs
- Levy-grant Schemes and a National Skills Fund which would increase the levels of investment in Education and Training and National Skills Development
- Provision and regulation of employment services and improvement of employment prospects through training and education
- A close liaison with the national specialised qualifications accreditation organisations (such as engineering, accounting, medicine, computer science, etc.).

5.2.3 Advantages

The qualifications framework is therefore also useful for students because it provides them with evidence as to the standard of their qualification and the level and type of work for which they are qualified. The other benefit of a qualifications framework is that it can detail how students (learners) can move between levels of education and/or across fields and occupations.

5.3 Aims of qualifications frameworks

As stated above, there are many different national qualifications frameworks, but they often have very similar aims.

Typically, a national qualifications framework is aimed at demonstrating pathways to and through formal qualifications [180,181] and may include information about non-traditional pathways to encourage the life-long learning of the workforce and provide a formal means of evaluating informal education or work experience [173–184]. Therefore, a national qualifications framework needs to be flexible enough to be relevant to a variety of different educational settings and purposes, while still providing set standards for different qualifications [173–184].

The national qualifications framework is part of the policies that are developed on a national or federal scale and are often seen as part of the governmental oversight of the quality of education institutions within a nation or region. The national qualifications framework therefore ensures that qualifications are recognised nationally and are all of equivalent standard [173–184].

In some instances, a stated aim of the national qualifications framework policy is to provide a means of comparing qualifications from different nations to allow for greater mobility of the workforce and also encourage life-long learning [172–181]. However, not all national qualifications framework organisations assess the equivalency of offshore degrees [180,183].

Finally, a national qualifications framework can be viewed as a means of developing national and international confidence in the qualifications being issued, which ensures that education will continue to contribute to the national and global economic performance [173,174]. Some national qualifications frameworks go further and seek to ensure that skills shortages in the labour market are being addressed by education institutions [180,181].

5.4 Comparative timelines of selected qualifications frameworks

The formulation of a national qualifications framework, and full implementation of such a framework, takes considerable time, because the national qualifications framework requires collaboration, active participation or engagement, and inputs from many stakeholders. The time needed has been graphically represented in Figure 5.1, where it can be easily seen that it can take up to a decade before full implementation of a national qualifications framework.

Indeed, the development of a national qualifications framework is technically, institutionally and financially demanding, especially for developing countries.

	1995	1996	2002	2003	2007	2008	2011	2013	2014	2015	2018
Australia	AQF Developed						Last Major Revision		AQF Fully Implemented		
European Union						EQF Adopted					
Hong Kong						HKQF Established			Credit Transfer Process Established		
Malaysia		National Accreditation Board (LAN) Established	Quality Assurance Division (QAD) Established	Malaysian Qualifications Framework (MQF) Established	MQF Adopted and LAN & QAD Dissolved						
South Africa	South African Qualifications Authority (SAQA) Act Established						South African National Qualifications Framework (SANQF) Established by SAQA				
India								National Skills Qualifications Framework (NSQF) was notified & all previous qualifications frameworks were superseded			End of the Trial Period to Compliance NSQF

Figure 5.1 Time history of major national qualifications framework implementation.

The Working Paper titled "National Qualifications Frameworks: Their feasibility for effective implementation in developing countries" published by the International Labour Organisation (ILO) in 2005 explored the potential benefits and challenges of national qualifications framework implementation in-depth [187]. The report concluded that setting up a national qualifications framework takes time and that additional time is needed before there is a measurable increase in the number of people participating in training and an improvement in the quality of that training [188]. Therefore, when developing a national qualifications framework, the report strongly suggested that not only consultation with all domestic stakeholders was vital, but that assistance from countries that already had well-developed and implemented national qualifications framework was also necessary.

5.5 Qualifications frameworks: basis and components

5.5.1 Basis

Across many countries, the NQFs are based on LOs and are predicated on the model of outcome-based education (OBE) and teaching [189]. Outcome-based assessment of qualifications is advantageous, because it naturally specifies the skills which a graduate of a particular qualification should be able to demonstrate (e.g. Australia, India, EU) upon completion of that particular qualification. The use and continuous improvement of OBE is therefore vital for all education institutions where a national qualifications framework exists. For details about OBE, see Chapter 2.

5.5.2 Components

NQFs typically comprise Qualification Type which refers to the title of the qualification and are typically generic (not discipline-specific). Within each qualification type, there is a [173–189]:

i. qualification type descriptor
ii. qualification level
iii. qualification level criteria
iv. context and sphere of influence.

5.5.2.1 Qualification type descriptor

The qualification type descriptor is typically the title of the qualification, and many NQFs cover most of the following types of qualifications, with very similar titles [173–189]:

- Doctoral/Doctorate Degree/Candidate Science
- Master's Degree
- Bachelor Honour Degree
- (Post) Graduate Certificate
- (Post) Graduate Diploma
- Graduate Certificate
- Graduate Diploma
- Professional Diploma
- Professional Certificate
- Professional Qualification
- Bachelor Degree
- Bachelor of Technology
- Bachelor of Vocation
- Associate Degree
- Polytechnic Diploma
- Tekhnikum Diploma
- Higher National Diploma
- Higher Diploma
- Higher Certificate
- Advanced Diploma
- National Diploma
- Advanced Certificate
- Diploma
- Certificate IV
- Certificate III
- Certificate II
- Certificate I
- Certificate
- Foundation Certificate
- Senior Secondary Certificate (Australia, with various titles, the EU, South Africa only)
- Grade/Class/Years 11, 10 and 9 (South Africa and the EU only).
- Primary School (EU).

It is easily seen that in many nations, the national qualifications framework spans different education sectors, from postgraduate education at a higher education institution to undergraduate education at a higher education institution, to vocational institution, polytechnic institution, TAFE, Tekhnikum and trade training, to high school, and even in the case of the EU, primary school. The implications of the national qualifications framework spanning different education institutions are examined in this chapter.

5.5.2.2 Qualification level and qualification level criteria

Within each NQF, every qualification title is given a level and each level has specific criteria which must be met for a qualification to be considered at that particular level. For example, in the Australian Qualifications Framework (AQF), Doctoral Degrees (PhD) are given level 10 and the criteria are expressed in terms of the required knowledge, skills and "application of knowledge and skills" a doctoral graduate should have at this level:

a. **Knowledge:** "Graduates at this level will have systemic and critical understanding of a substantial and complex body of knowledge at the frontier of a discipline or area of professional practice".
b. **Skills:** "Graduates at this level will have expert, specialised cognitive, technical and research skills in a discipline area to independently and systematically
    • engage in critical reflection, synthesis and evaluation
    • develop, adapt and implement research methodologies to extend and redefine existing knowledge or professional practice
    • disseminate and promote new insights to peers and the community
    • generate original knowledge and understanding to make a substantial contribution to a discipline or area of professional practice."
c. **Application of Knowledge and Skills:** "Graduates at this level will apply knowledge and skills to demonstrate autonomy, authoritative judgement, adaptability and responsibility as an expert and leading practitioner or scholar" [180].

Each qualification is thus examined in terms of its LOs to determine the level criteria it best matches. NQFs also provide a basis upon which to design new qualifications. Table 5.1 shows a more detailed example from the AQF, where all ten levels are clearly articulated in terms of **knowledge**, **skills** and **application of knowledge and skills**.

AQF levels and the AQF levels' criteria are an indication of the relative complexity and/or depth of achievement and the autonomy required to demonstrate that achievement. AQF level 1 has the lowest complexity, and AQF level 10 has the highest complexity.

The AQF level summaries are statements of the typical achievement of graduates who have been awarded a qualification at a certain level in the AQF.

Note also that different qualifications may be of the same level: for example, Bachelor Honours, Graduate Certificates and Graduate Diplomas are all considered to be Level 8. Such statement of equivalency allows for graduates to have their qualifications recognised, even if the actual title of the qualification is slightly different, thus allowing for national mobility.

Under AQF, the bachelor's degree with 3–4 years duration without research component is classified as AQF Level 7. However, a bachelor's degree with 3 years duration

Table 5.1 AQF's knowledge, skills and application of knowledge and skills levels

	Summary	Knowledge (K)	Skills (S)	Application of knowledge and skills
AQF level 1 – Certificate 1	Graduates at this level will have knowledge and skills for initial work, community involvement and/ or further learning	Graduates at this level will have foundational knowledge for everyday life, further learning and preparation for initial work.	Graduates at this level will have foundational cognitive, technical and communication skills to undertake defined routine activities identify and report simple issues and problems.	Graduates at this level will apply knowledge and skills to demonstrate autonomy in highly structured and stable contexts and within narrow parameters.
AQF level 2 – Certificate II		Graduates at this level will have basic factual, technical and procedural knowledge of a defined area of work and learning.	Graduates at this level will have basic cognitive, technical and communication skills to apply appropriate methods, tools, materials and readily available information to: undertake defined activities provide solutions to a limited range of predictable problems.	Graduates at this level will apply knowledge and skills to demonstrate autonomy and limited judgement in the structured and stable contexts and within narrow parameters.
AQF level 3 – Certificate III	Graduates at this level will have theoretical and practical knowledge and skills for work and/or further learning.	Graduates at this level will have factual, technical, procedural and some theoretical knowledge of a specific area of work and learning.	Graduates at this level will have a range of cognitive, technical and communication skills to select and apply a specialised range of methods, tools, materials and information to complete routine activities and to provide and transmit solutions to predictable and sometimes unpredictable problems.	Graduates at this level will apply knowledge and skills to demonstrate autonomy and judgement and to take limited responsibility in known and stable contexts within established parameters.

(Continued)

Table 5.1 (Continued) AQF's knowledge, skills and application of knowledge and skills levels

	Summary	Knowledge (K)	Skills (S)	Application of knowledge and skills
AQF level 4 – Certificate IV	Graduates at this level will have theoretical and practical knowledge and skills for specialised and/ or skilled work and/or further learning.	Graduates at this level will have broad factual, technical and some theoretical knowledge of a specific area or a broad field of work and learning.	Graduates at this level will have a broad range of cognitive, technical and communication skills to select and apply a range of methods, tools, materials and information to: complete routine and non-routine activities provide and transmit solutions to a variety of predictable and sometimes unpredictable problems.	Graduates at this level will apply knowledge and skills to demonstrate autonomy, judgement and limited responsibility in known or changing contexts and within established parameters.
AQF level 5 – Diploma	Graduates at this level will have specialised knowledge and skills for skilled/ paraprofessional work and/or further learning.	Graduates at this level will have technical and theoretical knowledge in a specific area or a broad field of work and learning.	Graduates at this level will have a broad range of cognitive, technical and communication skills to select and apply methods and technologies to analyse information to complete a range of activities and to provide and transmit solutions to sometimes complex problems transmit information and skills to others.	Graduates at this level will apply knowledge and skills to demonstrate autonomy, judgement and defined responsibility in known or changing contexts and within broad but established parameters.

(Continued)

Table 5.1 (Continued) AQF's knowledge, skills and application of knowledge and skills levels

	Summary	Knowledge (K)	Skills (S)	Application of knowledge and skills
AQF level 6 – Advanced diploma, associate degree	Graduates at this level will have broad knowledge and skills for paraprofessional/ highly skilled work and/or further learning.	Graduates at this level will have broad theoretical and technical knowledge of a specific area or a broad field of work and learning.	Graduates at this level will have a broad range of cognitive, technical and communication skills to select and apply methods and technologies to: analyse information to complete a range of activities; interpret and transmit solutions to unpredictable and sometimes complex problems; transmit information and skills to others.	Graduates at this level will apply knowledge and skills to demonstrate autonomy, judgement and defined responsibility: in contexts that are subject to change within broad parameters to provide specialist advice and functions.
AQF level 7 – Bachelor degree	Graduates at this level will have broad and coherent knowledge and skills for professional work and/or further learning.	Graduates at this level will have broad and coherent theoretical and technical knowledge with depth in one or more disciplines or areas of practice.	Graduates at this level will have well-developed cognitive, technical and communication skills to select and apply methods and technologies to: analyse and evaluate information to complete a range of activities; analyse, generate and transmit solutions to unpredictable and sometimes complex problems; transmit knowledge, skills and ideas to others.	Graduates at this level will apply knowledge and skills to demonstrate autonomy, well-developed judgement and responsibility: in contexts that require self-directed work and learning within broad parameters to provide specialist advice and functions.

(Continued)

Table 5.1 (Continued) AQF's knowledge, skills and application of knowledge and skills levels

	Summary	Knowledge (K)	Skills (S)	Application of knowledge and skills
AQF LEVEL 8 – Bachelor honours degree, graduate certificate, graduate diploma	Graduates at this level will have advanced knowledge and skills for professional or highly skilled work and/or further learning.	Graduates at this level will have advanced theoretical and technical knowledge in one or more disciplines or areas of practice.	Graduates at this level will have advanced cognitive, technical and communication skills to select and apply methods and technologies to: analyse critically, evaluate and transform information to complete a range of activities analyse, generate and transmit solutions to complex problems transmit knowledge, skills and ideas to others.	Graduates at this level will apply knowledge and skills to demonstrate autonomy, well-developed judgement, adaptability and responsibility as a practitioner or learner.
AQF level 9 – Master's degree	Graduates at this level will have specialised knowledge and skills for research, and/or professional practice and/or further learning.	Graduates at this level will have advanced and integrated understanding of a complex body of knowledge in one or more disciplines or areas of practice.	Graduates at this level will have expert, specialised cognitive and technical skills in a body of knowledge or practice to independently: analyse critically, reflect on and synthesise complex information, problems, concepts and theories Research and apply established theories to a body of knowledge or practice interpret and transmit knowledge, skills and ideas to specialist and non-specialist audiences.	Graduates at this level will apply knowledge and skills to demonstrate autonomy, expert judgement, adaptability and responsibility as a practitioner or learner.

(Continued)

Table 5.1 (Continued) AQF's knowledge, skills and application of knowledge and skills levels

	Summary	Knowledge (K)	Skills (S)	Application of knowledge and skills
AQF level 10 – Doctoral degree	Graduates at this level will have systematic and critical understanding of a complex field of learning and specialised research skills for the advancement of learning and/or for professional practice.	Graduates at this level will have systemic and critical understanding of a substantial and complex body of knowledge at the frontier of a discipline or area of professional practice.	Graduates at this level will have expertise, specialised cognitive, technical and research skills in a disciplined area to independently and systematically engage in critical reflection, synthesis and evaluation; develop, adapt and implement research methodologies to extend and redefine existing knowledge or professional practice; disseminate and promote new insights to peers and the community generate original knowledge and understanding to make a substantial contribution to a discipline or area of professional practice.	Graduates at this level will apply knowledge and skills to demonstrate autonomy, authoritative judgement, adaptability and responsibility as an expert and leading practitioner or scholar.

Source: Adapted from Ref. [180].

plus 1 year research is considered AQF Level 8. Australian engineering bachelor's degree program which is of 4 years duration is also considered AQF Level 8 if the engineering degree includes at least 1 year equivalent embedded research. Table 5.2 shows a comparative AQF Levels 7 and 8 criteria and their descriptors. The fourth column in Table 5.2 shows the fundamental difference between Level 7 and Level 8.

The bachelor degree qualifications without honours must be designed and accredited to enable graduates to demonstrate the LOs expressed as knowledge, skills and the application of knowledge and skills specified in the level 7 criteria and the bachelor degree descriptor [180]. Similarly, the bachelor honours degree qualifications must be designed and accredited to enable graduates to demonstrate the LOs expressed as knowledge, skills and the application of knowledge and skills specified in the level 8 criteria, and the bachelor degree descriptor (see Table 5.2) [180]. The AQF levels progression from Certificate I (AQF Level 1) to PhD degree (AQF Level 10) is shown in Figure 5.2.

The taxonomic approach therefore enables consistency, on a national scale, in the way in which qualifications are described. The classifications also provide clarity about the differences and relationships between qualification types, helping students to continuously improve and develop their qualifications as well as providing employers with a framework within which to describe available positions [179].

Another example of a qualifications framework is shown in Table 5.3, which shows the knowledge, skills and application of knowledge and skills required by the European Qualifications Framework (EQF) as defined by the European Union.

The EQF, like AQF, specifies levels and criteria of increasing complexity and/or depth of achievement, and the autonomy required to demonstrate that achievement. EQF level 1 has the lowest complexity and EQF level 8 has the highest.

Similar to the AQF, note also that different qualifications may be of the same level, for example, Bachelor Honours, Graduate Certificates and Graduate Diplomas are all considered to be Level 8. Such a statement of equivalency allows for graduates to have their qualifications recognised, even if the actual title of the qualification is slightly different, allowing for international mobility within the European Union and beyond.

Global mobility for graduates can then be demonstrated through the comparison of these two NQFs as shown in Table 5.4. For example, the Australian Associate Degree can be seen to be equivalent to the EU Higher Professional Qualification. Tables 5.1–5.4 represent the "best case" scenario, where the individual NQFs have similar types of criteria (e.g. skills, knowledge and application of skills and knowledge); however, if all NQFs do not use the same type of descriptive criteria, equivalences can be more difficult to establish.

To demonstrate this, Table 5.5 gives the criteria of the Indian National Skills Qualifications Framework (NSQF). Here, it can be noted that the criteria for each level are slightly different from those used by the AQF or the EQF. The NSQF uses knowledge and skills, just as the AQF and EQF do, but it then specifies "core skills" and degrees of "responsibility", neither of which figure prominently in the AQF or the EQF.

The Hong Kong Qualifications Framework (HKQF) is another example which demonstrates the variation in the number of levels and level criteria that can exist. This system has seven levels, and each level is described by criteria grouped into four categories: "knowledge and intellectual skills"; "processes"; "autonomy and accountability" and "communication, ICT and numeracy". While these categories

Table 5.2 AQF level 7 & 8 criteria and descriptors bachelor degree without and with honours

	AQF level 7 criteria for the bachelor degree without honours	AQF level 8 criteria for the bachelor degree with honours	Comments
Summary	Graduates at this level will have broad and coherent knowledge and skills for professional work and/or further learning	Graduates at this level will have advanced knowledge and skills for professional or highly skilled work and/or further learning	**L7:** Broad and coherent knowledge **L8:** Advanced knowledge
Knowledge	Graduates at this level will have broad and coherent theoretical and technical knowledge with depth in one or more disciplines or areas of practice	Graduates at this level will have advanced theoretical and technical knowledge in one or more disciplines or areas of practice	**L7:** Broad and coherent theoretical and practical knowledge **L8:** Advanced theoretical and practical knowledge
Skills	Graduates at this level will have well-developed cognitive, technical and communication skills to select and apply methods and technologies to: Analyse and evaluate information to complete a range of activities Analyse, generate and transmit solutions to unpredictable and sometimes complex problems Transmit knowledge, skills and ideas to others	Graduates at this level will have advanced cognitive, technical and communication skills to select and apply methods and technologies to: Analyse critically, evaluate and transform information to complete a range of activities Analyse, generate and transmit solutions to complex problems Transmit knowledge, skills and ideas to others	**L7:** Cognitive skills and analysis skills **L9:** Advanced cognitive skills and critical analysis skills
Application of knowledge and skills	Graduates at this level will apply knowledge and skills to demonstrate autonomy, well-developed judgement and responsibility: In contexts that require self-directed work and learning Within broad parameters to provide specialist advice and function	Graduates at this level will apply knowledge and skills to demonstrate autonomy, well-developed judgement, adaptability and responsibility as a practitioner or learner	**L7:** Mostly self-directed working skills **L8:** Self-directed working skills as practitioner

(Continued)

Table 5.2 (Continued) AQF level 7 & 8 criteria and descriptors bachelor degree without and with honours

	Bachelor degree without honours qualification type descriptor	Bachelor degree with honours qualification type descriptor	Comments
Purpose	The bachelor degree qualifies individuals who apply a broad and coherent body of knowledge in a range of contexts to undertake professional work and as a pathway for further learning	The bachelor honours degree qualifies individuals who apply a body of knowledge in a specific context to undertake professional work and as a pathway for research and further learning	**L7:** Coherent knowledge in broad area **L8:** Knowledge in specialised area and research
Knowledge	Graduates of a bachelor degree will have a broad and coherent body of knowledge, with depth in the underlying principles and concepts in one or more disciplines as a basis for independent lifelong learning	Graduates of a bachelor honours degree will have coherent and advanced knowledge of the underlying principles and concepts in one or more disciplines and knowledge of research principles and methods.	**L7:** Coherent and broad body of knowledge **L8:** Advanced knowledge and knowledge of research principles and methods
Skills	Graduates of a Bachelor Degree will have: Cognitive skills to review critically, analyse, consolidate and synthesise knowledge Cognitive and technical skills to demonstrate a broad understanding of knowledge with depth in some areas Cognitive and creative skills to exercise critical thinking and judgement in identifying and solving problems with intellectual independence Communication skills to present a clear, coherent and independent exposition of knowledge and ideas	Graduates of a Bachelor Honours Degree will have: Cognitive skills to review, analyse, consolidate and synthesise knowledge to identify and provide solutions to complex problems with intellectual independence Cognitive and technical skills to demonstrate a broad understanding of a body of knowledge and theoretical concepts with advanced understanding in some areas Cognitive skills to exercise critical thinking and judgement in developing new understanding Technical skills to design and use research in a project Communication skills to present a clear and coherent exposition of knowledge and ideas to a variety of audiences	**L7:** Cognitive and technical skills to solve problems **L8:** Cognitive and technical skills to solve complex problems with research capabilities

(Continued)

Table 5.2 (Continued) AQF level 7 & 8 criteria and descriptors bachelor degree without and with honours

	Bachelor degree without honours qualification type descriptor	Bachelor degree with honours qualification type descriptor	Comments
Application of knowledge and skills	Graduates of a bachelor's degree will demonstrate the application of knowledge and skills: With initiative and judgement in planning, problem-solving and decision-making in professional practice and/or scholarship To adapt knowledge and skills in diverse contexts With responsibility and accountability for own learning and professional practice and in collaboration with others within broad parameters	Graduates of a Bachelor Honours Degree will demonstrate the application of knowledge and skills: With initiative and judgement in professional practice and/or scholarship To adapt knowledge and skills in diverse contexts With responsibility and accountability for own learning and practice and in collaboration with others within broad parameters To plan and execute project work and/or a piece of research and scholarship with some independence	**L7:** Application of knowledge and skills in diverse context with responsibility and judgement **L8:** Application of knowledge and skills in diverse context with responsibility, judgement, research and scholarship
Volume of learning	The volume of learning of a bachelor's degree is typically 3–4 years	The volume of learning of a bachelor honours degree is typically 1 year following a bachelor's degree. A bachelor honours degree may also be embedded in a bachelor degree, typically as an additional year (3 + 1 = 4 years) or 4 years engineering program	**L7:** Study time 3–4 years **L8:** Study time 3 years + 1 year or 4 years with equivalent 1-year embedded research

Source: Adapted from Ref. [180].

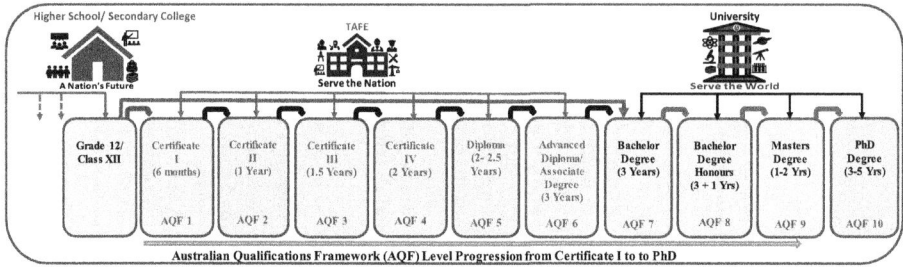

Figure 5.2 AQF level progression from Certificate I to PhD degree.

have some similarity with the other NQFs, the detail of the HKQF actually specifies a volume or notional total learning hours, which is the total number of hours an average learner/student needs to complete that qualification [188].

A more detailed national qualifications framework is the Malaysian Qualifications Framework (MQF), which categorises the level criteria according to [185]:

- depth, complexity and comprehension of knowledge
- cognitive skills
- application of functional skills as well as the breadth and sophistication of practice
- personal skills
- ethics and professionalism
- scope and complexity of application, and responsibilities.

The MQF also specifies the number of credits required to successfully complete each type of award but does not include foundation or university preparatory programs. The MQF was also designed to provide pathways for individuals to progress their education throughout their career [185].

Even more diverse is the South African National Qualifications Framework (SANQF), which uses level descriptors with quite extensive criteria grouped into the following categories [190]:

- scope of knowledge
- knowledge literacy
- method and procedure
- problem-solving
- ethics and professional practice
- accessing, processing and managing information
- producing and communicating of information
- context and systems
- management of learning
- accountability

It is noted that while an NQF harmonises qualifications across a single nation or region, when professionals are required to practise across multiple regions, there can be

Table 5.3 EQF's levels with descriptors

	Knowledge (K) (theoretical and/or factual)	Skills (S) (cognitive - use of logical, intuitive and creative thinking) and practical – manual dexterity, use of methods, materials, tools and instruments)	Application of knowledge and skills (ability to apply knowledge and skills autonomously and with responsibility)
EQF Level 1 – Primary school	Basic general knowledge	Basic skills required to carry out simple tasks	Work or study under direct supervision in a structured context
EQF Level 2 – Secondary school with no diploma	Basic factual knowledge of a field of work or study	Basic cognitive and practical skills required to use relevant information in order to carry out tasks and to solve routine problems using simple rules and tools	Work or study under supervision with some autonomy
EQF Level 3 – Secondary diploma/ vocational diploma	Knowledge of facts, principles, processes and general concepts, in a field of work or study	A range of cognitive and practical skills required to accomplish tasks and solve problems by selecting and applying basic methods, tools, materials and information	Take responsibility for completion of tasks in work or study; adapt own behaviour to circumstances in solving problems
EQF Level 4 – Higher national certificate/ upper secondary diploma	Factual and theoretical knowledge in broad contexts within a field of work or study	A range of cognitive and practical skills required to generate solutions to specific problems in a field of work or study	Exercise self-management within the guidelines of work or study contexts that are usually predictable, but are subject to change; supervise the routine work of others, taking some responsibility for the evaluation and improvement of work or study activities
EQF Level 5 – Higher national diploma	Comprehensive, specialised, factual and theoretical knowledge within a field of work or study and an awareness of the boundaries of that knowledge	A comprehensive range of cognitive and practical skills required to develop creative solutions to abstract problems	Exercise management and supervision in contexts of work or study activities where there is unpredictable change; review and develop performance of self and others

(Cotinued)

Table 5.3 (Continued) EQF's levels with descriptors

	Knowledge (K) (theoretical and/or factual)	Skills (S) (cognitive - use of logical, intuitive and creative thinking) and practical – manual dexterity, use of methods, materials, tools and instruments)	Application of knowledge and skills (ability to apply knowledge and skills autonomously and with responsibility)
EQF Level 6 – Bachelor degree/diploma	Advanced knowledge of a field of work or study, involving a critical understanding of theories and principles	Advanced skills, demonstrating mastery and innovation, required to solve complex and unpredictable problems in a specialised field of work or study	Manage complex technical or professional activities or projects, taking responsibility for decision-making in unpredictable work or study contexts; take responsibility for managing professional development of individuals and groups
EQF Level 7 – Master's degree/diploma	Highly specialised knowledge, some of which is at the forefront of knowledge in a field of work or study, as the basis for original thinking and/or research Critical awareness of knowledge issues in a field and at the interface between different fields	Specialised problem-solving skills required in research and/or innovation in order to develop new knowledge and procedures and to integrate knowledge from different fields	Manage and transform work or study contexts that are complex, unpredictable and require new strategic approaches; take responsibility for contributing to professional knowledge and practice and/or for reviewing the strategic performance of teams
EQF Level 8 – Doctoral degree (PhD)/candidate science	Knowledge at the most advanced frontier of a field of work or study and at the interface between fields	The most advanced and specialised skills and techniques, including synthesis and evaluation, required to solve critical problems in research and/or innovation and to extend and redefine existing knowledge or professional practice	Demonstrate substantial authority, innovation, autonomy, scholarly and professional integrity and sustained commitment to the development of new ideas or processes at the forefront of work or study contexts including research

Source: Adapted from Ref. [186].

Table 5.4 AQF and EQF levels mapping

AQF	AQF Levels	EQF Levels	EQF
Doctoral degree (PhD)	10	8	Doctorate Degree (PhD), third cycle higher professional qualifications including chartered engineer
Master's degree	9	7	Master's degree, second cycle higher professional qualifications including engineering manager
Bachelor Honours degree/ graduate certificate/ graduate diploma	8	6	Bachelor's degree/honours bachelor's degree, first cycle higher professional qualifications including "Master Craftsman (certified)"
Bachelor's degree	7		
Associate degree/ advanced diploma	6	5	Short-cycle higher education (SCHE) qualifications/higher professional qualifications
Diploma	5		
Certificate IV	4	4	Upper secondary general education certificates/vocational education and training (VET) qualifications
Certificate III	3	3	Secondary education certificates/VET qualifications
Certificate II	2	2	Lower-secondary education/basic VET qualifications
Certificate	1	1	Primary Education Certificates/Basic VET qualifications

Source: Adapted from Ref. [189].

difficulties in assessing the equivalency of qualifications, depending on the respective NQFs that are being compared.

5.5.2.3 Context and sphere of influence for NQFs

A significant feature of most NQFs is that they operate and regulate qualifications which span different education institutions.

In the Australian context, the AQF covers all four of the national education sectors:

i.   Higher education
ii. Vocational education and training
iii. Dual sector education and training
iv. General (high school education).

These types of education institutions are similar to others across the world, except, perhaps, for the "dual sector" education and training, which requires further explanation. Dual sector education institutions offer both higher education and vocational education. An example is RMIT University in Melbourne, Australia, which offers qualifications from Certificate 1 (Level 1) to PhD (Level 10). The AQF can accommodate this by clear specifications of the level and level descriptors, and in addition,

Table 5.5 The NSQF levels and level descriptors

Level	Process required	Professional knowledge	Professional skill	Core skill	Responsibility
Level 1	Prepares person to carry out process that are repetitive on regular basis require no previous practice	Familiar with common trade terminology, instructional words meaning and understanding	Routine and repetitive, takes safety and security measures	Reading and writing, addition subtraction personal financing, familiarity with social and religious diversity, hygiene and environment	No responsibility; always works under continuous instruction and close supervision
Level 2	Prepares person to carry out process that are repetitive on regular basis with little application of understanding, more of practice	Material tools and application in a limited context, understands context of work and quality	Limited service skill used in limited context, select and apply tools, assist in professional works with no variables differentiates good and bad quality	Receive and transmit written and oral messages, basic arithmetic personal financing understanding of social political and religious diversity, hygiene and environment	No responsibility works under instruction and close supervision
Level 3	Person may carry put a job which may require limited range of activities routine and predictable	Basic facts, processes and principles applied in trade of employment	Recall and demonstrate practical skill, routine and repetitive in narrow range of application	Communication written and oral, with minimum required clarity, skill of basic arithmetic and algebraic principles, personal banking, basic understanding of social and natural environment	Under close supervision some responsibility for own work within defined limit

(Continued)

Table 5.5 (Continued) The NSQF levels and level descriptors

Level	Process required	Professional knowledge	Professional skill	Core skill	Responsibility
Level 4	Work in familiar, predictable, routine, situation of clear choice	Factual knowledge of field of knowledge or study	Recall and demonstrate practical skill, routine and repetitive in narrow range of application, using appropriate rule and tool, using quality concepts	Language to communicate written or oral, with required clarity, skill to basic arithmetic and algebraic principles, basic understanding of social political and natural environment	Responsibility for own work and learning
Level 5	Job that requires well developed skill, with clear choice of procedures in familiar context	Knowledge of facts, principles, processes and general concepts, in a field of work or study.	A range of cognitive and practical skills required to accomplish tasks and solve problems by selecting and applying basic methods, tools, materials and information	Desired mathematical skill, understanding of social, political and some skill of collecting and organising information, communication	Responsibility for own work and learning and some responsibility for other's works and learning
Level 6	Demands wide range of specialised technical skill, clarity of knowledge and practice in broad range of activity involving standard non-standard practices	Factual and theoretical knowledge in broad contexts within a field of work or study	A range of cognitive and practical skills required to generate solutions to specific problems in a field of work or study	Reasonably good in mathematical calculation, understanding of social, political and, reasonably good in data collecting organising information, and logical communication	Responsibility for own work and learning and full responsibility for other's works and learning

(Continued)

Table 5.5 (Continued) The NSQF levels and level descriptors

Level	Process required	Professional knowledge	Professional skill	Core skill	Responsibility
Level 7	Requires a command of wide ranging specialised theoretical and practical skill, involving variable routine and non-routine context	Wide ranging, factual and theoretical knowledge in broad contexts within a field of work or study	Wide range of cognitive and practical skills required to generate solutions to specific problems in a field of work or study	Good logical and mathematical skill understanding of social political and natural environment good in collecting and organising information, communication and presentation skill	Full responsibility for output of group and development
Level 8	Comprehensive, cognitive, theoretical knowledge and practical skills to develop creative solutions, to abstract problem. Undertakes self-study, demonstrates intellectual independence, analytical rigour and good communication			Exercise management and supervision in the context of work/study having unpredictable changes, responsible for development of self and others	
Level 9	Advanced knowledge and skill for critical understanding of the subject, demonstrating mastery and innovation, completion of substantial research and dissertation			Responsible for decision-making in complex technical activities, involving unpredictable study/work situations	
Level 10	Highly specialised knowledge and problem-solving skill to provide original contribution to knowledge through research and scholarship			Responsible for strategic decisions in unpredictable complex situations of work/study	

Source: Adapted from Ref. [173].

AQF 5, 6 and 8 are qualifications which can be awarded within both the higher education and vocational education systems.

The SANQF was developed by the South African Qualifications Authority in 2008. The SANQF is more comprehensive, in which it includes levels for junior high school grades or secondary school certificate (Grades 9, 10) as well as the senior high school years or higher secondary certificate (Grades 11 and 12). This is similar to the EQF system, which has eight levels, from primary school to doctorate qualifications. Figure 5.3 indicates the mapping of the SANQF and how this relates to different educational options within the South African educational system.

The Indian context is quite complicated because there are numerous education institutions and training providers in the public and private sectors, and their qualifications are very diverse. The Indian NSQF has therefore been designed with a view to bring all qualifications providers (education institutions and training organisations) into the same system. In India, the qualifications are provided at different levels including: (a) secondary schools, polytechnics and higher education institutions including 49 central, 367 state and 123 deemed (24 IITs, 31 NITs, etc.) and 282 private universities (total 821 universities); (b) 13,000 industrial training institutes (ITIs, 80% of which are private and offering long-term courses); (c) National Skill Development Corporation-funded private training providers offering short-term training (over 6,000 such providers); (d) 16 different Ministries providing mostly short-term training; and (e) employers offering enterprise-based training. As mentioned, the principal goal of India's NSQF is to integrate education and training to allow for the movement between general education and technical education, something previous education systems have not been able to achieve [174]. If these mushrooming qualifications are not regulated by the NQF, their quality, recognition and inter-disciplinary mobility would be extremely hard to achieve.

The MQF spans three different training sectors:

- **Skills sector**
  Awards: Malaysian Skills Certificate 1–3, Malaysian Skills Diplomas 4, Malaysian Skills Advanced Diploma 5
- **Vocational and Technical sector**
  Awards: Certificate, Diploma, Advanced Diploma

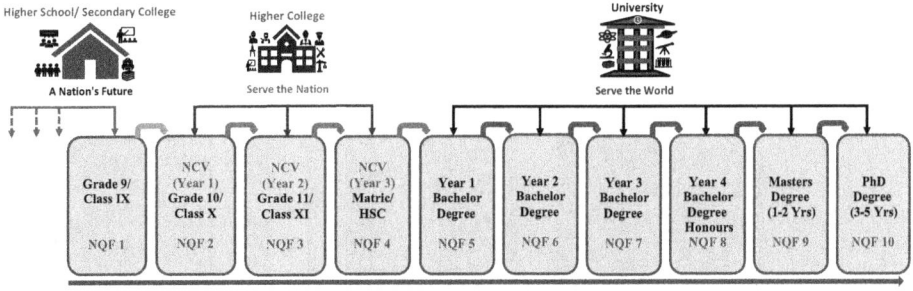

South African National Qualifications Framework (NQF) Level Progression from Grade 9 to PhD

Figure 5.3 SANQF mapping. (Adapted from Refs. [190,191].)

- **Higher Education sector**
  Awards: Certificate, Diploma, Advanced Diploma, Graduate Certificate and Diploma, Bachelor's Degree, Postgraduate Certificate and Diploma, Master's Degree, Doctoral Degree. It is to be noted that, like Australia, there are Malaysian education institutions which would be categorised as "dual sector", with award levels which can be achieved in either.

NQFs are administered and managed by different bodies in different nations. In Australia and Malaysia, there is a federal or national government department in either education or human development which oversees the NQF, while in India, there is a separate body called the National Skill Development Agency that approves accreditation norms [173].

An example of the administration of an NQF comes from Australia, where, in 2008, the Federal Government reviewed the higher education sector (*Bradley Report 2008*) and found that there was a need for a new, independent regulatory body. In the 2010–2011 budget, the Tertiary Education Quality and Standards Agency (TEQSA) was established by dissolving the Australian Universities Quality Agency as the regulatory and quality assurance agency for higher education. Part of its role is to accredit courses and programs of study against the relevant national qualifications framework criteria for the relevant standard. TEQSA also considers the risks associated with higher education providers in terms of their regulation, student load, staff profile (qualifications and experience) and financial viability [192]. The general review process used by TEQSA can be seen in Figure 5.4.

5.6 Comparisons between the AQF and Engineers Australia's stage 1 accreditation criteria

The cross-mapping between different qualifications frameworks and/or accreditation criteria is rarely publicly available. After much discussion within Australia, an alignment between the AQF and the International Engineering Alliance (i.e. Engineers Australia's stage 1 competency standard) awards has been developed, as shown in Table 5.6.

A typical course mapping of a 4-year full-time Bachelor of Engineering (Honours) program at AQF Level 8, together with Engineers Australia stage 1 competencies

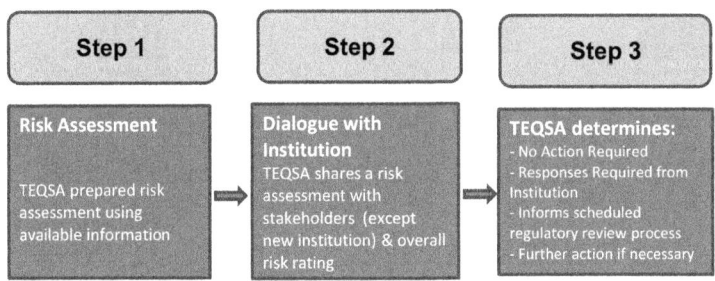

Figure 5.4 Key steps in risk assessment process of TEQSA. (Adapted from Ref. [192].)

Table 5.6 Engineering Qualifications under AQF and IEA Accords

IEAust (EA) grade	Qualification	AQF level	International Accords
Engineering Associate (senior technician)	Associate Degree or Advanced Diploma	6	Dublin
Engineering Technologist	Bachelor Degree	7	Sydney
Professional Engineer	Bachelor Honours Degree	8	Washington
	Master's Degree	9	Washington

Source: Adapted from Ref. [193].

and the higher education institution's graduate attributes (GA), is shown in Table 5.7. The table also shows how various core (compulsory) courses address AQF descriptors, EA stage 1 competencies and the higher education institution's GAs. The mapping shows if there are any deficiencies in the course design. This type of mapping helps the program designer to enhance the program structure and delivery sequence.

The individual AQF GAs are listed in Table 5.1. The typical higher education institute GAs are as follows:

GA1   Work Ready
GA2   Global in Outlook and Competence
GA3   Environmentally Aware and Responsive
GA4   Culturally and Socially Aware
GA5   Active and Lifelong Learners
GA6   Innovative

Under the requirements of the AQF, during the accreditation of Bachelor's (Honours) degree programs (qualifications), the accrediting authorities/organisations must ensure the following [180]:

- Graduates of a Bachelor Honours Degree qualification will achieve LOs at level 8.
- All the LOs (knowledge, skills and the application of knowledge and skills) of the Bachelor Honours Degree qualification type are evident in each qualification accredited as this type. Some may have more emphasis than others in different Bachelor Honours Degree qualifications depending on their purpose.
- Generic LOs are explicitly identified in the qualification and aligned with the level of the qualification type, the purpose of the qualification and the discipline. Generic LOs fall into four broad categories: fundamental skills, people skills, thinking skills and personal skills. In the higher education sector, they are generally known as GAs and are defined by each higher education provider.
- The relationship between the LOs in the level 8 criteria, the qualification type descriptor and the discipline is clear.

Table 5.7 Cross mapping of AQF, university GAs, EA stage 1 competencies and relevant courses for a typical bachelor of engineering (honours) program

PLOs (EA stage 1 competencies)	AQF	University GA	Year 1	Year 2	Year 3	Year 4
1. Knowledge and skills base						
1.1 Comprehensive, theory-based understanding of the underpinning natural and physical sciences and the engineering fundamentals applicable to the engineering discipline.	K1	GA1, GA5	Course 01 Course 02 Course 03	Course 09 Course 10 Course 11	Course 14 Course 15 Course 16	
1.2 Conceptual understanding of the, mathematics, numerical analysis, statistics and computer and information sciences which underpin the engineering discipline.	K1	GA1, GA5	Course 02 Course 04 Course 05	Course 12	Course 16 Course 17	
1.3 In-depth understanding of specialist bodies of knowledge within the engineering discipline.	S2	GA1	Course 02	Course 11 Course 13	Course 15 Course 16 Course 17 Course 18 Course 19	Course 22 Course 23 Course 24
1.4 Discernment of knowledge development and research directions within the engineering discipline.	K2, S4	GA1			Course 16 Course 17	Course 22 Course 23
1.5 Knowledge of contextual factors impacting the engineering discipline.	S1	GA1	Course 03 Course 06 Course 07		Course 18 Course 20 Course 21	Course 22 Course 23 Course 24
1.6 Understanding of the scope, principles, norms, accountabilities and bounds of contemporary engineering practice in the specific discipline.	A1	GA1	Course 06		Course 18 Course 20 Course 21	Course 22 Course 23
2. Engineering application ability						
2.1 Application of established engineering methods to complex engineering problem-solving.	S1	GA1	Course 03	Course 09 Course 10 Course 11	Course 14 Course 16 Course 17 Course 18 Course 19 Course 21	Course 22 Course 23 Course 24

(Continued)

Table 5.7 (Continued) Cross mapping of AQF, university GAs, EA stage I competencies and relevant courses for a typical bachelor of engineering (honours) program

PLOs (EA stage I competencies)	AQF	University GA	Year 1	Year 2	Year 3	Year 4
2.2 Fluent application of engineering techniques, tools and resources.	S2	GA1	Course 01 Course 02 Course 03 Course 07 Course 08	Course 09 Course 10 Course 12 Course 13	Course 15 Course 16 Course 17 Course 18 Course 19 Course 20	Course 22 Course 23 Course 24
2.3 Application of systematic engineering synthesis and design processes.	S3	GA1, GA6	Course 06	Course 09 Course 11 Course 13	Course 18 Course 17 Course 20 Course 21	Course 22 Course 23
2.4 Application of systematic approaches to the conduct and management of engineering projects	A4	–		Course 09	Course 21	Course 22 Course 23
3. Professional and personal attributes						
3.1 Ethical conduct and professional accountability.	A1	GA1	Course 06		Course 18 Course 20 Course 21	Course 22 Course 23
3.2 Effective oral and written communication in professional and lay domains.	S5	GA1	Course 01 Course 03 Course 07 Course 08	Course 09 Course 10	Course 21	Course 22 Course 23
3.3 Creative, innovative and proactive demeanour.	A2	GA2, GA3, GA4		Course 09 Course 13	Course 18	Course 22 Course 23
3.4 Professional use and management of information.	A4	GA1	Course 06	Course 09 Course 10	Course 18 Course 20	Course 22 Course 23 Course 24
3.5 Orderly management of self- and professional conduct.	A3	GA1, GA5	Course 06	Course 13	Course 20 Course 21	Course 22 Course 23
3.6 Effective team membership and team leadership.	K2, A3	GA6, GA2	Course 06	Course 09	Course 20	Course 22 Course 23

- The design of the components of the qualification will provide coherent LOs for the level and qualification type and will enable graduates to demonstrate them.
- The volume of learning is sufficient for graduates to achieve the LOs for a qualification of this level and type.

It may be noted that the title of "honours" in an Australian degree is typically achieved by 1 year of honours study, after 3 years of a Bachelor degree. However, there are also examples of "embedded honours", where research activities are embedded throughout the 4-year program. This is the case with the Bachelor of Engineering (Honours) degrees in Australia. Practically, it means that there must be a minimum amount of credit focused on research throughout the whole length of the program. Typically, the research-focused LOs are concentrated in the last 2 years of study, when the students have fully developed their foundational skills.

After obtaining successful accreditation, the accredited program (qualification) must be placed on the AQF Register under the AQF Qualifications Register Policy [180]. In Australia, a Bachelor Honours Degree qualification may only be issued by an organisation that is authorised by an accrediting authority to do so and which meets any Australian government standards for higher education. The issuing higher education institution is responsible for ensuring the quality of the LOs of the program and that the graduate has satisfactorily completed any requirements for the awarding of the qualification. The issuing higher education institutions must issue qualifications consistent with the AQF Qualifications Issuance Policy [180].

It is the responsibility of the issuing higher education institutions to maintain a register of the AQF qualifications they have issued consistent with the AQF Qualifications Register Policy [180].

5.7 Alignment of national qualification framework with international qualifications framework

The national and international compatibility, recognition and alignment of qualification standards/frameworks are vital for having global relevance of qualifications including national and international portability. The international compatibility of qualifications and alignment with other qualifications frameworks are important objectives of any sovereign nation. As discussed in Chapter 1, the international mobility of graduates and professionals is on the rise. To support this mobility, mutual recognition and compatibility of national qualifications frameworks with other countries or regions' qualifications frameworks are extremely beneficial. It is advisable that the governing body of each country's national qualifications framework should have developed principles and processes for guiding discussions about alignment of its NQF with other countries' NQFs.

5.7.1 Benefits of international alignment

The benefit of international alignment of NQF ranges from economic gains at a national or regional level to benefits for individuals. Some major benefits of international alignment of national qualifications framework include [180]

- providing a systematic basis for improving mutual trust and the recognition of qualifications between nations or regions,
- facilitating transparency and reliability of information about qualifications and the qualifications framework in each nation or region,
- increasing international understanding, comparability, confidence and recognition of qualifications for both study and employment,
- contributing to the credibility and robustness of each nation's or region's qualifications systems, including knowledge and understanding of the various quality assurance systems and processes supporting the qualifications frameworks,
- assisting the international mobility of students and skilled professionals by increasing confidence that their qualifications will be understood and recognised nationally and internationally (own country and other countries),
- improving employers' understanding of qualifications to assist with skills supply, and
- providing a comparative benchmark for the AQF.

5.7.2 *Principles of international alignment of national qualifications framework*

The general international alignment principles set out the expectations for each nation or region in the alignment process. The overarching principles are core considerations in any alignment process as follows [180]:

- Alignment with other nations' or regions' qualifications frameworks should be undertaken only where there is a demonstrable benefit
- Alignment should enhance any existing relationships and arrangements between these nations or regions.
- The national qualifications framework of one country should not be adapted to suit another nation's or region's requirements.
- Alignment of national or regional qualifications frameworks is generally not an automatic recognition of one country's qualifications framework in other country. However, it makes much easier to have formal mutual recognitions agreement(s).
- If a nation or region does not yet have a formal national or regional qualifications framework, the internationally recognised and appreciated national qualifications frameworks of other countries may be used for the development and alignment of national qualifications framework.

The general international alignment principles for national qualifications framework with other countries are as follows [180]:

a. The legitimacy and responsibilities of all relevant national or regional bodies involved in the alignment process are clearly determined and transparent.
b. The national and/or regional quality assurance system for education and training are integral to the qualifications framework and is consistent with international quality assurance principles.
c. There is a clear and demonstrable link between the qualifications levels in the national or regional qualifications framework.

d. The national or regional qualifications framework and its qualifications are based on the principles and objectives of LOs that are comparable.

e. The procedures for inclusion of qualifications in the national and/or regional qualifications framework and/or describing the place of qualifications in the qualifications system are transparent.

f. National and/or regional policies for the validation of all learning, and credit systems where these exist, are an integral component of the national or regional qualifications frameworks.

g. The alignment process includes the stated agreement of the relevant accrediting and/or quality assurance bodies for each nation or region.

h. The alignment process involves international experts to support and assist the development of trusted outcomes.

i. One comprehensive report, setting out the alignment and the evidence supporting it, is jointly published by the relevant national authorities in each nation or region and addresses separately each of the principles.

For international alignment of national qualifications framework, usually a high-powered committee consisting of internationally recognised national experts in professional and general education is formed to undertake negotiation with counterparts of other countries' governing bodies for national qualifications frameworks.

Chapter 6

International quality rankings of higher education institutions

6.1 Background

The 21st century is the era of globalisation, and the higher education institutions are not immune from this influence. In education, globalisation starts with the expansion of academic networks through the internet, emerging technologies, and increasing mobility of students, graduates, academics/faculty members and knowledge creation for economic and social development. The higher education institutions in the developed and emerging nations have been undergoing rapid transformations in their operation, management and delivery of education and research. To be in the top 100 elite global higher education institutions ranking table, numerous quality assurance exercises, professional accreditations, Q1 (high ranking) journal publications and high h-indexes must be demonstrated by a higher education institution. This relentless pursuit of enhanced performance has reshaped the operation modes of such institutions so that they resemble business ventures or corporations more than not-for-profit organisations that work for social good. The global higher education institution rankings have become an all-pervasive feature of higher education landscapes [194,195]. They generate discourses of difference and distinction that have far-reaching effects in the lives of academics/faculty members and students. Indeed, rankings can now affect the investment decisions of governments. Rankings are a "calculative technology" par excellence. They make legible the tangible, and intangible features of universities draw them into fields of equivalence and generate imaginative geographies of institutional difference. They are, then, critical tools in constructing the reputation and influence that an institution has [194,196].

The reputation of higher education institutions is a key feature, with images of quality and prestige differentiating institutions [197]. Nevertheless, there has been an amplification of the "reputation race" that involves a shift from local to global competition. [196,198]. One key feature of this increased emphasis on reputation has been the move from relatively diverse institutional discourses to a narrower range of metric-based assessments [194,199]. This includes the higher education institution ranking, national and international benchmarking, accreditation systems, research assessment exercises and the myriad internal systems for monitoring and auditing institutions [200]. These are calculative practices – that is, systems of measurement that make the characteristics, actions and positions of individuals in higher education institutions accountable to stakeholders [194,201].

The global higher education institutions ranking has gained popularity over the last two decades as an indicator of quality. The ranking shapes the future of the higher education institutions in the emerging global knowledge economy [202], even though those institutions generate a wide range of outputs that are not marketable and are unamenable to market valuation [202,203].

A detailed identification and quantification of the various output components produced by a higher education institution is extremely difficult. The use of weighting as an indicator or a number to capture the higher education institution's performance of generated output components is a challenging and highly contentious task. The components of a typical higher education institution output are [202,203] as follows:

a. Educational output that improves students' cognitive and social skills necessary for higher productivity and therefore higher economic value.
b. Informational output that reports student's academic performance and other attributes to the prospective employers, students and other stakeholders.
c. Research output that creates knowledge and art which may directly and indirectly contribute towards a nation's productivity and prosperity.
d. Consumption benefits which refer to the students' experiences.

The important dimensions of quality education and research are to foster knowledgeable, work-ready graduates, who are citizens of strong values and ethics. Unfortunately, some of these dimensions are grossly neglected in the parameters of the global higher education institutions ranking [204].

Seeking world-class university status has become a dream for not only higher education institutions in developed nations but also in emerging nations [205–207]. This "making a world class institution dream" inspires national governments and funding organisations and agencies to develop world-class higher education institutions through an accelerated implementation of "concentration and selection" policies. This aspiration creates a range of common issues and problems related to funding, research, market forces, autonomy and accountability, globalisation of science, academic freedom and the academic profession [205–208]. Many governments in the developed countries have managed to support their leading higher education institutions' increasing cost of operating with a world-class research-orientation by concentrated funding. However, there are two issues related to this approach. First, due to a recent economic shortfall, many developed countries have been reducing their public expenditure (funding) on higher education, while most developing and transition economics still have a fairly low higher education spending as a share of Gross Domestic Product (GDP) [209]. This creates a concern: to what extent can the funding of world-class higher education institutions be sustainable? In addition, while the top end of the higher education system has had significant funding through national initiatives, other higher education institutions at the bottom of the same systems might not obtain adequate financial support, and this might, in turn, undermine the overall quality of mass higher education [205,210]. Policymakers at a national level should ask how many world-class higher education institutions are desirable and affordable as a public sector investment [211]. From the perspective of research and innovation, there is a trade-off between quantity and quality [205].

Currently, national ranking systems are functioning in more than 70 countries [199], with the ranking of higher education institutions being in vogue in the US for nearly 90 years. There are four major global higher education institution ranking systems: Times Higher Education (THE) World University Rankings, the Quacquarelli Symonds or QS World Ranking, Shanghai's Academic Ranking of World Universities or ARWU and Cybermetrics Lab of Spanish National Research Council's Webometrics ranking. Apart from Webometrics, the other three ranking systems release global higher education institutions ranking data every 6 months, using a range of methodologies and parameters. However, all ranking systems essentially uphold the supremacy of the Anglo-American research-focused higher education institution model [202,212,213]. The THE, QS and ARWU have gained the most in terms of their use and credibility since their inception.

6.2 Global higher education institution ranking systems

In 2019, there were over 18,000 higher education institutions in the world. Global ranking provides a means of determining quality competitively so that institutions, students, employers, quality assurance organisations or bodies, governments and other stakeholders can determine where to provide support: this may mean employers using such rankings to make employment decisions, students using rankings to decide where to study and even governments considering rankings to influence funding levels [199].

The global ranking systems typically include just little over 5% of all higher education institutions by listing the "top" 1,000 institutions out of 18,000 institutions. However, the perception is often that it is only those "top" 20, 50 or 100 education institutions which are commendable.

While there has been a criticism of the rankings' methodologies and sources of data, such international ranking schemes have a wide range of influence and are being increasingly linked to international competitiveness, the geopolitical knowledge landscape, and reputation. The rankings are perhaps a symptom of our global society and are a result of both societies' and industries' pursuit of mobile talent and financial gain. The result is that those at the top of the rankings attract more stakeholder support via enrolments, stipends and research funding.

The formal global ranking system was pioneered by the Shanghai Jiao Tung University in 2003, the "Shanghai Academic Rankings of World Universities" (ARWU), and it continues to be used as a measure for higher education institutions. Since then, three other main global ranking systems have been evolved: (a) the THE, (b) the QS and (c) Webometrics or WR. This chapter discusses and compares all four global higher education institution ranking systems. Finally, some perspectives will be provided on the development of new ranking systems based on the United Nation's Sustainable Development Goals (SDGs).

6.3 Historical context

The first so-called ranking system was the prototype of the WR. This scheme was developed by the Cybermetrics Lab, and quantitative studies of the presence of academic content on the web have occurred since the mid-1990s. In 1999, the European Union

(EU) supported a project to examine the web data from European higher education institutions [214], but the system was not used in a formal sense until later.

The ARWU was first published formally in 2003 by the Centre for World-Class Universities within the Graduate School of Education of Shanghai Jiao Tung University in China. The initial purpose of the ARWU was to articulate the global significance of Chinese Universities; however, since its establishment, it has received a great deal of attention from governments, universities and the global media. In 2011, the ARWU established an International Advisory Board which meets every 2 years to provide the ARWU with feedback and advice on its current practice and future directions [215].

The second formal world university ranking system was the QS, in association with the UK-based THE. These two organisations worked together from 2004 to 2009, but in 2010, the QS split from the THE and started its own QS ranking system. The QS ranking survey assures the quality of its ranking by being the only international ranking scheme receiving International Ranking Expert Group approval.

Splitting from QS ranking, the THE scheme began collaboration with Thomson Reuters in 2010 and has developed its own ranking system [216]. The THE ranking system obtains feedback via external auditing. For example, in 2019, Pricewaterhouse-Coopers (PwC) audited the THE rankings for that year.

The Webometrics ranking is released once or twice a year and is still performed by the Cybermetrics Lab, which is part of the Spanish National Research Council [214]. The Webometrics ranking also ranks institutions worldwide, as well as within specific world regions, including the Oceania region.

6.4 Ranking criteria

Each higher education institution ranking system seeks to measure the degree of influence of different higher education institutions, using criteria which fall broadly into five different categories:

i.   Research Publications, Citations and Impact
ii. Teaching
iii. International Profile
iv. Presence on the Internet
v.   Employer Reputation.

The first three criteria are used across all ranking systems, while the last two are used by only one individual system, thereby highlighting the degree of variation which may occur between different ranking schemes. If stakeholders are going to use such rank-ordering, then the system which uses the most appropriate criteria for that stakeholder needs to be chosen. The obvious result is that different stakeholders may rely on different schemes, resulting in potentially conflicting strategic goals for individual higher education institutions. Each of these criteria is discussed in the following sub-sections.

6.4.1 Research publications, citations and impact (criterion 1)

All four ranking systems use different measures for the research impact. These measures are summarised in Table 6.1. The weighting factors show that the research weighed between 90% of the total score and 30% of the total and that different indicators are used to evaluate this criterion. It can be seen that the ARWU uses primarily research in its overall ranking. Such a ranking system could have limited relevance when seeking only undergraduate qualifications. In addition, the ARWU criteria place a special emphasis on particular publications, which may not be relevant to all disciplines. Since 2016, the ARWU has been addressing this by including engineering disciplines [217]. Further discipline areas are added with the information gained from an international survey of chairs and heads of departments and schools. The survey asks the experts to list the top-tier journals and internationally recognised awards in their discipline area. The survey is in the process of continual updating, with feedback welcomed by the ARWU from the top 100 universities. For the ARWU, "highly cited" researchers are identified by Clarivate Analytics.

The THE uses citations as its highest valued criterion. The citations are based on the data from Elsevier, using the Scopus-indexed journals database. Each time a ranking is issued, the citations are collected over a certain time frame (usually 5 years). The final metric used is the average number of times an education institution's work is cited [216]. The citation data are normalised such that the average citation rate within each discipline area is taken into account, and an estimate of the cumulative probability of

Table 6.1 Weighting for ranking criterion 1 (research publications, citations and impact criteria) for all four ranking systems

System	Research publications, citations and impact criteria	Weighting to overall ranking (%)	Total weighting for criterion 1 (%)
ARWU (Shanghai)	Number of "highly cited" researchers in the disciplines of natural sciences, engineering, life sciences, medical sciences and social sciences	20	90
	Papers published in *Science* and *Nature*	20	
	Papers indexed in science citation index-expanded and social science citation index	20	
	Per capita academic performance	10	
	Alumni winning Nobel Prizes or Fields medals	10	
	Staff winning Nobel Prizes or Fields medals	10	
Times higher education	Research reputation survey	18	62.5
	Research income	6	
	Research productivity	6	
	Research influence: citations	30	
	Industry income (innovation)	2.5	
QS	Academic reputation survey	40	60
	Citations per academic staff/faculty	20	
Webometrics	Data from SCImago	35	35

achieving a particular citation rate for that discipline is used in the final assessment. In addition, the THE allows institutions to provide, and sign off on, their data, and higher education institutions can be excluded from the THE rankings if they do not teach undergraduates, thereby removing those institutions which specialise in post-graduate education only [216,218]. Higher education institutions can also be excluded from the THE ranking if the institution has published fewer than 1,000 relevant articles within the survey time frame, or if more than 80% of the institutions' research are not concentrated in one of the THE's 11 subject areas:

a.   Arts and Humanities
b.   Business and Economics
c.   Clinical, Pre-clinical and Health
d.   Computer Science
e.   Education
f.   Engineering and Technology
g.   Law
h.   Life Sciences
i.   Psychology
j.   Physical Sciences

The academic reputation survey is used, in effect, to peer-review the research performed at different higher education institutions and has the second highest weighting in THE's ranking system. For research income, the THE uses income per academic staff/faculty member, with adjusted figures in terms of purchasing power parity (PPP). PPP is a flexible measure because it can be affected by an individual country's national policy, and the national economy, which are outside the control of the individual higher education institution. However, research income is scaled according to the discipline area, reflecting the fact that grants in the scientific disciplines are typically of a much higher monetary value than grants in the social sciences, arts and humanities.

Research productivity is measured by using the Scopus database and counting the number of publications per scholar, taking account of the size of the higher education institution and normalised by discipline [216]. The difficulty with such a measure is that not all publications are well-captured by the Scopus database system.

The industry income criterion takes the total amount of research income earned from industry and scales it against the number of faculty member/academic staff. It is suggested that this is a reasonable measure of knowledge transfer and the institution's ability to receive funding from the commercial/business sector.

The QS ranking uses a survey to determine the reputation of each institution in terms of both research and teaching. The survey seeks opinions of over 80,000 individual academic staff/faculty members and is considered to be the largest survey of academic opinion in the world.

The QS also uses citations per faculty member/academic staff as a measure of research impact. This measure is taken over a 5-year period for the papers being cited and a 6-year timeframe for the citations to occur. The Scopus database is used to develop the citations data. In addition, the citations are normalised, according to the discipline, by taking account of the rate of publication within different discipline fields.

The Webometrics ranking system uses Google Scholar and SCImago Institutions Rankings (SIR) to collect data on publication rates of different higher education institutions [214]. Webometrics utilises four metrics: presence, visibility, transparency (openness) and excellence (scholar) (Table 6.2). The SIR is a classification of academic and research-related institutions, ranked by a composite indicator that combines three different sets of indicators that are based on research performance, innovation outputs and societal impact. These indicators are measured by their web visibility (Figure 6.1).

6.4.2 Teaching (criterion 2)

Both THE and QS have a criterion for teaching in their overall ranking systems. The details of weighting for various factors of the teaching criterion for the THE and the QS ranking systems are shown in Table 6.3. There are no weightings for teaching allocated in the other two higher education institution ranking systems, ARWU and Webometrics.

The THE's academic reputation survey covers both research activities and teaching activities at the higher education institutions being reviewed, and reputation has been allocated the highest weighting within the teaching criterion. It should be noted that the survey measures perceived prestige of the institutions being examined. Disciplines and countries have weighted responses such that the responses reflect the actual distribution of scholars within each region and institution.

Table 6.2 Current calculation of indicators of webometrics ranking system

Indicators	Meaning	Methodology	Source	Weighting (%)
Presence	Public knowledge shared	Size (number of pages) of the main web domain of the institution. It includes all the subdomains that share the same (central/main) web domain	Google	5
Visibility	Web contents impact	Number of external networks (subnets) linking to the institution's webpages (normalised and then average value)	Ahrefs Majestic	50
Transparency (or openness)	Top cited researchers	Number of citations from top 110 authors (excl. top 10 outliers)	Google Scholar Profiles	10
Excellence (or scholar)	Top cited papers	Number of papers amongst the top 10% most cited in each one of the 26 disciplines of the full database. Data for the 5 year period: 2013–2017	SCImago	35

Source: Adapted from Ref. [214].

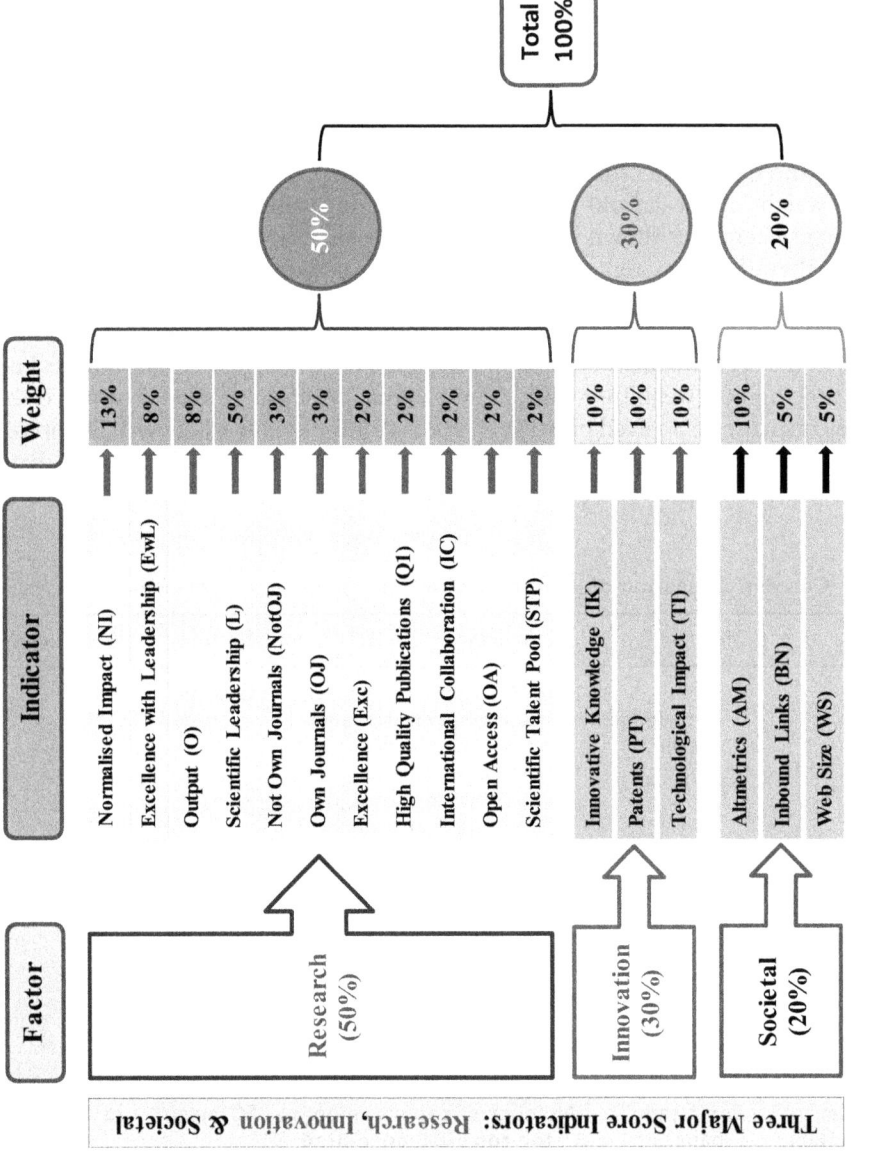

Figure 6.1 SIR indicators and weighting. (Adapted from Ref. [219].)

Table 6.3 Weighting for teaching (criterion 2)

Ranking scheme	Teaching criteria	Weighting to overall ranking (%)	Total weighting for criterion 2 (%)
ARWU	-	-	-
Time higher education (THE)	Reputation survey	15	30.25
	Academic staff to student ratio	4.5	
	Doctorate to bachelor ratio	2.5	
	Doctorates awarded to academic staff	6	
	Institutional income	2.25	
QS	Academic staff/faculty member to student ratio	20	20
Webometrics	-	-	-

While the staff-student ratio is self-explanatory, the doctorate (PhD) student-bachelor student ratio and the doctorates awarded to academic staff/faculty member ratio are used to provide a measure of how an institution is involved in developing the next generation of academics (Table 6.3). It is also assumed that a high proportion of postgraduate research students means that the teaching is at the highest level and is therefore attractive to graduates. The number of doctorates awarded is normalised to take account of the practice within each discipline, because the volume of doctorates awarded varies accordingly. Institutional income is also scaled with respect to the number of academic staff/faculty members and PPP.

The QS solely relies on the academic staff/faculty member to student ratio as a measure of teaching quality. By doing so, it assumes that the higher the academic staff-to-student ratio, the easier it is for students to access academic staff/faculty members and receive a high-quality education. In addition, the academic staff/faculty member-to-student ratio is used to determine how high the teaching burden is on individual academic staff/faculty members.

6.4.3 International profile (criterion 3)

The THE and QS consider the "international profile" or "international outlook" for each higher education institution. The metrics used for this criterion (Criterion 3) are listed in Table 6.4.

The THE assumes that the ability of a higher education institution to attract both academic staff/faculty member and students (undergraduate and postgraduate) from overseas is a key indicator of the quality.

The "International Collaboration" measure is determined by calculating the proportion of the journal publications which have at least one international co-author. Normalisation of the data also occurs, dependent on the discipline areas within each academic institution [216].

The QS also uses the international student ratio and the international/ethnically diverse academic staff/faculty member ratio as indicators of the importance of the higher education institution on the global stage. For high values for these ratios, it is assumed that the higher education institution provides a multinational environment,

Table 6.4 Weighting for international profile (criteria 3)

Ranking scheme	International profile criteria	Weighting (%)	Total weighting for criterion 3 (%)
ARWU	-	-	-
THE	Proportion of international students	2.5	7.5
	Proportion of international staff	2.5	
	International collaboration	2.5	
QS	International student ratio	5	10
	International faculty ratio	5	
Webometrics	-	-	-

providing students with an awareness of global issues: a vital transferable skill highlighted by employers [218,220].

6.4.4 Presence on the internet (criterion 4)

The THE, QS and ARWU do not allocate any weighting for the presence on the internet (Criterion 4). However, the Webometrics (Spain) ranking is quite different to the other three, with its original aim to assess the presence of different academic institutions on the web. This ranking scheme assumes that the presence on the internet is well-correlated with the institution's dissemination of knowledge through open-access initiatives [214]. The Webometrics ranking does not evaluate the useability of the institutions' websites, nor their popularity. The weighting indicators for Criterion 4 of the Webometrics ranking are as follows [214,218]:

- Presence (public knowledge shared): size (number of pages) of the main web-domain of the institution. It includes all the subdomains that share the same (central/main) web-domain, data from Google (**5%**).
- Visibility (web contents impact): number of external networks (subnets) linking to the institution's webpages (normalized and then average value), data from Ahrefs-Majestic (**50%**).
- Transparency or openness (top-cited researchers): number of citations from top 110 authors (excl. top 10 outliers), data from Google Scholar Profiles (**10%**).
- Excellence or Scholar (top-cited papers): number of papers amongst the top 10% most cited in each one of the 26 disciplines of the full database, for example, data for the 5-year period: 2013–2017, data collected from SCImago (**35%**).

6.4.5 Employer reputation (criterion 5)

The QS is the only global higher education institution ranking that applies a 10% weighting to employer reputation. Employer reputation is determined via a survey of employers. The survey asks employers to identify which higher education institutions produce graduates who are the most competent and work-ready. Typically, over 40,000 responses from employers are received. The QS claims that this survey is the largest of its kind in the world.

6.5 Comparative weighting for all four ranking systems

The total points for the ranking schemes vary notably. Each ranking system puts emphasis on different issues (Tables 6.1–6.5). The total weighting for ARWU is 90, while the total is 100 for TTHE, QS and Webometrics. Considering all four criteria and their sub-categories that are being used by ARWU, THE, QS and Webometrics, the THE and QS ranking systems use more comprehensive and balanced approaches. The ARWU is highly research-focused, while Webometrics predominantly looks at

Table 6.5 Total comparative weighting of four world higher education institution ranking systems against all five criteria

1.0	Criterion 1: research publications, citations and impact	Weighting to overall ranking (%)	Weighting for criterion 1 (%)
ARWU (Shanghai)	Number of "highly cited" researchers in the disciplines of natural sciences, engineering, life sciences, medical sciences and social sciences	20	90
	Papers published in *Science* and *Nature*	20	
	Papers indexed in science citation index-expanded and social science citation index	20	
	Per capita academic performance	10	
	Alumni winning Nobel Prizes or Fields medals	10	
	Staff winning Nobel Prizes or Fields medals	10	
Times higher education	Research reputation survey	18	62.5
	Research income	6	
	Research productivity	6	
	Research influence: citations	30	
	Industry income (innovation)	2.5	
QS	Academic reputation survey	40	60
	Citations per academic staff/faculty	20	
Webometrics	Data from Google Scholar	30	30
2.0	Criterion 2: teaching	Weighting to overall ranking (%)	Weighting for criterion 2
ARWU (Shanghai)	-	0	0
Time higher education (THE)	Reputation survey	15	30
	Academic staff to student ratio	4.5	
	Doctorate to bachelor ratio	2.5	
	Doctorates awarded to academic staff	6	
	Institutional income	2.0	
QS	Academic staff/faculty member to student ratio	20	20
Webometrics	-	0	0

(Continued)

Table 6.5 (Continued) Total comparative weighting of four world higher education
institution ranking systems against all five criteria

3.0	International profile criteria	Weighting (%)	Weighting for criterion 3 (%)
ARWU (Shanghai)	-	0	0
Time higher education (THE)	Proportion of international students	2.5	7.5
	Proportion of international staff	2.5	
	International collaboration	2.5	
QS	International student ratio	5	10
	International faculty ratio	5	
Webometrics	-	0	0

4.0	Criterion 4: presence on the internet	Weighting (%)	Weighting for criterion 4 (%)
ARWU (Shanghai)	-	0	0
Time higher education (THE)	-	0	0
QS	-	0	0
Webometrics	Presence (public knowledge shared), data from Google	5	65
	Visibility (web contents impact), data from AhrefsMajestic	50	
	Transparency or openness (top cited researchers), data from Google Scholar profiles	10	

5.0	Criterion 5: employer reputation	Weighting (%)	Weighting for criterion 5 (%)
ARWU (Shanghai)	-	0	0
Time higher education (THE)	-	0	0
QS	Employer perception via survey on higher education institutions that produces employable (quality) graduates	10	10
Webometrics	-	0	0

the web presence. The THE has started to use the United Nation's SDGs as new parameters for its higher education institutions' ranking. The details about these SDGs parameters are discussed in Section 6.6.

In summary, the THE uses 13 indicators grouped into five core higher education institution performance indicators: teaching, research, citations, international outlook and industry income (as a proxy for knowledge transfer), which are assigned 30%, 30%, 30%, 7.5% and 2.5%, respectively. For the measurement of teaching performance, 15% is based on reputation survey, 4.5% on academic staff/faculty member-to-student ratio, 2.25% on doctorate student-to-bachelor student ratio and 2.25% on higher education institutional income. For research performance measurement, 18% is based on reputation survey and 6% each on research income (grants and royalty) and research productivity. Regarding international outlook, 7.5% is allocated, which consists of 2.5% to international-to-domestic student ratio, 2.5% to the proportion of international academic staff/faculty member to domestic academic staff, and 2.5% to international collaboration.

The QS Ranking uses six metrics. They are academic reputation (40%), faculty member/academic staff-to-student ratio (20%), citations per faculty/academic from Scopus (20%), employer reputation from the global survey (10%), proportion of international students (5%) and proportion of international academic staff/faculty members (5%).

For the ARWU ranking, four categories of indicators are used to assess the excellence of higher education institutions. They are quality of education, indicated by the alumni of the institution winning Nobel Prizes (20%) and Field Medals (10%) and by the existing academic staff/faculty members. The quality of the academic staff/faculty members is measured by the most cited researchers in 21 broad subject categories which are compiled by Thomson Reuters (20%). Finally, there is a 20% weighting to papers published in *Nature* and *Science*.

In regard to research performance, 20% is allocated to research papers indexed in the Science Citation Index-expanded and the Social Science Citation index. Another 10% is allocated to per capita academic performance of a higher education institution.

The Webometrics uses four metrics. They are as follows: (i) presence (public knowledge shared), data from Google (5%); (ii) visibility (web content impact), data from AhrefsMajestic (50%); (iii) transparency or openness (top-cited researchers), data from Google Scholar Profiles (10%) and excellence or scholar (most-cited papers), data from SCImago (35%).

6.6 Emerging nation higher education institutions ranking

Since 2014, the THE has started a separate ranking for higher education institutions in developing countries. This new ranking incorporates geographic factors and the level of economic development of the nation in which the higher education institution is based. The average overall score of emerging nations in the ranking is based on government investment in higher education as a percentage of GDP. The separate emerging economies' higher education institutions' ranking is undertaken in part to address a common criticism of international league tables: their focus on wealthy universities in rich countries in the Global North [221,222]. Indeed, the top 10 institutions of any standard ranking system are invariably based in the UK or the USA. Typically, these institutions have long histories of education and research, large endowments and well-established local and international partnerships.

Therefore, the new emerging economies' higher education institutions' ranking gives an opportunity to highlight leading institutions in the emerging world. This new ranking also offers higher education institutions in developing countries an opportunity to benchmark themselves against peers operating in similar economic environments. Over 530 higher education institutions from 47 countries were featured in the 2020 emerging nations ranking. The THE expects increasing visibility of higher education institutions in emerging countries as a result of their performance in the rankings, because that performance should assist these institutions to cultivate partnerships with leading institutions in other countries [221,222].

The 2020 emerging countries' higher education institutions' ranking has revealed that there is little correlation between ranking performance and higher education investment or university access. The Financial Times Stock Exchange (FTSE) classification of a country based on 21 parameters for the evaluation of its equity capital market also shows little correlation to higher education institutions' ranking performance. The FTSE equity market classification is shown in Table 6.6.

The 2020 emerging nations' higher education institutions' ranking also indicates that many of the top performing institutions in terms of the overall score are from Europe. In contrast, higher education institutions in Africa and Latin America generally receive lower rankings. It is believed that emerging countries from Europe benefit significantly by collaborating with neighbouring and regional higher education institutions that have stronger traditions of higher education and research [221,222].

Table 6.6 The FTSE classification of equity markets as of September 2019

Developed nations	Advanced emerging nations	Secondary emerging nations	Frontier nations
Australia	Brazil	Chile	Argentina
Austria	Czech Republic	China	Bahrain
Belgium/Luxemburg	Hungary	Colombia	Bangladesh
Canada	Malaysia	Egypt	Botswana
Denmark	South Africa	India	Bulgaria
Finland	Mexico	Indonesia	Cote d'Ivoire
France	Taiwan	Kuwait	Croatia
Germany	Thailand	Pakistan	Cypris
Hong Kong	Turkey	Peru	Estonia
Ireland		Philippines	Ghana
Israel		Qatar	Iceland
Italy		Russia	Jordan
Japan		Saudi Arabia	Kazakhstan
Netherlands		United Arab Emirates	Kenya
New Zealand			Lithuania
Norway			Morocco
Poland			Nigeria
Portugal			Oman
Singapore			Palestine
South Korea			Republic of North Macedonia
Spain			Romania
Sweden			Serbia
Switzerland			Slovak Republic
UK			Slovenia
USA			Sri Lanka
			Tunisia
			Vietnam
			Tanzania

Source: Adapted from Ref. [223].

6.7 UN Sustainable development goals and global institution ranking

In 2015, all United Nations Member States have adopted "The 2030 Agenda for Sustainable Development", which offers a shared blueprint for peace and prosperity for people and the planet, now and into the future. In this 2030 agenda, there are 17 SDGs, which comprise an urgent call for action by all countries – developed and developing – in a global partnership. All members of the United Nations Organisation (UN) recognise that ending poverty and other deprivation must go hand-in-hand with strategies that improve health and education, reduce inequality, and spur economic growth – all while tackling climate change and working to preserve our oceans and forests [224]. All 17 SDGs are shown in Figure 6.2.

The THE ranking system has taken into consideration 11 of these objectives to develop a new ranking scheme in 2019. The goals indicated by an asterisk in the list below are adopted by the THE ranking system.

    i. No Poverty
   ii. Zero Hunger
  iii. Good Health and Well Being*
  iv. Quality Education*
   v. Gender Equality*
  vi. Clean Water and Sanitation
 vii. Affordable and Clean energy
viii. Decent Work and Economic Growth*
  ix. Industry, Innovation and Infrastructure*
   x. Reduced Inequalities*
  xi. Sustainable Cities and Communities*
 xii. Responsible Consumption and Production*
xiii. Climate Action*
xiv. Life below water
 xv. Life on Land
xvi. Peace, Justice and Strong Institutions*
xvii. Partnerships for the Goals*

The aim of the new ranking system is to provide insight into the institutions' work towards equality and climate action as well as sustainable living. The data sources are still from the higher education institutions themselves, Elsevier and Vertigo Ventures [227,239]. This newly developed THE ranking system has more flexibility, allowing a wider variety of higher education institutions to participate, including those which have never before taken part in a global ranking system [228].

The important flexibility of this new ranking system of the THE is the calculation of the final score. The calculation is made by taking the score for 17 SDGs (Partnerships for the Goals) at a weighting of 22%, with the top three of the remaining 10 goals being weighted at 26% each. The score for each goal is scaled to a maximum of 100 to ensure that, irrespective of which sustainability goals an institution selects, all are treated equally.

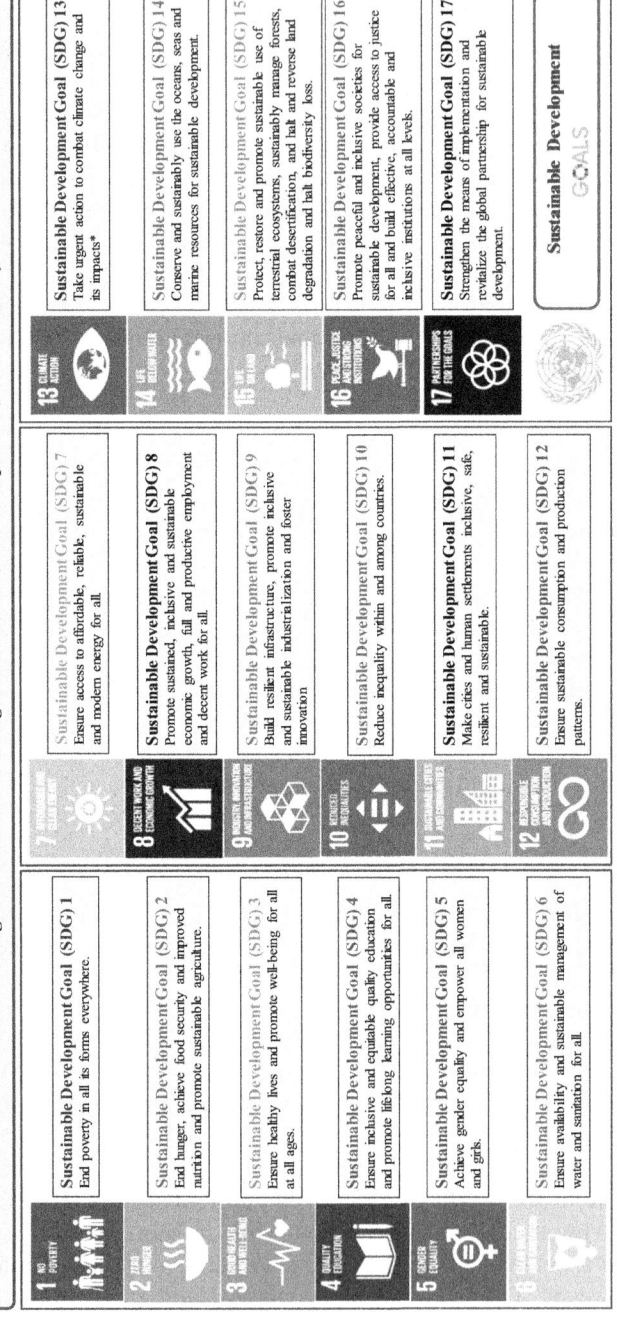

Figure 6.2 UN SDGs. (Adapted from Refs. [225–226].)

Table 6.7 Weighting for SDGs in THE's new ranking system

SDGs	Weighting	Sub-weighting
SDG 17 – Partnerships for the goals	Research (27%)	Proportion of academic publications with co-author from other country (14%)
		Number of publications that relate to the 11 SDGs (13%)
	Relationships to support the goals (23%)	Policy development with government or NGOs (4.6%)
		Promoting cross-sectoral dialogue with government or NGOs (4.6%)
		Collaborating internationally to capture data relating to SDGs (4.6%)
		Working internationally to promote best practice around SDGs (4.6%)
		Supporting the education of NGOs with respect to the SDGs (4.6%)
	Publication of SDG reports (50%)	Publication of specific data on university's performance against each of the 10 SDGs (excluding SDG 17 on partnerships for the goals)
		Data are obtained from universities

Source: Adapted from Ref. [228].

In addition, the THE publishes results for each individual sustainability goal, so that higher education institutions can participate according to how many goals they are aligned with, although these will not appear in the overall ranking table [228]. Each goal has its own internal weighting criteria. An example is given in Table 6.7.

The data for research and publications are derived from the information supplied by Elsevier and Vertigo Ventures, and typically, publications are confined to within a 5-year period. Policies and initiatives form part of the "continuous metric" of the ranking scheme, and the higher education institutions need to provide evidence to support their achievement claim. The THE ranking system expects such evidence to be publicly available and should demonstrate best practice.

To be included in the THE ranking system, the higher education institution must teach undergraduate students and the institutions need to provide and sign off on the data they supply to THE.

The other three ranking systems, ARWU, QS and Webometrics, are still considering the UN SDGs in their respective world higher education institutions' ranking system.

6.8 State-sponsored pursuit for global institutions league table

The global competition for securing a position in the top "100 higher education institutions list" is not limited to English-speaking developed nations. It has now spread to Europe, South East Asia and North Asia. The national governments have undertaken a range of strategies and approaches in pursuit of academic excellence.

The North Asian nations of China, South Korea, Taiwan and Hong Kong are among the first in Asia to implement strategic funding programs in pursuit of excellence. The government of the People's Republic of China has adopted a national policy for developing globally prominent higher education institutions. Under this policy, the Chinese government launched several specific targeted national initiatives and competitive funding programs, including the 211 Project and the 985 Project [205]. The 211 Project aims at developing 100 higher education institutions in major discipline areas by the early 21st Century. To further strengthen the development of excellence, the Chinese government also started the 985 Project, which emphasises the exploration of new mechanisms for higher education governance, with a view to transforming a select group of universities to world-class status [205,229]. These government-initiated projects provided funding and other resources to this group of higher education institutions to boost teaching and research capabilities, quality and performance, and institutional governance and management flexibility [205,229].

As the world's third largest economy, the government of Japan did not want its higher education institutions to fall behind in the global higher education ranking competition, and since 2001, the Japanese government has developed competitive funding schemes to foster a world-class standard at local higher education institutions. Regardless of government changes in Tokyo, the funding commitment and focus to pursue excellence in Japanese higher education institutions remain unaltered [205,230].

With over 201 universities (45 public and 156 private) and 2.2 million enrolled university students, South Korea – an engineering powerhouse and the fourth-largest economy in Asia – wants its higher education institutions to excel in the global list of elite higher education institutions. The government started a series of initiatives, including Brain Korea 21, World-Class University Initiatives and the BK21 PLUS project [205,231]. Across the region, similar government-sponsored projects, such as the Development Plan for World-Class Universities and Research Centres of Excellence in Chinese Taipei (Taiwan), The World-Class Universities program in Singapore and the Accelerated Program for Excellence in Malaysia, have been undertaken [205,230].

Like North and South East Asia, European nations, led by Germany, France, Spain and Russia, have also joined the race to global elite rankings of their higher education institutions. Germany undertook one of the earliest strategic funding programs in Europe. Administered by German federal and state governments since 2005, the "Excellence Initiative" is intended to enhance research in Germany, to support and promote elite higher education institutions, with the goal of improving its higher education institutions' performance at global level [205,232].

Inspired by the German initiative, and in order not to fall behind the elite league competition, the government of France launched a structural support program, "Investment Programme for the Future", in 2009, to boost higher education and research capabilities. This initiative is additional to the existing "Plan Campus" Program [205,233].

Overcoming the difficulties of the collapse of the former Soviet Union, and intent on regaining the lost reputation of some Russian world-class higher education institutions, the government of the Russian Federation has undertaken a series of projects since the early 2000s. The primary objectives of these projects are to strengthen Russian higher education institutions' research capacity. The Russian president, Vladimir Putin, in

2012, signed a decree that by 2020 there should be at least five Russian higher education institutions in the top 100 world university ranking list [205,234].

Other examples of special programs in Europe are the "Centres of Excellence" program (Denmark). Finland initiated "Centres of Excellence in Research" and Norway the "Centres of Excellence Scheme". Spain also has the "International Campus of Excellence" program [205].

6.9 Collaboration between developed and developing countries' higher education institutions

The higher education institutions in developing nations are severely under-funded and are lacking in infrastructure and research-active academic staff/faculty members. Furthermore, the reluctance of developed nations' higher education institutions to collaborate with developing countries' institutions makes it harder for developing nations' higher education institutions to build their research profile and footprint. However, even with limited resources and manpower, these higher education institutions can still make progress by utilising the global diaspora network, undertaking research and publishing jointly with regional and developed nations' higher education institutions. For developed nations' higher education institutions, such collaborations provide opportunities to use their research findings to change the lives of millions in tangible ways as well as assist improvement of the expertise and in-house research and teaching infrastructure of institutions in less developed higher education and research systems [235]. Developing partnerships between higher education institutions of developed nations and developing nations will allow the transfer of knowledge and experience without compromising developed nations' higher education institutions' reputations.

The 5 years' research outputs (scholarly books, book chapters, peer-reviewed journal articles, conference papers, etc.) from 2014 to 2018 from the top Least Developing Countries (LDCs) are shown in Figure 6.3. The figure also indicates the number

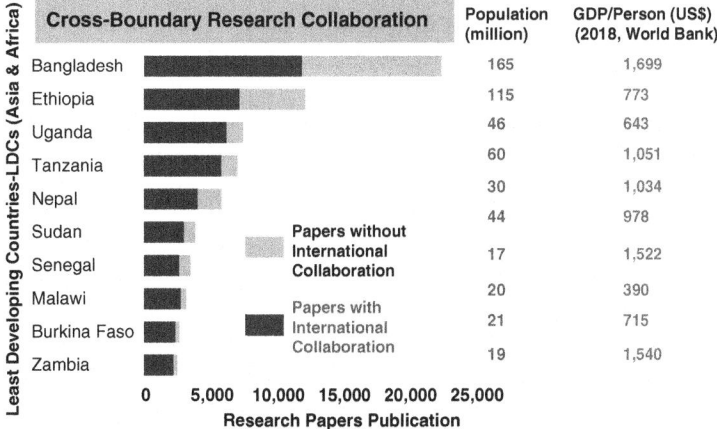

Figure 6.3 Research publications of the top 10 LDCs in 2014–2018. (Adapted from Refs. [235–239].)

of papers published with and without international collaboration. The figure clearly demonstrates that international and regional collaboration is vital. Countries such as China and India are utilising their diaspora connections and taking various initiatives for brain regain and recirculation. Bangladesh, Vietnam, Pakistan and the Philippines are also utilising their diaspora connections. However, it is strongly suggested that every higher education institution from emerging or developing countries should be proactive in international research, teaching and learning collaboration with regional and developed countries' higher education institutions, regardless of their diaspora connections.

Developed nations can allocate their aid funds, in collaboration with the participation of the developing countries' higher education institutions, such that the higher education institutions are assisted in building their capacity in research and teaching and learning, resulting in more effective use of aid money. At present, most aid money is spent inefficiently because a significant percentage of allocated money is spent covering the costs of foreign experts and/or consultants as well as unproductive or useless projects. Through joint research, however, experts can be produced locally, and they can not only contribute to their economy but also make a bridge between aid-receiving and aid-providing countries because they know the local context. At the same time, developed nations' higher education institutions raise their research profile through life-changing research that addresses the UN SDGs.

To achieve the SDGs, partnerships of technical, social, cultural and environmental experts, government policymakers and social workers from developed and developing nations are of paramount importance. Collaboration between the higher education institutions of developed and developing countries will play a vital role in these partnerships.

6.10 Ranking systems for public good

The four ranking systems use different indicators and weighting criteria. The result is that any stakeholder should be well aware of the differences between such systems and use the one which best-fits their purpose. This means that the stakeholder, whether a higher education institution, a prospective student or academic staff/faculty member or an employer or government, should not use such a rank as the single indicator of quality in higher education.

It is envisaged that higher education institutions will use such rankings as part of an overall quality assurance system. Education institutions should also provide publicly available information about the benefits they give to society. Engagement with the media and the public in general to improve the understanding of ranking systems would also be highly beneficial.

Incorporating the SDGs in the ranking of global higher education institutions by the THE is certainly warranted. It is highly desirable that the other three ranking systems should also include the SDGs.

Chapter 7

Academic (internal) quality assurance

7.1 Introduction

Academic quality, in higher education, is a broad framework of the institution's standards, mission and objectives in its academic courses, programs and disciplines. Academic quality assurance is generally an encompassing term referring to an ongoing continuous process of evaluating (assessing, monitoring, guaranteeing, maintaining and improving) the quality of a higher education system, institutions, programs and courses. Therefore, it is the activity for validating the performance of a higher education institution. Usually, there are three types of academic quality assurance: (a) institutional (internal) quality assurance, (b) national quality assurance and international quality assurance (Figure 7.1).

Academic quality assurance (institutional and national) is also a process of demonstration and/or verification that a desired level of quality of an academic activity has been attained or sustained or is highly likely to be attained or sustained [240]. Academic activities generally are (i) teaching and learning (undergraduate and postgraduate levels), (ii) research (academic staff and postdoctoral research fellows) and (iii) research training for higher degrees by researchers (postgraduate level). The mechanisms (e.g., systems, processes and activities) employed to verify such attainments are typically known as quality assurance systems, quality systems, institutional quality assurance or just "quality assurance" [240]. The quality assurance processes are equally applicable to any aspect of a higher education institution [240].

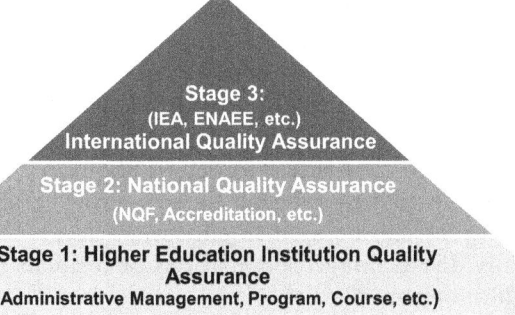

Figure 7.1   Academic quality assurance stages.

Today, the higher education institutions in the developed nations, and in many developing countries, have quality assurance structures and mechanisms in place to undertake activities for achieving "continuous improvement" as an integral part of academic quality assurance. Continuous improvement is typically based on an on-going reflective feedback cycle involving monitoring, review and consequent evidence-based improvements of the institution's management efficiency and academic courses and programs. The course/program quality may also include a review of policies and procedures [240].

Frequently, higher education institutions undertake benchmarking or external referencing for quality assurance. The benchmarking process allows collecting and reporting critical operational data to conduct comparisons of performances of different higher education institutions' internal management, disciplines, programs and courses to establish good practice [241]. The benchmarking or external referencing is not done with reference to the National Quality Assurance Scheme but can be done with respect to a model university with the same operating environment.

Throughout the subsequent discussion, the term "course" will be used to refer an individual course, model or subject, and the term "program" will be used to refer to a specific degree or qualification.

7.2 Institutional (internal) quality assurance

The institutional (also called internal) quality assurance examines organisational capacity to sustain an advanced academic program through financial and human resources, infrastructure, policies and/or effective management practices. The primary objective of institutional quality assurance is to demonstrate that the higher education institution's intrinsic motivation is to pursue the public good, not private gain [242].

Institutional quality assurance is the systematic organisational structure for implementing continuous quality assurance functions in all activities of the higher education institution (leadership, management, student, course and program administration). If the internal academic quality assurance activities are undertaken appropriately, generally no major deficiency arises during the auditing process undertaken by external quality assurance organisations.

The institutional quality assurance report of a higher education institution is a vital source of information for all stakeholders. The report and performance indicators are used to evaluate the outcomes of program(s) and the institutional capacity to support the learning environment and to achieve graduate work-readiness. Reports on the financial health of the higher education institution, its physical resources, including infrastructure, teaching, learning and research facilities, and library resources, very relevant and useful for prospective students when they consider where to invest their time and money [242]. For policymakers, institutional quality assurance can be used to gain access to details about institutional performance and be used to justify increasing or decreasing funding. Standards on admissions or research publications can be used to encourage access for under-represented, socio-economically disadvantaged populations or to focus the institution's attention on economic development [242].

In addition to strategic planning, a higher education institution should ensure strategic positioning of courses and programs with an access to external industry engagement. The leadership and management of program teams are critical, and there should be clear workload and performance management processes. Research also needs to be strategic and should have appropriate links to the teaching and learning activities of the institution. Facilities and physical resources also need constant monitoring, as do student profiles and admission and entry requirements [243–245].

Additional support services typically include career development and employment opportunities, counselling and health services, housing/accommodation advisory services and other services such as counselling and legal advice.

7.2.1 Program quality assurance

There are at least two essential prerequisites to academic program quality assurance. The first is that the characteristics of quality that are being sought need to be defined. These qualities are inputs (entry standards and staff qualifications), processes (cycle time for an enrolment process or time to get feedback from assignments), outputs (completion rates) and outcomes (knowledge and skills acquired and including lifelong learning skills). The second is that a judgement of attainment needs to be made. This may involve quantitative measures, or qualitative judgements, or both. A presupposition of academic quality assurance is that judgements about academic quality are made by someone (or some process) that is competent to do so [240].

The higher education institutions in the developed nations generally undertake academic program quality assurance through external and internal engagement. This allows getting constructive and independent feedback about the quality of the program(s) and benchmarking for further improvement [240,243].

7.2.1.1 Program quality assurance through external engagement

Academic program quality assurance through external engagement is pivotal because it provides important feedback on the quality, relevance and visibility of academic programs and courses. There are various ways the external engagement is undertaken. The most fundamental and vital one is the Program Advisory Committee (PAC) or Industry Advisory Committee (IAC). Others are periodic institution-led Graduate Employment Surveys, national graduate employment surveys and tapping industry expertise through the appointment of renowned external experts as Adjuncts.

The national graduate employment survey provides data on graduates, from all higher education institutions within the country, about their employment. In Australia, the Department (Ministry) of Education, Skills and Employment, Australian Government, assesses quality through the Quality Indicators for Learning and Teaching (QILT) surveys for higher education (diploma, bachelor and masters by coursework) that cover the student life cycle from commencement to employment: (a) the Student Experience Survey (SES), (b) the Course Experience Questionnaire (CEQ), (c) the Graduate Outcomes Survey (GOS) and (d) the Graduate Outcomes Survey – Longitudinal (GOS-L) [246].

The SES is conducted for commencing and final-year enrolled students (not yet graduated) at Australian higher education institutions for diploma, bachelor and masters by coursework programs. The SES measures and reports on teaching and learning outcomes, and student learning experience.

The CEQ collects information from recent graduates (approximately 4 months after their graduation) about the quality of education programs (qualifications) that Australian higher education institutions offered them.

The GOS, along with the CEQ, is completed by graduates from Australian higher education institutions around 4 months after completing their educational programs (qualifications). The GOS provides information on the labour market outcomes and further study activities of graduates.

The GOS-L supplements the GOS by measuring the medium-term employment outcomes of graduates 3 years after their graduation.

The Department (Ministry) of Education, Skills and Employment, Australian Government, also conducts the Employer Satisfaction Survey to obtain information about the quality of education, the generic skills, technical skills and work readiness of the graduate employed in their workplace [246].

In summary, these surveys provide four important data sets [246]:

- Quality of the overall educational experience of current students
- Overall satisfaction of recent graduates
- Outcomes of students moving into full-time employment after graduation
- Average salary received by recent graduates

The QILT survey data are used to benchmark the national standard and also classify the higher education institutions that perform higher or below the national average. The institutions that are below the national average need to develop strategies for improvement. The QILT survey data are annually collected and are available for public access from the QILT website [246].

Adjunct appointments of eminent industry or professional practitioners and researchers at Professor and Associate Professor levels aim to create opportunities for joint supervision of research students, participation in joint projects and the embedding of industrial experience into the learning and teaching environment. Such adjunct appointments are typically initiated by the unit or discipline head, endorsed by higher management, and finally approved by the institution's academic council. The duration of an adjunct appointment is generally 3 years and does not create an employment relationship with the higher education institution. The adjunct appointment has additional benefits in that it helps the higher education institution build community connections and get an external perspective on teaching and research.

The following sections explore the Program Advisory Committee and the Industry Advisory comment in more detail, before quality assurance processes via internal engagement are examined.

7.2.1.1.1 Program advisory committee/industry advisory committee

The Program Advisory Committee (PAC) or Industry Advisory Committee (IAC) are constituted by members of the industry and associated professional organisations. Typically, the academic board or a similar committee appoints these members after consultation with the appropriate unit or discipline head.

These appointees are well-known practising professionals well-versed in contemporary engineering and current and future industry needs. The committee reviews and evaluates academic programs on a regular basis (at least twice a year). Minor program amendments (less than 20% content change), major program amendments (over 20% program content change) and new program introduction and/or old program termination are all discussed and finalised in PAC/IAC meetings. Depending on the size of the academic program, the PAC/IAC committee generally consists of five to ten members including some from the discipline/unit of the higher education institution. The PAC/IAC meetings are always chaired by the external member. The PAC/IAC assesses the quality, relevance and viability of new programs, proposes developments and continuously monitors existing programs from an external stakeholder (industry) perspective [247].

7.2.1.2 Program quality assurance through internal engagement

Academic program quality assurance through internal engagement is paramount, as corrective actions are taken in situ. There are various mechanisms used for internal academic quality assurance, including program annual review (PAR), the SES on the overall student experience of the program, course assessment committees (CACs), program assessment boards (PABs) and the program curriculum review. Student complaints and resolution committees also form part of the internal engagement which can be used for quality assurance.

7.2.1.2.1 Program annual review

The academic PAR is considered to be central for quality assurance and ongoing quality improvement. Generally, its cycle is once per year. The following information or feedback is taken into consideration during the PAR:

a. Student and graduate surveys' consolidated data from individual CES, program-specific SES and the national CEQ
b. Input/feedback from PAC/IAC and outcomes of Industry Forums
c. Program Professional Accreditation reports and recommendations
d. Trends and issues outside the scope or responsibility of the program team or unit or discipline
e. Strategic institutional plan, budget, student profile management, quality, financial viability, etc.
f. Any informal feedback from research collaborators, students, graduates and employers
g. Staff-Student Consultative Committee (SSCC) minutes
h. Program team review reports
i. Student complaints on quality delivery and relevance.

The sole purpose of academic PAR is to aid design and delivery program content such that it helps students equip themselves with required knowledge and graduate capabilities so that they can work effectively immediately after graduation. The PAR is also used to ensure an outstanding learning environment within the higher education institution. The recommendations or directions for improvement from the PAR are then cascaded down to individual courses, units, modules or subjects. The principal lecturers or coordinators can then revise the course material and the assessment with these recommendations in mind, while still maintaining alignment with the required learning outcomes.

In short, the academic PAR:

a.   informs ongoing improvements to the program,
b.   provides a systematic review of program quality which informs profile and work planning and
c.   ensures that the program is aligned with the higher education institution's strategic objectives.

7.2.1.2.2 Student experience survey

Some higher education institutions conduct a regular (twice a year) SES on the overall program education quality. This SES provides vital data from the student perspective about program delivery, resources materials, infrastructure or facilities and relevance. The SES does not provide data on individual courses, units, modules or subjects. Nevertheless, the SES data are useful for the program quality improvement.

7.2.1.2.3 Course assessment committee and program assessment board

The CAC and PAB, also known as the student progress committee, looks at students' performance in individual courses, subjects and units, as well as in the program. It reviews assessment, grading and remedial actions to be taken for poorly performing students. The review of course delivery, assessment types and rubrics, the marking scheme and moderation for individual courses, units, modules or subjects is also undertaken at CAC and PAB meetings. The recommendations or directions of CAC and PAB help course delivery improvement and the student experience.

7.2.1.2.4 Student complaints and resolution

Higher education institutions generally have special independent units, appeal committees and student rights officers (usually from the students' union) to deal with complaints lodged by students about individual courses, units, modules or subject and/or other related matters. Any issues related to teaching and learning, including program, course, unit, module, subject, class timetables, facilities, infrastructure, occupational health and safety (OH&S) and other related matters, are taken into consideration in program quality assurance, the unit or discipline and the institution's strategic and operational planning. Again, the remedial actions from such efforts help improve program quality and the student learning experience.

7.2.1.2.5 Program curriculum review

Higher education institutions need to undertake periodic comprehensive review of the curriculum in all undergraduate programs to ensure the programs and their content are of high quality, and with work (industry) relevance. This is typically done by reviewing and mapping graduate attributes, course or unit contents and their currency and feedback from all stakeholders, especially the PAC/IAC. The curriculum review committee also examines graduate work readiness, student electives, work-integrated learning (WIL), industrial placement and student exchange opportunities for global learning experience.

In addition, the program review committee looks at the assessment of student education (OBE). Well-designed assessment is vital for effective delivery of an academic program. Academic staff/faculty members need to be fully aware of the different student assessment types and how to select appropriate assessment types for the evaluation of students' learning outcomes. Academic staff/faculty members also need to be fully familiar with (a) the institution's assessment policy, procedures and guidelines; (b) the grading and feedback mechanism; (c) reviewing assessment quality and (d) academic integrity and ethics.

It is worth noting that assessment is a fundamental and integral part of outcome-based learning. Teaching and practising are not enough; outcomes need to be measured to verify the achievement of graduate course and program-specific competencies. Assessment enables the lecturer/faculty member to measure the effectiveness of their teaching by linking student performance to specific learning objectives. Therefore, by analysing students' performance in assessments, lecturers/faculty members can develop an effective pedagogy.

In professional qualifications such as engineering, a set of competencies formulated by the national competency standards and/or professional organisations are used to assess learning outcomes. Individual students are measured against these standards in order to receive credit for their learning experience. The idea is to ensure that students are not simply earning a degree for time spent in the classroom but also can demonstrate their learning through authentic assessments of the skills they have gained [242,248].

Therefore, academic quality assurance at the program level ensures that the curriculum will lead to a worthwhile academic credential or qualification. Recognition via a quality assurance review is also necessary for admission into advanced academic programs or to practise as a registered or licensed/ chartered member of a profession [242,248].

7.2.2 Course/unit/module/subject quality assurance

Course-based quality assurance is a labour-intensive activity and forms a central part of the internal quality assurance activities of individual courses, units, modules and subjects. Course-based quality assurance is fundamental for competency-based education, and it is a strategy to ensure quality outcomes for an individual program [249]. It is ensured through the CES for each course and the SSCC meetings.

7.2.2.1 The course experience survey

The course experience survey (CES) is one of the indicators of quality for a course, unit, subject or module from a student's perspective. The higher education institutions in the developed nations and also in emerging nations have constituted the CES as an integral part of academic program's quality assurance system.

The CES obtains feedback about students' learning experiences in all active courses, subjects, modules and units of a higher education institution. This feedback is used to inform local improvement planning, course review and course delivery pedagogy. The CES is based on a definition of good teaching and can be used by academic staff/ faculty members to identify areas where most improvements might be needed. The CES generally contains around 10–20 questions on various aspects of course delivery and staff involved in it. Typical CES questions are shown in Table 7.1. Most CESs are designed so that they can be completed in 10–15 minutes.

Table 7.1 Typical CES questions

Question	Strongly disagree	Disagree	Neutral	Agree	Strongly agree
The learning objectives in this course are clear					
This course gives me confidence in tackling unfamiliar problems					
The teaching staff are good at explaining things					
The teaching staff provide feedback/comments on my work					
Overall, I am satisfied with the quality of this course					

In addition to the set questions, students can also write their individual comments as free responses. The survey is open to students at the end of the academic semester. A set of typical CES is shown in Figure 7.2.

The higher education institution's central survey centre collects the survey data and processes using various weightings for the students' responses to different survey questions.

The results are then provided to the relevant course coordinator, lecturer, unit or discipline head and other higher management at the end of the semester or academic term. The results include distributions of student satisfaction for each question, as well as derived overall indicators, such as the percentage agreement Good Teaching Score (GTS) and Overall Satisfaction Index (OSI).

In most developed nations' higher education institutions, the CES data are not only used to improve course delivery quality but also for individual academic/faculty member annual performance evaluation and career progression (academic promotion). As mentioned earlier, the processed survey data are sent to upper management for consideration, and remedial action may be recommended if an individual academic staff/faculty member's GTS and OSI are substantially below the set benchmark.

The GTS and OSI scores are considered key parameters for teaching and are documented and reviewed as part of the academic staff/faculty member's annual key performance indicators. Academic staff/faculty members who need to improve their GTS/OSI score are generally asked to make an improvement plan for achieving higher scores in the next delivery of their unit, module, course or subject. They can also be advised to observe the course or unit delivery of high-achieving/-performing senior academic staff/faculty members or to be mentored by such members. They can also be asked by the management to attend specialised pedagogical short courses or workshops.

7.2.2.2 Staff-student consultative committee

The SSCC is where student groups, or representatives of student cohorts, express their learning experience in individual courses. Typically, the only academic present is the program manager, although if the program manager also teaches a course, then a replacement academic is used in the meeting. SSCC meetings are held at least twice in a particular semester or term, to provide their experience in individual courses, and their opinion of educational quality.

Course Experience Survey (CES)

Academic staff/ faculty member(s) of this course will use survery results to make improvements in the delivery of this course. The academic staff/ faculty member(s) may also use the survey feedback to support their career progression endeavour and research

The survey is confidential and your individual feedback is not published. The institution only publishes aggregate/total survey results. However, please be aware that unsolicited comments may not be considered confidential if they are threatening or intimidating and may be investigated.

Course/Subject Code:

Shade circles like this: ●
Do not tick or cross the circles

Course/Subject Name:

Section One

This section asks you about your experience in your course.
Thinking about this course, please read the following statements and shade one response only.

	strongly disagree	disagree	neither agree nor disagree	agree	strongly agree
1. The learning objectives in this course are clear to me	O	O	O	O	O
2. The teaching staff are extremely good at explaining things	O	O	O	O	O
3. The teaching staff normally give me helpful feedback on how I am going in this course	O	O	O	O	O
4. This course contributes to my confidence in tackling unfamiliar problems	O	O	O	O	O
5. Assessment tasks in this course require me to demonstrate what I am learning	O	O	O	O	O
6. The amount of work required in this course is about right	O	O	O	O	O
7. The teaching staff in this course motivate me to do my best work	O	O	O	O	O
8. The teaching staff work hard to make this course interesting	O	O	O	O	O
9. The staff make a real effort to understand difficulties I might be having with my work	O	O	O	O	O
10. The staff put a lot of time into commenting on my work	O	O	O	O	O
11. I can see how this course will help me in the workplace	O	O	O	O	O
12. This course prepares me for working in a global or international setting	O	O	O	O	O
13. Overall, I am satisfied with the quality of this course	O	O	O	O	O

What are the best aspects of this course?   What aspects of this course are most in need of improvement?

Section Two

In order to aggregate the results of this survey by student group we need to know something about you. This information is confidential and will not be used to identify any individual persons.

Are you?
O A full-time student
O A part-time student

Are you an international student?
O Yes
O No

What is your age?
O 20 years or under
O 21-24 years
O 25-34 years
O 35-44 years
O 45 years or over

In the last week how many hours, outside of class, did you study for this course?
O 0-2 hours
O 3-4 hours
O 5-6 hours
O 7-10 hours
O 11 or more hours

Figure 7.2 Typical paper-based CES questionnaires.

The committee is a unique platform for students and academic staff/faculty members involved in course delivery, as it provides a mechanism by which the higher education institution can continuously improve student experience in terms of both course delivery and general resources. Good pedagogical practices that students value can also be disseminated in the unit or discipline and beyond for effective delivery of courses and programs.

Usually, each committee meeting is held in a friendly environment so that students can express their honest opinion about the individual course delivery and support system without any fear of punishment. All discussions and required actions are documented at each meeting, and specific issues relating to the performance of each course are discussed directly by the relevant lecturer/faculty member and other relevant people.

7.3 National academic quality assurance

National quality assurance is generally undertaken by sovereign government quality assurance organisations (e.g. TEQSA in Australia, the Bangladesh Accreditation Council-BAC/University Grants Commission – UGC in Bangladesh, the National Assessment and Accreditation Council – NAAC/UGC in India, the Quality Assurance Agency – QAA in the UK, the European Network for Quality Assurance – ENQA in the EU, etc.). The ENQA is now called the European Association for Quality Assurance in Higher Education. Every sovereign state has its own national academic quality assurance agency or organisation. These organisations seek to ensure that higher education institutions are at the appropriate national standard. They also verify performance, issues and make summative judgments of institutional fitness against societal needs and/or public policy demands [242,248,250]. Thus, higher education institutions that do not perform according to national standards and public expectation receive a performance enhancement roadmap developed or recommended by the external academic quality assurance organisation. Quality assurance is not a once-off issue. The main purpose is to develop a mechanism to undertake continuous quality enhancement. Quality assurance in a higher education institution has two primary functions [242,248,250]. First, it establishes the legitimacy of an institution and the programs of study it offers. Second, it informs students, policymakers and other stakeholders about program purposes and outcomes [242].

The outcomes of the quality assurance process suggest three alternative ways of looking at the activity. First, the accreditation model of quality assurance is designed to make a go/no-go assessment of the institution. A positive decision means the institution can continue to operate with all the privileges it has earned through the process. A negative decision typically represents an existential crisis leading to closure or dramatic changes in access to students or funding. The assessment model of quality assurance is more of a formative process, intended to provide feedback to the institution for improvement. The goal here is to identify weaknesses and ensure these will be promptly corrected. Rankings are the third model of quality assurance. Whether focusing on the higher education institutions in a particular country, or making international comparisons, rankings use a relatively simple set of factors to order institutions from the "best" to the "worst". The rankings can be quite influential with policymakers [242,250].

7.4 International academic quality assurance

International academic quality assurance is generally undertaken through bilateral and multilateral agreements between national program quality assurance organisations and program accreditation organisations. The two such major organisations are the International Engineering Alliance (IEA) and the European Network for Accreditation of Engineering Education (ENAEE). The mutual recognition of academic qualifications and jurisdictions of the IEA and ENAEE are discussed in detail in Chapter 4. International Quality ranking systems for higher education are examined in Chapter 6.

Appendix A

Sample program guide for B.Eng. (Mechanical Engineering)

This program guide lists the major details and sub-details which should be included in a program guide.

AI Program guide

Program:	XXXX Bachelor of Engineering (Mechanical Engineering) (Honours)
Plan:	XXXX Bachelor of Engineering (Mechanical Engineering) (Honours)
Campus:	AUSNN Melbourne Campus
Version:	XX
Status:	Approved

Last Updated: 06/02/2020, 13:54

AI.I Program details

Award Title:	Bachelor of Engineering (Mechanical Engineering) (Honours)
Award Abbreviation:	BEng (Mech Eng) (Hons)
Total Credit Points:	384
Career:	UGRD
Duration:	4 years full time; 8 years part-time
Location:	Melbourne Campus
Owning School:	Engineering (XXXX)
Owning School URL:	XXXXXX
ASCED Code:	######
CRICOS Code:	######B
Proposed Introduction:	Semester 2, 2020
Program Proposer Details:	
Name:	Dr/Associate Professor/Professor XXXX
Email:	XXXX

AI.2 National accreditation and industry links

AI.2.1 External accreditation

This section describes:

- The accreditation status of the program (full/provisional/nil) and under system accreditation were achieved;
- The accrediting body;
- Any international agreements covered by the accreditation status;
- Opportunities for graduates of the program to be members of professional organisations.

AI.2.2 Industry links

This section describes:

- Any formal links to individual industry representatives;
- Any University Committees which seek industry feedback on qualifications;
- The membership of any such University Committees;
- The role of such University Committee(s) in the development and maintenance of the program.

AI.3 Purpose of the program

This section describes:

- Overall objective of the program
- Discipline area of the program
- Level of qualification
- Context of the qualification in terms of career, relevant industries and location of these industries
- Abilities a successful graduate will have acquired by graduation, including both transferable and specific technical skills
- Pedagogy used in delivery of the program
- Main mode of delivery
- Content areas
- Experience and qualifications of the staff delivering the program
- Student opportunities for interacting with industry during the program of studies
- Student opportunities for independent research and design innovation.

A1.4 *Program learning outcomes*

The program-learning outcomes should be mapped across relevant criteria. It is advantageous if multiple criteria sets can be included in the same map as per the example below, which maps PLOs against both Australian Qualifications Framework criteria and University Graduate Attributes. In the example given, the PLOs are the graduate attributes required by Engineers Australia.

Program learning outcomes

EA 1 Knowledge and Skill Base

EA 1.1 Comprehensive, theory-based understanding of the underpinning natural and physical sciences and the engineering fundamentals applicable to the engineering discipline.

EA 1.2 Conceptual understanding of mathematics, numerical analysis, statistics and computer and information sciences which underpin the engineering discipline.

EA 1.3 In-depth understanding of specialist bodies of knowledge within the engineering discipline.

EA 1.4 Discernment of knowledge development and research directions within the engineering discipline.

EA 1.5 Knowledge of contextual factors impacting the engineering discipline.

EA 1.6 Understanding of the scope, principles, norms, accountabilities and bounds of contemporary engineering practice in the specific discipline.

EA 2 Engineering Application Ability

EA 2.1. Application of established engineering methods to complex engineering problem-solving.

EA 2.2. Fluent application of engineering techniques, tools and resources.

EA 2.3. Application of systematic engineering synthesis and design processes.

EA 2.4. Application of systematic approaches to the conduct and management of engineering projects.

EA 3 Professional and Personal Attributes

EA 3.1. Ethical conduct and professional accountability

EA 3.2. Effective oral and written communication in professional and lay domains.

EA 3.3. Creative, innovative and proactive demeanour.

EA 3.4. Professional use and management of information.

EA 3.5. Orderly management of self- and professional conduct.

EA 3.6. Effective team membership and team leadership. [29]

A1.5 Program-learning outcomes matrix

Program-learning outcomes / Bachelor of engineering	AQF LOADs	RMIT s GAs	Year 1	Year 2	Year 3	Year 4
1. Knowledge and skill base						
1.1. Comprehensive, theory-based understanding of the underpinning natural and physical sciences and the engineering fundamentals applicable to the engineering discipline.	K1	GA1, GA5	CCCC1004 FFFF1007 EEEE1006	AAAA2001 CCCC2003 GGGG1008 AAAA2101	CCCC3003 GGGG3008 DDDD3005	GGGG4008
1.2. Conceptual understanding of the mathematics, numerical analysis, statistics and computer and information sciences which underpin the engineering discipline.	K1	GA1, GA5	MMMM1002 MMMM1102	MMMM2002 AAAA2001 AAAA2101	GGGG3008 CCCC3103 DDDD3005	GGGG4008
1.3. In-depth understanding of specialist bodies of knowledge within the engineering discipline.	S2	GA1	EEEE1006	GGGG1008 HHHH2009 AAAA2101	CCCC3003 GGGG3008 HHHH3009 GGGG3108 CCCC3103 DDDD3005	DDDD4005 GGGG4008
1.4. Discernment of knowledge development and research directions within the engineering discipline.	K2, S4	GA1			CCCC3103 AAAA3001 DDDD3005	AAAA4001 AAAA4101
1.5. Knowledge of contextual factors impacting the engineering discipline.	S1	GA1	AAAA1001 DDDD1005 FFFF1007	DDDD2005	HHHH3009 AAAA3101	AAAA4001 AAAA4101 DDDD4005
1.6. Understanding of the scope, principles, norms, accountabilities and bounds of contemporary engineering practice in the specific discipline.	A1	GA1	AAAA1001 BBBB1003		HHHH3009 AAAA3101 AAAA3001	AAAA4001 AAAA4101 DDDD4005
2. Engineering application ability						
2.1. Application of established engineering methods to complex engineering problem-solving.	S1	GA1	FFFF1007	AAAA2001 CCCC2003 GGGG1008 AAAA2101 DDDD2005	CCCC3003 HHHH3009 GGGG3108 CCCC3103 AAAA3101 DDDD3005	AAAA4001 AAAA4101 DDDD4005 GGGG4008

Program-learning outcomes Bachelor of engineering	AQF LOADs	RMITs GAs	Year 1	Year 2	Year 3	Year 4
2.2. Fluent application of engineering techniques, tools and resources.	S2	GA1	CCCC1004 DDDD1005 FFFF1007 BBBB1003 EEEE1006	MMMM2002 AAAA2001 CCCC2003 HHHH2009 AAAA2101 DDDD2005	GGGG3008 HHHH3009 GGGG3108 CCCC3103 DDDD3005	AAAA4001 AAAA4101 DDDD4005 GGGG4008
2.3. Application of systematic engineering synthesis and design processes.	S3	GA1, GA6	AAAA1001	AAAA2001 GGGG1008 HHHH2009 OENG1206 DDDD2005	HHHH3009 GGGG3108 AAAA3101	AAAA4001 AAAA4101
2.4. Application of systematic approaches to the conduct and management of engineering projects.	A4		AAAA1001	AAAA2001 DDDD2005	AAAA3101 AAAA3001	AAAA4001 AAAA4101
3. Professional and personal attributes						
3.1. Ethical conduct and professional accountability.	A1	GA1	AAAA1001		HHHH3009 AAAA3101 AAAA3001	AAAA4001 AAAA4101
3.2. Effective oral and written communication in professional and lay domains.	S5	GA1	AAAA1001 CCCC1004 DDDD1005 FFFF1007 BBBB1003	AAAA2001 CCCC2003 AAAA2101	AAAA3101 AAAA3001	AAAA4001 AAAA4101
3.3. Creative, innovative and proactive demeanour.	A2	GA2, GA3, GA4	AAAA1001	AAAA2001 MIET2420	HHHH3009	AAAA4001 AAAA4101
3.4. Professional use and management of information.	A4	GA1	AAAA1001	AAAA2001 CCCC2003 DDDD2005 HHHH2009	HHHH3009 AAAA3001	AAAA4001 AAAA4101 DDDD4005
3.5. Orderly management of self- and professional conduct.	A3	GA1 GA5	AAAA1001	AAAA2001	AAAA3101	AAAA4001 AAAA4101
3.6. Effective team membership and team leadership.	A3	GA1, GA5	AAAA1001	AAAA2001 DDDD2005	AAAA3101	AAAA4001 AAAA4101

LEGEND for core (compulsory) courses

Year 1

AAAA1001:	Introduction to Professional Engineering Practice
MMMM1002:	Engineering Mathematics C
BBBB1003:	Creative Engineering CAD
CCCC1004:	Mechanics and Materials 1
DDDD1005:	Applied Thermodynamics
MMMM1102:	Further Engineering Mathematics C
EEEE1006:	Advanced Manufacturing and Mechatronics: What We Make and How We Make It
FFFF1007:	Fluid Mechanics of Mechanical Systems

Year 2

MMMM2002:	Math & Stats for Aero, Mech & Auto
AAAA2001:	Mechatronics Principles
CCCC2003:	Mechanics and Materials 2
GGGG1008:	Engineering Dynamics
DDDD2005:	Thermal-Fluid System Design
AAAA2101:	Digital Fundamentals
HHHH2009:	Mechanical Design 1

Year 3

AAAA3001:	Research Methods for Engineers
CCCC3003:	Solid Mechanics 3
GGGG3008:	Mechanical Vibrations
DDDD3005:	Heat Transfer
HHHH3009:	Mechanical Design 2
GGGG3108:	Mechanics of Machines
CCCC3103:	Finite Element Analysis
AAAA3101:	Engineering and Enterprise

Year 4

AAAA4001:	Engineering Capstone Project Part A
AAAA4101:	Engineering Capstone Project Part B
GGGG4008:	Automatic Control
DDDD4005:	Renewable Energy Systems

Australian Qualification Framework learning outcome descriptors (AQF LODs) at level 8:

Knowledge

    K1 Coherent and advanced knowledge of the underlying principles and concepts in one or more disciplines

    K2 Knowledge of research principles and methods

Skills

    S1 Cognitive skills to review, analyse, consolidate and synthesise knowledge to identify and provide solutions to complex problems with intellectual independence

S2 Cognitive and technical skills to demonstrate a broad understanding of a body of knowledge and theoretical concepts with advanced understanding in some areas

S3 Cognitive skills to exercise critical thinking and judgement in developing new understanding

S4 Technical skills to design and use research in a project

S5 Communication skills to present a clear and coherent exposition of knowledge and ideas to a variety of audiences

Application of knowledge and skills

A1 Demonstrate application of knowledge and skills with initiative and judgement in professional practice and/or scholarship

A2 Adapt knowledge and skills in diverse contexts

A3 Demonstrate application of knowledge and skills with responsibility and accountability for own learning and practice in collaboration with others within broad parameters

A4 Demonstrate application of knowledge and skills to plan and execute project work and/or a piece of research and scholarship with some independence

RMIT graduate attributes (GAs)

GA1 Work ready

GA2 Global in outlook and competence

GA3 Environmentally aware and responsive

GA4 Culturally and socially aware

GA5 Active and lifelong learners

GA6 Innovative

A1.6 Program structure

Your weighted average mark will determine the honours level of your award once you have completed the program. If a course counts toward your weighted average mark, that fact will be stated in its course guide. In Enrolment Online, after you completed your course enrolment, you will be notified which of the enrolled courses will count toward the Year.

Year One of Program (Year 1)

Complete the following Eight (8) Courses:

Course title	Course code	Credit points	Campus
Introduction to Professional Engineering Practice	AAAA1001	12	####
Engineering Mathematics C	MMMM1002	12	####
Creative Engineering CAD	BBBB1003	12	####
Mechanics and Materials I	CCCC1004	12	####
Applied Thermodynamics	DDDD1005	12	####
Further Engineering Mathematics C	MMMM1102	12	####
Advanced Manufacturing and Mechatronics: What We Make and How We Make It	EEEE1006	12	####
Fluid Mechanics of Mechanical Systems	FFFF1007	12	####

Year Two of Program (Year 2)
Complete the following Seven (7) Courses:

Course title	Course code	Credit points	Campus
Math & Stats for Aero, Mech & Auto	MMMM2002	12	####
Mechatronics Principles	AAAA2001	12	####
Mechanics and Materials 2	CCCC2003	12	####
Engineering Dynamics	GGGG1008	12	####
Thermal-Fluid System Design	DDDD2005	12	####
Digital Fundamentals	AAAA2101	12	####
Mechanical Design 1	HHHH2009	24	####

And
Complete any One University Elective (one 12 Credit Point Course):
Year Three of Program (Year 3)
Complete the following Eight (8) Courses:

Course title	Course code	Credit points	Campus
Research Methods for Engineers	AAAA3001	12	####
Solid Mechanics 3	CCCC3003	12	####
Mechanical Vibrations	GGGG3008	12	####
Heat Transfer	DDDD3005	12	####
Mechanical Design 2	HHHH3009	12	####
Mechanics of Machines	GGGG3108	12	####
Finite Element Analysis	CCCC3103	12	####
Engineering and Enterprise	AAAA3101	12	####

Year Four of Program (Year 4)
Complete the following Four (4) Courses:

Course title	Course code	Credit points	Campus
Engineering Capstone Project Part A	AAAA4001	12	####
Engineering Capstone Project Part B	AAAA4101	12	####
Automatic Control	GGGG4008	12	####
Renewable Energy Systems	DDDD4005	12	####

And

Complete any Two (2) courses from following courses:

Course title	Course code	Credit points	Campus
Engineering Learning Factory Project	AAAA4201	12	####
Engineering Computer Graphics	CCCC4001	12	####
Mechanical Design 3	HHHH4009	12	####
Applied Heat and Mass Transfer	DDDD4105	12	####
Remote Area Power Supply	DDDD4205	12	####
Computational Engineering 1	CCCC4101	12	####
Computer Integrated Manufacturing	AAAA4301	12	####
Vehicle Power Systems	DDDD4205	12	####
Industrial and Vehicle Aerodynamics	DDDD4305	12	####
Mechatronic Design	AAAA4401	12	####
Advanced Robotics	AAAA4402	12	####
Advanced Engineering Computer Aided Design	CCCC4201	12	####
Computational Fluid Dynamics	DDDD4405	12	####

And

Complete any Two University Electives (two 12 Credit Point Courses)
Total Credit Points: 384
The value of the points used should be articulated here, distinguishing between directed learning and self-directed learning as appropriate.

A1.7 Work integrated learning

This section describes:

* How formal learning is linked to workplace experience;
* The courses/subjects with significant assessment involving external groups, businesses or organisations where work integrated learning occurs;
* In terms, the activities, assessments and opportunities for feedback from industry practitioners;
* The context in which the learning and work placement occur
* Any opportunities for undertaking a full-time work placement for credit.

A1.8 Approach to learning and assessment

This section describe the:

* flow of the curriculum through the program
* pedagogies used throughout the program
* staff profile
* engagement with relevant industries
* learning activities
* modes of delivery
* student responsibilities
* types and timings of assessments

- where to find the details of assessments for each course/module/subject
- availability of equitable learning services
- possibility of credit exemptions based on previous study and/or experience.

A1.9 Articulation and pathways

This section describes:

- any non-high school based entry pathways and any minimum requirements which need to be achieved;
- the possibility of credit transfer for non-standard enrolments;
- any opportunities for further study after the completion of the program.

A1.10 Entrance requirements

This section describes the prerequisites for applicants who have completed high school as well as any requirements for students who have studied English as a second language.

A1.11 Library, IT and specialist resources

This section describes:
Resources available from the Library, including the:

- Media types available, including electronic and internet resources and free sites
- Process for requesting special items
- Availability of student study space
- Availability of library staff for consultation and training
- Level of access to resources

In this section, it is also good to include a direct link to program-specific resources as well as a direct link to the library home page.
Online learning tools and content
This section identifies the main online tools relevant to the program, including the main learning management system.
Learning services available to you as a student at the University
List the other support services the University provides. These may be academic support; career development services and/or services which aid in the improvement and maintenance of personal well-being.

A1.12 Student expenses and charges in addition to fees

This section lists any additional charges the student may be expected to pay: e.g. costs for textbooks or consumables.

A1.13 Program transition plan

Where there has been a recent, substantial change to the program, it may be necessary to develop a transition plan or "pipeline" for specific cohorts. These plans should be clearly stated here.

Appendix B

Example of a typical course/unit/ subject/module guides

This sample lists the major details and sub-details which should be included in a course/subject/unit/module guide.

B1 Course information

Course ID:	######
Course Code:	GGGG1008
Course Title:	Engineering Dynamics
Status:	Published
School:	School of Engineering
Campus:	Melbourne
Teaching Period:	Semester 1, 2020
Credit Points:	12
Academic Career:	Undergraduate
Learning Mode:	Face to face

B1.1 Additional information

Primary Learning Mode:	List the major learning modes implemented
Learner Directed Hours:	as per the institution points system
Teacher Guided Hours:	as per the institution points system

B1.2 Course coordinator information

Course Coordinator Name:	The academic who coordinates the learning activities
Course Coordinator Phone:	+61 # ########
Course Coordinator Email:	as appropriate
Course Coordinator Location:	physical location
Course Coordinator Availability:	specify if an appointment is necessary

BI.3 Offering coordinator information

Offering Coordinator Name:	Academic delivering the bulk of the learning activities
Offering Coordinator Phone:	+6l # ########
Offering Coordinator Email:	as appropriate
Offering Coordinator Location:	physical location
Offering Coordinator Availability:	specify if an appointment is necessary
Additional Staff Contact Details:	List laboratory supervisors, tutors or guest lecturers here.

BI.4 Course information

BI.4.1 Course description

Briefly describes the course content in terms of the general knowledge area.

BI.4.2 Pre-requisites, co-requisites and assumed knowledge

Here list any prerequisites which must be successfully completed before undertaking the course. Co-requisites can be studied concurrently with the course and the assumed knowledge may refer to general knowledge or prior studies.

BI.4.3 Capabilities

List the program learning outcomes which the course addresses here. (See Tables 2.3 and 2.4.)

BI.4.4 Learning outcomes: course-learning outcomes (CLOs)

List the course-learning outcomes here.

BI.4.5 Overview of learning activities

List the learning activities, with examples of these and what each activity is designed to provide. There may also be a statement about how the learning activities relate to real-world problems or case studies.

BI.4.6 Details of learning activities

Detail the relationships between the different learning activities and state the expected level of attendance.

BI.4.7 Teaching schedule

Detail the curriculum week by week, as an approximate schedule.

B1.5 Overview of learning resources

Provide information on mandated texts and additional helpful references. Also list any other resources which may be available on the institution's learning management system.

B1.6 Overview of assessment type and weighting

State the types of assessment (Assignment, Class Test, Laboratory Practices, Homework, End of Term Examination, etc.), and for each one state, its:

- Weighting (%)
- Relation to the course learning outcomes
- Assessment work submission due date;
- Format and timing.

Detail how late submissions will be dealt with, including any penalties.

B1.6.2 Course grades available

This section lists:

- Grades available (e.g. High Distinction, Distinction, Credit, Pass, etc.)
- 7 Detailed descriptions of the standard of each grade
- Percentage range for each grade
- Any temporary grades and how these can be finalised
- Process for contesting marks
- Process whereby changes to assessment can be made during the semester.

B1.7 Other information

This section details the process for the granting of an extension of time due to personal circumstances.

Appendix C

Sample submission table of contents for bachelor of engineering program accreditation

THE INSTITUTION OF ENGINEERS AUSTRALIA (IEAust)

Submission for
Accreditation/Reaccreditation of
Bachelor of Engineering (Mechanical) Degree Program
to Meet the Engineers Australian's Academic Requirements for
Corporate Membership at the Washington Accord Level

Submitted by

University X

Faculty: Faculty of Engineering
Department: Mechanical Engineering, University X
Program: Bachelor of Engineering (Mechanical Engineering) (Honours)
Date of Visit: ....
Signed by: Date: ....

Professor ....
Dean, Faculty of Engineering
University X, Australia

The Engineers Australia (IEAust)
Level 31, 600 Bourke Street
Melbourne VIC 3000

Table of Contents for Submission

Preface

List of Tables

List of Appendices

Appendix 1 – Professional Development for Staff Member
Appendix 2 – Academic Calendar
Appendix 3 – Terms of Reference for Program Advisory Committees
Appendix 4 – Learning Outcomes Cross Reference
Appendix 5 – Example of Marking Guide and Rubrics
Appendix 6 – Samples of Approval Process for New and Amended Program(s)
Appendix 7 – School Guidebook on Engineering Experience
Appendix 8 – Sample Program Guides
Appendix 9 – Sample Annual Review Reports
Appendix 10 – Maps of Learning Outcomes and Assessments
Appendix 11 – Table(s) of Benchmark Comparisons
Appendix 12 – Individual Course Guides
Appendix 13 – Curriculum Vitae of Academic Staff /Faculty Members
Appendix 14 – Teaching Space, Laboratories and Special Rooms
Appendix 15 – Major Equipment and Computer Facilities
Appendix 16 – Teaching & Learning Academic Platforms & Lecture Captures Software
Appendix 17 – Library Facilities

Sample dual accreditation program submission table of contents to the host country's accreditation organisation

THE HONG KONG INSTITUTION OF ENGINEERS

SUBMISSION FOR
ACCREDITATION OR REACCREDITATION OF
ENGINEERING DEGREE PROGRAM
TO MEET THE HKIE'S ACADEMIC REQUIREMENTS FOR
CORPORATE MEMBERSHIP AT THE WASHINGTON ACCORD LEVEL

Submitted by

University X

Faculty: Engineering in collaboration with the
                  Local Partner Y in Hong Kong
Department: Mechanical Engineering, University X
Program: Bachelor of Engineering (Mechanical Engineering) (Honours)
Date of Visit: ....
Signed by:

Professor ....   Date: ....
Dean of Engineering
University X, Australia

The Hong Kong Institution of Engineers (HKIE)
9/F Island Beverley 1 Great George Street
Causeway Bay Hong Kong Tel: 2895 4446
Fax: 2577 7791

Table of Contents

References

Chapter 1

1. Public Broadcasting Service-PBS (2011), That Which Has Never Been, 12 February 2011, retrieved on 20 February 2020 from https://www.pbs.org/wgbh/nova/article/that-which-has-never-been/.
2. United Nations Educational, Scientific and Cultural Organisation - UNESCO (2010), Engineering: Issues, Challenges and Opportunities for Development, retrieved 20 February 2020 from http://unesdoc.unesco.org/images/0018/001897/189753e.pdf.
3. UNDESA (2018), SDG Indicators, retrieved on 20 February, 2020 from https://unstats.un.org/sdgs/indicators/database/.
4. UNESCO (2009), Institute of Statistics, UIS database, retrieved 10 December 2019 from http://www.uis.unesco.org/ev.php.
5. Roy, J. (2018), Engineering by the Numbers, the American Society for Engineering Education, retrieved on 9 February 2020 from https://ira.asee.org/wp-content/uploads/2019/07/2018-Engineering-by-Numbers-Engineering-Statistics-UPDATED-15-July-2019.pdf.
6. Dobbs, R., Roxburgh, C. and Lund, S. (2012), The World at Work: Jobs, Pay and Skills for 3.5 Billion People, McKinsey Global Institute, June, pp. 1–108, www.mckinsey.com/mgi.
7. Shook, E. and Knickrehm, M. (2018), Harnessing Revolution: Creating the Future Workforce, Accenture strategy, pp. 1–28, retrieved on 26 May 2019 from https://www.accenture.com/_acnmedia/pdf-40/accenture-strategy-harnessing-revolution-pov.pdf.
8. Giffi, C.A., Wellener, P. and Dollar, B. (2018), The Jobs Are Here, but Where Are the People? 2018 Deloitte and The Manufacturing Institute Skills Gap and Future of Work Study, accessed on 7 February 2020 from https://www2.deloitte.com/us/en/insights/industry/manufacturing/manufacturing-skills-gap-study.html.
9. Gartner (2019), https://www.gartner.com/en/newsroom/press-releases/2019-01-17-gartner-survey-shows-global-talent-shortage-is-now-the-top-emerging-risk-facing-organizations.
10. Binvel, Y., Franzino, M., Guarino, A., Laouchez, J-M. and Penk, W. (2018), The Global Talent Crunch, The Korn Ferry Institute, USA, pp. 1–50, https://www.kornferry.com/insights.
11. Marsh, R.R. and Oyelere, R.U. (2018), Global migration of talent: drain, gain and transnational impacts. In Dassin, J.R., et al. (Eds.), *International Scholarships in Higher Education*, Cham: Palgrave Macmillan, https://doi.org/10.1007/978-3-319-62734-2_11.
12. Forbes Magazine (2015), https://www.forbes.com/sites/niallmccarthy/2015/06/09/the-countries-with-the-most-engineering-graduates-infographic/#7cd649b1667d.
13. Lucena, J., Downey, G., Jesiek, B. and Elber, S. (2008), Competencies beyond countries: the re-organization of engineering education in the United States, Europe, and Latin America. *Journal of Engineering Education*, 97: 433–447.
14. Varghese, N.V. (2009), GATS and transnational mobility in higher education. In Bhandari, R. and Laughlin, S. (Eds.), *Higher Education on the Move: New Developments in Global Mobility*, New York: AIFS Foundation.

15. Alam, F., Alam, Q., Chowdhury, H. and Steiner, T. (2013), Transnational education: benefits, threats and challenges, *Procedia Engineering*, 56: 870–874.
16. Alam, F., Subic, A., Plumb, A., Shortis, M. and Chandra, R. (2012), An innovative offshore delivery of an undergraduate mechanical engineering program, in developments, In *Engineering Education Standards: Advanced Curriculum Innovations*. Hershey, PA: IGI Global, pp. 233–245.
17. Iliva, J. (2017), Do political events in host countries affect international education engagement? *International Education Conference (AICE)*, pp. 1–26, 10–13 October, Hobart, Australia.
18. Alam, F. (editor) (2014), *Using Technology Tools to Innovate Assessment, Reporting, and Teaching Practices in Engineering Education*, IGI Global, New York, p. 409.
19. Going Global (2014), Impacts of transnational education on host countries: academic, cultural, economic and skills impacts and implications of programme and provider mobility, British Council & German Academic Exchange Service (DAAD), pp. 1–76, accessed from https://www.britishcouncil.org/sites/default/files/tne_study_final_web.pdf
20. Ziguras, C. (2003), The impact of the GATS on transnational tertiary education: comparing experiences of New Zealand, Australia, Singapore and Malaysia, *Australian Education Researcher* 30: 89.
21. Greenwood, P. (2008), Mobility of Engineering Professionals. Standing Committee on Education and Training Report (CET), retrieved on 29 October 2019 from https://www.wfeo.org/wp-content/uploads/stc-education/Intropaper20_10.pdf.
22. Lozano, A., Sanchez, E. and Mucino, V.H. (2001), Engineering education across disciplines and cultures: A Mexico/USA industrial outreach program. Proceedings of the 2001 ASEE Annual Conference & Exposition. Albuquerque, NM: ASEE.
23. Francois, E.J (2016), What is transnational education?, In: Francois, E.J., Avoseh, M.B.M. and Griswold, W. (Eds.), *Perspectives in Transnational Higher Education*, . Rotterdam: Sense Publishers, https://doi.org/10.1007/978-94-6300-420-6_1, pp. 3–22
24. Chowdhury, H., Alam, F., Biswas, S.K., Islam, M.T. and Islam A.K.M. S. (2013), Quality assurance and accreditation of engineering education in Bangladesh, *Procedia Engineering*, 56: 864–869.
25. Abanteriba, S. (2005), Development of strategic international industry links to promote undergraduate vocational training and postgraduate research programmes. *European Journal of Engineering Education*, 31(3): 283–301.
26. IDP (2011), Employment Outcomes of International Students in Australia. Presentation to the Asia Pacific Association for International Education Conference, Taiwan.
27. Knight, J. (2006), Higher Education Crossing Borders: A Guide to the Implications of the General Agreement on Trade in Services (GATS) for Cross-border Education, Commonwealth of Learning (COL)/UNESCO, Paris (France), pp. 1–76, retrieved on 10 March 2020 from https://unesdoc.unesco.org/ark:/48223/pf0000147363.
28. Mapchart (2020), retrieved on 22 March 2020 from https://mapchart.net/world.html.
29. Calderon, A. (2010), Emerging countries for student recruitment in tertiary education. The IMHE OECD Conference on Higher Education in a World Changed Utterly: Doing More with Less. Paris, p. 6.
30. IIE Open Doors Report on International Education Exchange, retrieved on 18 January 2020 from http://www.iie.org/opendoors.
31. International Institute of Education-IIE (2020), retrieved on 3 January 2020 from https://www.iie.org/
32. Allan, M. and Chisholm, C.U. (2008), *The Development of Competencies for Engineers within a Global Context*. Loughborough, UK: Higher Education Academy Engineering Subject Centre and the UK Centre for Materials Education.
33. Dolby, N. (2008), Global citizenship and study abroad: a comparative study of American and Australian undergraduates, *Journal of Study Abroad. V. XVII*, Fall 2008: 51–67.
34. Urry, J. (2000), *Sociology beyond Societies: Mobilities for the Twenty-first Century*, Routledge, London.
35. Rizvi, F., Lingard, B. (2010), *Globalizing Education Policy*, Routledge, New York.

36. Skidmore, M. (2011), The Future of Transnational Education, Observatory on Border-less Higher Education (OBHE), retrieved 17 March 2019 from http://www.obhe.ac.uk/newsletters/borderless_report_november_2011/future_transnational_education.
37. Lien, D. (2008), Economic analysis of transnational education, *Education Economics*, 16(2): 149.
38. OECD (2010), Education at a Glance, retrieved 24 March 2011 from http://www.oecd.org/document/.
40. Alam, F., Sarkar, R., La Brooy. R. and Chowdhury, H. (2016), Engineering Education in 21st Century, AIP Proceedings 1754, 020002, https://doi.org/10.1063/1.4958344
41. Van Mol, C. and Ekamper, P. (2016), Destination cities of European exchange students, *Geografisk Tidsskrift-Danish Journal of Geography*, 116(1): 85–91.
42. Study International (2018), Which Country Is Home to the Largest International Student Population? retrieved 28 September 2018 from https://www.studyinternational.com/news/country-home-largest-international-student-population/.
43. Mok, K. H. (2009), The Quest for Regional Hub of Education: Searching for New Govern-ance and Regulatory Regimes in Singapore, Hong Kong and Malaysia, East-West. Senior Seminar on Quality Issues in the Emerging Knowledge Society, Malaysia.
44. Hunter, B., White, G.P. and Godbey, G.C. (2006), What does it mean to be globally competent? *Journal of Studies in International Education*, 10: 267–285.
45. US News & World Report (2020), Arab Region Branch Campuses, retrieved 10 February 2020 from https://www.usnews.com/education/arab-region-universities/branch-campuses?page=3.
46. Lu, X. (2018), Transnational Education: Sino-Foreign Cooperative Universities in China, *World Education News & Reviews*, 14 August, retrieved 2 March 2019 from https://wenr.wes.org/2018/08/sino-foreign-cooperative-universities.
47. Docquier, F. and Rapoport, H. (2012), Globalization, brain drain and development, *Journal of Economic Literature*, 50(3): 681–730.
48. Bezrukov, A., Ziyatdinova, J., Sanger, P., Ivanov, V.G. and Zoltareva, N. (2018), Inbound international faculty mobility programs in Russia: best practices, In: Aucer, M.E. et al. (Eds.), *Teaching and Learning in a Digital World, Advances in Intelligent Systems and Computing*, New York: Springer, https://doi.org/10.1007/978-3-319-73210-7_31, pp. 715.
49. Docquier, F., Lowell, L. and Marfouk, A. (2009), A gendered assessment of highly skilled emigration, *Population and Development Review*, 35(2): 297–321.
50. Capuano, S. and Marfouk, A. (2013), African brain drain and its impact on source coun-tries: what do we know and what do we need to know? *Journal of Comparative Policy Analysis: Research and Practice*, 15(4): 297–314.
51. Collier, P. (2013), *Exodus: Immigration and Multiculturalism in the 21st Century*, Oxford University Press, Oxford, p. 320.
52. Beine, M., Docquier, F. and Rapoport, H. (2008), Brain drain and human capital forma-tion in developing countries: winners and losers, *The Economic Journal*, 118(5): 631–652.
53. Times Higher Education –THE (2019), retrieved 20 December 2019 from https://www.timeshighereducation.com/news/v-c-overseas-student-recruitment-weakening-developing-world#survey-answer.
54. Alam, F., Dilla, E., Subic, A. and Tu, J. (2007), A three-step teaching and learning method in laboratory experiments for a thermal fluid course, *World Transactions of Engineering and Technology Education*, 6(1): 13–18.
55. Alam, F., Tang, H. and Tu, J. (2004), The development of an integrated experimental and computational teaching and learning tool for thermal fluid science, *World Transactions on Engineering and Technology Education*, 3(2): 249–252.
56. Chowdhury, H., Alam, F. and Mustary, I. (2019), Development of an innovative technique for teaching and learning of laboratory experiments for engineering courses, *Energy Procedia*, 160: 806–811.
57. Wang, H. (2013), *Global Talent Blue Book- Annual Report of Chinese Returnee Develop-ment*, China Social Science Academy Press, Beijing.
58. OECD Better Life Index, retrieved 20 November 2019 from http://www.oecdbetterlifeindex.org.

59. Michael Page Professional Consulting (2016), The World's Most in Demand Professions, retrieved 22nd June 2019 from https://www.michaelpage.co.uk/minisite/most-in-demand-professions/.

60. Dixon, M. (2016) Migration of engineers and the gender dimension. In Triandafyllidou, A. and Isaakyan I. (Eds.), *High-Skill Migration and Recession. Migration, Diasporas and Citizenship*, London: Palgrave Macmillan.

61. The Institution of Engineers Australia, retrieved 14 March 2019 from https://www.engineersaustralia.org.au/Engineering-Registers/International-Registers/APEC-Engineer.

62. International Engineering Alliance – IEA (2019), retrieved 26 September 2019 from http://www.ieagreements.org/agreements/.

63. European Network for Accreditation of Engineering Education – ENAEE (2019), retrieved 4 July 2019 from https://www.enaee.eu/about-enaee/#the-founder-members-of-ESOEPE.

64. Dixon, M. (2013), *Skills, Professional Regulation, and International Mobility in the Engineering Workf*or*ce*, pp. 1–13, Washington, DC: Migration Policy Institute.

65. European Federation of National Engineering Associations – FEANI (2019), retrieved 30 October 2019 from https://www.feani.org/feani/eur-ing-title/what-eur-ing-title.

66. Warnick, G. (2011), Global Competence: Its Importance for Engineers Working in a Global Environment, American Society of Engineering Education, Paper No. AC2011-350, pp. 1–30, https://www.asee.org/public/conferences/1/papers/350/view.

67. Doerry, E., Doerry, K. and Bero, B. (2003), The global engineering college: exploring a new model for engineering education in a global economy. Proceedings of the 2003 ASEE Annual Conference & Exposition. Nashville, TN: ASEE.

68. Brustein, W.I. (2007), Paths to Global Competence: Preparing American College Students to Meet the World, retrieved 23 July, 2016 from http://www.iienetwork.org/page/84657/.

69. Mariasingam, M., Smith, T. and Courter, S. (2008), Internationalization of engineering education. Proceedings of the ASEE Annual Conference & Exposition. Pittsburgh, PA: ASEE.

70. Zamrik, S. (2007), Workforce issues and partnerships in mechanical engineering. Proceedings of the Middle East Mechanical Expo Conference and Exhibit. Manama, Kingdom of Bahrain: Mechanical Engineering.

71. Parkinson, A., Magleby, S. and Harb, J. (2009), Developing global competence in engineers: what does it mean? What is most important? Proceedings of the 2009 ASEE Annual Conference and Exposition. Austin, TX: ASEE.

72. Galloway, P.D. (2008), *The 21st Century Engineer: A Proposal for Engineering Reform*. Reston, VA: ASCE Press.

73. Reimers, F. (2008), Educating for global competency. In Cohen, J.E. and Malin, M.B. (Eds.), *International Perspectives on the Goals of Universal Basic and Secondary Education*, Cambridge, MA: American Academy of Arts and Sciences.

74. Lohmann, J.R., Rollins, H.A. and Hoey, J.J. (2006), Defining, developing and assessing global competence in engineers, *European Journal of Engineering Education*, 31: 119–131.

75. Caligiuri, P. and Santo, V.D. (2001), Global Competence: What Is It, and Can It Be Developed through Global Assignments? retrieved 24 June 2016 from http://www.entrepreneur.com/tradejournals/article/print/81626936.html.

76. Georgia Institute of Technology (2005), Strengthening the Global Competence and Research Experiences of Undergraduate Students, retrieved 20th July 2016 from http://www.assessment.gatech.edu/wp-content/uploads/QEP.pdf.

77. Hunter, W.D. (2004), *Knowledge, Skills, Attitudes, and Experiences Necessary to Become Globally Competen*t. Bethlehem, PA: Unpublished Doctoral Dissertation.

78. Renganathan, V., Gerhardt, L.A. and Greenwood, A.G. (2008), Incorporating global perspectives in U.S. engineering education. Proceedings of the 2008 ASEE Annual Conference & Exposition. Pittsburgh, PA: ASEE.

79. Zhao, Y. (2009), Needed: global villagers. *Teaching for the 21st Century* 67(1): 60–65.

80. Gilleard, J. and. Gilleard, J.D. (2002), Developing cross-cultural communication skills. *Journal of Professional Issues in Engineering Education and Practice*, 128: 187–200.

81. Chowdhury, H. and Alam, F. (2012), Engineering education in Bangladesh: An indicator of economic development, *European Journal of Engineering Education*, 37(2): 217.

Chapter 2

82. Laguador, J.M. and Dotong, C.I. (2014), Knowledge versus practice on the outcomes-based education implementation of the engineering faculty members in LPU, *International Journal of Academic Research in Progressive Education and Development*, 3(1): 63–74.

83. Lorcke, A.M., Doran, T. and Eika, B. (2013), Outcome (competency) based education: an exploration of its origins, theoretical basis, and empirical evidence, *Advances in Health Science Education*, 18: 851–863.

84. Weegar, M.A. and Pacis, D. (2012), A Comparison of Two Theories of Learning Behaviorism and Constructivism as Applied to Face-to-Face and Online Learning, *E-Leader Manila 2012*, pp. 1–20, retrieved on 24 January 2018 from https://www.g-casa.com/conferences/manila/papers/Weegar.pdf.

85. Altbach, P.G. (2015), AHELO: the myth of measurement and comparability, *International Higher Education*, 82 Fall: 1–2.

86. Spady, W.G and Mitchell, D.E. (1977), Competency based education: organizational issues and implications, *Educational Researcher*, 6(2): 9–15.

87. Wright, K. (2011), Reality without scare quotes, *Journalism Studies*, 12(2): 156–171.

88. Sessums, C.D. (2019), D2L Desire 2 Learn, retrieved on 8 May 2019 from https://www.d2l.com/en-apac/blog/what-is-obe/.

89. Spady, W.G. (1994), *Outcome-Based Education: Critical Issues and Answers*, American Association of School Administrators, ERIC, Arlington, VA.

90. OECD (2011), A Tuning - AHELO Conceptual Framework of Expected Desired/Learning Outcomes in Engineering, OECD Education Working Papers, No. 60, OECD, p.54.

91. Alam, F., Sarkar, R., La Brooy, R. and Chowdhury, H. (2016), Engineering education in 21st century, *AIP Conference Proceedings*, 1754 (1), 020002; https://doi.org/10.1063/1.4958344.

92. Brandt, R. (1998), An Overview of Outcome-Based Education, Curriculum Handbook, Association for Supervision and Curriculum Development, retrieved 2 September 2019 from http://www.ascd.org/publications/curriculum_handbook/413/chapters/An_Overview_of_Outcome-Based_Education.aspx.

93. Donnelly, K. (2007), Australia's adoption of outcomes based education – a critique, *Issues in Educational Research*, 17 (2): 1–21, retrieved 20 June 2019 from http://www.iier.org.au/iier17/donnelly.html.

94. Allais, S. (2007), Education service delivery: the disastrous case of outcomes-based qualifications frameworks, *Progress in Development Studies*, 7(1): 65–78.

95. Austin, T.L. (2014), Goals 2000 - The Clinton Administration Education Program, retrieved 10 September 2018 from https://www3.nd.edu/~rbarger/www7/goals200.html.

96. Kennedy, K. (2011), Conceptualising quality improvement in higher education: policy, theory and practice for outcomes based learning in Hong Kong, *Journal of Higher Education Policy & Management*, 33(3): 205–218.

97. Mohayidin, M.G., Suandi, T., Mustapha, G., Konting, M.M., Kamaruddin, N., Man, N.A., Adam, A. and Abdullah, S.N. (2008), Implementation of Outcome-Based Education in Universiti Putra Malaysia: A Focus on Students' Learning Outcomes, *International Education Studies*, 1(4): 147–160, retrieved 16 November 2018 from https://files.eric.ed.gov/fulltext/EJ1065417.pdf.

98. King, R., Howard, P., Brodie, L., Male, S. and Hoffmann, P. (2015), Systematic approaches to improving engineering education in Australia. Proceedings of the 3rd Convention of the Federation of Engineering Institutions for Asia and the Pacific (FIEAP), Taipei, 7–9 July, Taiwan.

99. IEA Graduate Attributes and Professional Competencies (2013), Ver 3, retrieved 6 May 2017 from http://www.ieagreements.org/assets/Uploads/Documents/Policy/Graduate-Attributes-and-Professional-Competencies.pdf.

100. AMS-MAN-10 (2018), Version 1.0, Accreditation Management System: Accreditation Criteria User Guide – Higher Education, Engineers Australia (EA), 18 April.

101. Green, M.F. (2015), Mapping the Landscape: Accreditation and the International Dimensions of U.S. Higher Education, NAFSA: Association of International Educators, pp. 1–28.

102. Hossain A.S.M.D. (2016), Alignment of regional and ABET accreditation efforts: an efficient approach to assessment of student learning outcomes, *Technology Interface International Journal*, 16(2): 5–12.
103. AMS-POL-01 (2019), Version 2.0 Accreditation Management System: Accreditation Principles, Engineers Australia, accessed from https://www.engineersaustralia.org.au/sites/default/files/2019-02/AMS-POL-01_Accreditation_Principles_v2.0.pdf
104. Webster, J. (2000), Engineering education in Australia, *International Journal of Engineering Education*, 16(2): 146–153.
105. Greenwood, P. (2011), Updated Information Paper on Mobility Prepared for WFEO Standing Committee on Education in Engineering (CEIE), accessed May 8, 2019, https://www.wfeo.org/wp-content/uploads/stc-education/MobInfPupdateVDec.2011.pdf.
106. AMS-STD-10 (2017), Version 1.0 Accreditation Management System: accreditation Standard-Higher Education, Engineers Australia, accessed from https://www.engineersaustralia.org.au/sites/default/files/2019-08/AMS-STD-10_Accreditation_Standard-Higher_Education_v1.0.pdf
107. Gqibani, S., Clarke, N. and Nel, A.L. (2017), Moving from content-based to outcomes-based curricula: implications for assessment, teaching, learning and throughput. IEEE Global Engineering Education Conference (EDUCON), 25–28 April, Athens, pp. 1062–1068.
108. Hanrahan, H. (2016), Toward Global Recognition of Engineering Qualifications Accredited in Different Systems, ENAEE, pp. 1–8.
109. Freeston, I. (2012), International frameworks for accrediting engineering education. 4th International Symposium for Engineering Education, The University of Sheffield, July, pp. 1–6.
110. Schwann, C. and Spady, W. (1998), Why change doesn't happen and how to make sure it does, *Educational Leadership*, 55(7): 45–47.
111. Brawley, S., Clark, J., Dixon, C., Ford, L., Nielsen, E., Ross, S. and Upton, S. (2015), History on trial: evaluating learning outcomes through audit and accreditation in a national standards environment, *Teaching & Learning Inquiry*, 3(2): 89–105.
112. Bradley, D., Noonan, P., Nugent, H., and Scales, B. (2008), Review of Australian higher education: final report, Commonwealth of Australia, Canberra, December, 978-0-642-77804-8.
113. RMIT University (2019), Graduate Attributes, https://www.rmit.edu.vn/graduate-attributes.
114. RMIT University (2020), Course Overview: Engineering Dynamics, http://www1.rmit.edu.au/courses/029182.
115. Anderson, L.W., Krathwohl, D.R., Airasian, P.W., Cruikshank, K.A., Mayer, R.E., Pintrich, P.R., Raths, J. and Wittrock, M.C. (2000), *A Taxonomy for Learning, Teaching, and Assessing: A Revision of Bloom's Taxonomy of Educational Objectives*, Pearson Education, London, pp. 1–336.
116. Bloom, B.S., Engelhart, M.D., Furst, E.J., Hill, W.H. and Krathwohl, D.R. (1956). Taxonomy of educational objectives: the classification of educational goals. *Handbook I: Cognitive Domain*. New York: David McKay Company.
117. Shane, H.G. (1981), Significant writings that have influenced the curriculum: 1906–1981, *Phi Delta Kappan*. 62(5): 311–314.
118. Lewis, B. (2020), Using Bloom's Taxonomy for Effective Learning, *ThoughtCo*, 29 January2020, retrieved 11 February 2020 from http://www.thoughtco.com/blooms-taxonomy-the-incredible-teaching-tool-2081869.

Chapter 3

119. European Association of Institutions in Higher Education (EURASHE), Bologna (1999), Bologna Declaration, retrieved 21 February 2020 from https://www.eurashe.eu/library/modernising-phe/Bologna_1999_Bologna-Declaration.pdf.
120. Alam, F., Sarkar, R., La Brooy, R. and Chowdhury, H. (2016), Engineering education in 21st century, *AIP Conference Proceedings*, 1754(1), 020002; https://doi.org/10.1063/1.4958344.

121. European network for Accreditation of Engineering Education (ENAEE), retrieved 6 May 2019 from www.enaee.eu/accredited-engineering-degrees.
122. European network for Accreditation of Engineering Education (ENAEE), retrieved 6 May 2019 from https://www.enaee.eu/accredited-engineering-courses-html/engineering-schools/engineering-accreditation-degree/.
123. European Commission (EC), retrieved 9 May 2019 from http://ec.europa.eu/education/ects/users-guide/key-features_en.htm#ectsTop.
124. EUR-ACE Framework Standards and Guidelines-EAFSG (2015), ENAEE, retrieved 1 May 2019 from https://www.enaee.eu/up-assets-enaee/uploads/2017/11/EAFSG-Doc-Full-status-8-Sept-15-on-web-fm.pdf.
125. Augusti, G. (2007), Accreditation of engineering programmes: European perspectives and challenges in a global context, *European Journal of Engineering Education*, 32(30): 273–283.
126. 25 years Washington Accord 1989–2014, International Engineering Alliance (IEA), retrieved 29 April 2019 from http://www.ieagreements.org/assets/Uploads/Documents/History/25YearsWashingtonAccord-A5booklet-FINAL.pdf.
127. Chowdhury, H., Alam, F., Biswas, S.K., Islam, M.T. and Islam A.K.M. S. (2013), Quality assurance and accreditation of engineering education in Bangladesh, *Procedia Engineering*, 56: 864–869.
128. Thebuwana, H., Hadgraft, H. and Alam, F. (2017), Addressing graduate competencies: understanding the contextual factors impacting the engineering discipline, *Energy Procedia*, 110: 359–364.
129. Li, T.L. (2018), What is the Washington Accord for Engineers, *EduAdvisor*, retrieved 23 January 2020 from https://eduadvisor.my/articles/what-is-the-washington-accord-for-engineers/.
130. Graduate Attributes and Professional Competencies – IEA (2013), Version 3, retrieved 6 May 2017 from http://www.ieagreements.org/assets/Uploads/Documents/Policy/graduate-Attributes-and-Professional-Competencies.pdf.
131. Holger, D.K. (2016), A History of the International Engineering Alliance and Its Constituent Agreements, IEA, retrieved 10 May 2019 from https://www.ieagreements.org/accords/washington/http://www.ieagreements.org/assets/Uploads/Documents/History/IEA-History-1.1-Final.pdf.
132. Kootsookos, A., Alam, F., Chowdhury, H. and Jollands, M. (2017), Offshore engineering education: assuring quality through dual accreditation, *Energy Procedia*, 110: 537–542.
133. Green, M.F. (2015), Mapping the Landscape: Accreditation and the International Dimensions of U.S Higher Education, NAFSA: Association of International Educators, p. 34, https://shop.nafsa.org/.
134. AMS-POL-01 (2017), Version 1.0 Accreditation Management System: Accreditation Principles, Engineers Australia, https://www.engineersaustralia.org.au/.
135. G03 (2008), General Review Process: Accreditation Management System: Education Programs at the Level of Professional Engineer, Engineers Australia, https://www.engineersaustralia.org.au/.
136. AMS-MAN-10 Version 1.0 Accreditation Management System: Accreditation Criteria User Guide – Higher Education, Engineers Australia, 18 April 2018, https://www.engineersaustralia.org.au/.
137. Engineers Australia (2011), Stage 1 Competency Standard for Professional Engineers, retrieved 21 February 2020 from https://www.engineersaustralia.org.au/resource-centre/resource/stage-1-competency-standard-professional-engineer.
138. AMS-STD-10 Version 1.0 Accreditation Management System: Accreditation Standard - Higher Education, Engineers Australia, 2017, https://www.engineersaustralia.org.au/.

Chapter 4

139. UNESCO-OECD Guidelines for Quality Provision in Cross-border Higher Education (2005), pp. 1–42, retrieved 27 February 2020 from http://www.oecd.org/education/skills-beyond-school/35779480.pdf.

140. Alam, F., Hadgraft, R. and Alam, Q. (2014), eLearning – challenges and opportunities. In Alam, F. (ed.), *Using Technology Tools to Innovate Assessment, Reporting, and Teaching Practices in Engineering Education*, New York: IGI Global, p. 409.
141. Cross-Border Education Research Team -CBERT (2020), retrieved 27 February 2020 from http://cbert.org/
142. Kinser, K. and Lane, J.E. (2016), International branch campuses: evolution of a phenomenon, *International Higher Education*, 85: 3–5.
143. Alam, F., Alam, Q., Chowdhury, H. and Steiner, T. (2013), Transnational education: benefits, threats and challenges, *Procedia Engineering*, 56: 870–874.
144. Kinser, K. and Lane J.E. (2017), An Overview of Authorization and Quality Assurance of Higher Education Institutions, UNESCO Global Education Monitoring Report, ED/GEMR/MRT/2017/P1/3/REV, pp. 1–27.
145. Organisation for Economic Cooperation and Development (OECD), retrieved 27 February 2020 from https://www.oecd.org/about/members-and-partners/.
146. Kinser, K. and Lane, J.E. (2013), The problems with cross-border quality assurance, *International Higher Education*, 73: 18–19.
147. UNESCO-OECD guidelines for quality provision in cross-border higher education, retrieved 28 February 2020 from https://www.oecd.org/general/unescooecdguidelines-forqualityprovisionincross-borderhighereducation.htm.
148. Alam, F., Subic, A., Plumb, G., Shortis, M. and Chandra, R. (2012), An innovative offshore delivery of an undergraduate mechanical engineering program in developments. In Rasul, M. (Ed.), *Engineering Education Standards: Advanced Curriculum Innovations*, New York: IGI Global, pp. 233–245.
149. AMS-POL-01 Version 2.0 Accreditation Management System: Accreditation Principles, Engineers Australia, 2019, accessed from https://www.engineersaustralia.org.au/sites/default/files/2019-02/AMS-POL-01_Accreditation_Principles_v2.0.pdf
150. Green, M.F. (2015), Mapping the Landscape: Accreditation and the International Dimensions of U.S. Higher Education, NAFSA: Association of International Educators, pp. 1–34, retrieved 22 May 2019 from https://shop.nafsa.org/detail.aspx?id=134E.
151. OECD (2011), A tuning-AHELO Conceptual Framework of Expected Desired/Learning Outcomes in Engineering, OECD Education Working Papers, No. 60, OECD, pp. 1–54.
152. Roser, C. (2015), A Critical Look at Industry 4.0, December, retrieved 20 January 2020 from www.AllAboutLean.com.
153. Hossain, A.S.M.D. (2016), Alignment of regional and ABET accreditation efforts: an efficient approach to assessment of student learning outcomes, *Technology Interface International Journal*, 16(2): 5–12.
154. Kootsookos, A., Alam, F., Chowdhury, H. and Jollands, M. (2017), Offshore engineering education: assuring quality through dual accreditation, *Energy Procedia*, 110: 537–542.
155. AMS-MAN-10 (2018), Version 2.0 Accreditation Management System: Accreditation Criteria User Guide – Higher Education, Engineers Australia, accessed from https://www.engineersaustralia.org.au/sites/default/files/2019-09/AMS-MAN-10_Accreditation_Criteria_User_Guide-Higher_Education_v2.0.pdf
156. Altbach, P.G. (2015), AHELO: the myth of measurement and comparability, *International Higher Education Number*, 82: 1–2.
157. RMIT University (2019), http://www1.rmit.edu.au/courses/036649.
158. RMIT University (2019), http://www1.rmit.edu.au/courses/049376.
159. RMIT University (2019), http://www1.rmit.edu.au/courses/014884.
160. RMIT University (2019), http://www1.rmit.edu.au/courses/014903.
161. International Engineering Alliance (IEA), International Engineering Alliance: Educational Accords, retrieved 10 December 2017 from http://www.ieagreements.org/assets/Uploads/Documents/Policy/Accord-Rules-and-Procedures-July-2017-version-2017.1.pdf.
162. Hong Kong Institution of Engineers – HKIE (2013), Professional Accreditation Handbook (Engineering Degrees), retrieved 10 December 2017 from https://www.hkie.org.hk/en/quali/criteria_development/upload/page/95/self/59ba2214bb703.pdf.

163. Laguador, J.M. and Dotong, C.I. (2014), Knowledge versus practice on the outcomes-based education implementation of the engineering faculty members in LPU, *International Journal of Academic Research in Progressive Education and Development*, 3(1): 63–74.

164. Thandapani, D., Gopalakrishnan, K., Devadasan, S.R., and Murugesh, R. (2013), Implementation of European quality award in engineering educational institutions IVA accreditation board for engineering and technology, *International Journal of Business Excellence*, 6(1): 59–76.

165. Gqibani, S., Clarke, N. and Nel, A.L. (2017), Moving from content-based to outcomes-based curricula: implications for assessment, teaching, learning and throughput. IEEE Global Engineering Education Conference (EDUCON), 25–28 April, Athens, pp. 1062–1068.

166. May, D. and Terkowsky, C. (2014), What should they learn? A short comparison between different areas of competence and accreditation boards' criteria for engineering education. IEEE, Global Engineering Education Conference (EDUCON), 3–5 April, Military Museum and Cultural Enter, Harbiye, Istanbul, pp. 146–150.

167. Mutereko, S. (2017), Analysing the accreditation of engineering education in South Africa through Foucalt's panoptican and governmentality lenses, *Assessment and Evaluation in Higher Education*, 143(2): 235–247.

168. Fergus, J.W. (2016), Recent and upcoming changes in ABET accreditation, *Journal of Materials*, 68(4): 1055–1057.

169. Freeston, I. (2012), International frameworks for accrediting engineering education. 4th International Symposium for Engineering Education, The University of Sheffield, July, pp. 1–6.

170. Male, S., Alam, F., Baillie, C., Crispin, S., Hancock, P., Leggoe, J., MacNish, C. and Ranmuthugala, D. (2016). Students' experiences of threshold capability development with intensive mode teaching. In Davis, M. and Goody, A. (Eds.), *Research and Development in Higher Education: The Shape of Higher Education*, Perth: Higher Education Research and Development Society of Australasia (HERDSA), pp. 192–201.

171. Cameron, I., Hadgraft, R. and Wright, S. (2010), Learning and Teaching Academic Standards Project: Engineering and ICT Learning and Teaching Academic Standards Statement, Australian Learning and Teaching Council (ALTC), Department of Education, Employment and Workplace Relations, Commonwealth of Australia, pp. 1–28, retrieved 29 June 2018 from http://www.acds-tlcc.edu.au/wp-content/uploads/sites/14/2016/11/altc_standards_ENGINEERING_090211.pdf.

Chapter 5

172. Chowdhury, H. and Alam, F. (2012), Engineering education in Bangladesh - an indicator of economic development, *European Journal of Engineering Education*, 37(2): 217–228.

173. Ministry of Skill Development and Entrepreneurship, Government of India, retrieved 7 May 2019 from https://www.msde.gov.in/nsqf.html.

174. Mehrotra, S. K. and Pratap, A. (2018), The Promise and the Reality of the National Skills Qualification Framework, The Wire India, retrieved 27 December 2018 from https://thewire.in/government/the-promise-and-the-reality-of-the-national-skills-qualification-framework.

175. Malaysian Qualifications Agency (2017), Malaysian Qualifications Framework 2nd Edition, retrieved 1 May 2019 from http://pps.utem.edu.my/phocadownloadpap/2018%20MQF%202nd%20Edition%2002042018.pdf.

176. Alam, F., Sarkar, R., La Brooy, R. and Chowdhury, H. (2016), Engineering education in 21st century, *AIP Conference Proceedings*, 1754 (1), 020002; https://doi.org/10.1063/1.4958344.

177. Tuck, R. (2007), An Introductory Guide to National Qualifications Frameworks: Conceptual and Practical Issues for Policy Makers, Skills and Employability Department, International Labour Organisation, pp. 76, retrieved 29 April 2019 from http://www.ilo.org/wcmsp5/groups/public/@ed_emp/@ifp_skills/documents/instructionalmaterial/wcms_103623.pdf.

178. McInnis, C. (2010), The Australian qualifications framework. In Dill, D.D. and Beerkens, M. (Eds.), *Public Policy for Academic Quality, Higher Education 141 Dynamics 30*, Dordrecht: Springer, pp. 1–271.

179. Comparative Analysis of the Australian Qualifications Framework and the European Qualifications Framework for Lifelong Learning: Joint Technical Report (2016), European Union, pp. 1–75, accessed from https://internationaleducation.gov.au/News/Latest-News/Documents/ED16-0165%20-%20693040%20-%20Joint%20Technical%20Report_ACC.pdf

180. Australian Qualifications Framework -AQF (2013), Second Edition, January, Australian Qualifications Framework Council, pp. 1–111, retrieved on 20 March 2019 from https://www.aqf.edu.au.

181. European Centre for the Development of Vocational Training (CEDEFOP), http://www.cedefop.europa.eu/en/events-and-projects/projects/national-qualifications-framework-nqf.

182. Hong Kong Qualifications Framework –HKQF (2012), retrieved 16 December 2018 from https://www.hkqf.gov.hk/filemanager/en/content_16/HKQF_ATS_E_2012_10.pdf

183. South African Qualifications Authority (SAQA), retrieved 22 March 2029 from http://www.saqa.org.za/.

184. Engineering Council UK, retrieved 12 January 2020 from https://www.engc.org.uk/standards-guidance/.

185. Malaysian Qualifications Framework (2017), retrieved 29 April 2019 from http://pps.utem.edu.my/phocadownloadpap/2018%20MQF%202nd%20Edition%2002042018.pdf.

186. European Commission (2018), Learning Opportunities and Qualifications in Europe, retrieved 18 August 2019 from https://ec.europa.eu/ploteus/content/descriptors-page.

187. International Labour Organization (ILO) (2007) Report on An Introductory Guide to National Qualifications Frameworks: Conceptual and Practical Issues for Policy Makers, International Labour Office, CH-1211 Geneva 22, Switzerland, ISBN 978-92-2-118612-0, pp. 1–76.

188. Qualifications Framework (2015), Government of Hong Kong Special Administrative Region, (Last Revised October 2018), retrieved 1 May 2019 from https://www.hkqf.gov.hk/filemanager/en/content_13/The%20revised%20GLD%20and%20the%20Explanatory%20Notes_Eng_April_2018.pdf.

189. The European Qualifications Framework: supporting learning, work and cross-border mobility (2018), European Union, Luxembourg, ISBN 978-92-79-80382-6, doi:10.2767/385613, KE-01-18-211-EN-N, 1–32.

190. SAQA (2012), The South African Qualifications Authority Level Descriptors for the South African National Qualifications Framework, retrieved 1 May 2019 from http://www.saqa.org.za/docs/misc/2012/level_descriptors.pdf.

191. DGMT South African Youth Website (2020), retrieved 3 January 2019 from http://youth.dgmt.co.za/wp-content/uploads/sites/2/2016/11/DGMT-Pathways-from-school-to-work2.pdf.

192. TEQSA Risk Assessment Framework (2019), Version 2.3, retrieved 22 October 2019 from https://www.teqsa.gov.au/sites/default/files/teqsa-risk-assessment-framework-v2-3-2-horizontal-layout.pdf?v=1551933858.

193. King, R., Howard, P., Brodie, L., Male, S. and Hoffmann, P. (2015), Systematic Approaches to Improving Engineering Education in Australia, proceedings of the 3rd Convention of the Federation of Engineering Institutions for Asia and the Pacific (FIEAP), Taipei, 7–9 July 2015.

Chapter 6

194. Collins, F.L. and Park, G.-S. (2016), Ranking and the multiplication of reputation: reflections from the frontier of globalizing higher education, *Higher Education*, 72: 115–129.

195. Hazelkorn, E. (2011), *Rankings and the Reshaping Of Higher Education: The Battle for World-Class Excellence*.Palgrave Macmillan, London, pp. 1–259.

196. Vught, F.V. (2008), Mission diversity and reputation in higher education, *Higher Education Policy*, 21: 151–174.

197. Bourdieu, P. (1984), *Distinction: A Social Critique of the Judgement of Taste*. Harvard University Press, Cambridge, pp. 1–632.

198. Marginson, S. (2007), Global university rankings: implications in general and for Australia, *Journal of Higher Education Policy and Management*, 29(2): 131–142.

199. Hazelkorn, E. (2019). University Rankings: There is Room for Error and "Malpractice". Elephant in the Lab. https://doi.org/10.5281/zenodo.2592196, from https://elephantinthelab. org/the-accuracy-of-university-rankings-in-a-international-perspective/.
200. Lewis, N. (2011), Political projects and micro-practices of globalising education: building an international education industry in New Zealand, *Globalisation, Societies and Education*, 9(2): 225–246.
201. Miller, P. (2004), Governing by numbers: why calculative practices matter. In Amin, A. and Thrift, N. (Eds.), *The Blackwell Cultural Economy Reader*, Malden, MA: Blackwell, pp. 179–190.
202. Chattopadhyay, S. (2019), World ranking of universities: what does it entail for the future. In Bhushan, S. (Ed.), *The Future of Higher Education in India*, Singapore: Springer Nature, pp. 55–76.
203. Stiglitz, J.E. (1975), The theory of screening, education, and the distribution of income, *The American Economic Review*, 65(3): 283–300.
204. Nandi, E., and Chattopadhyay, S. (2012), Quality, accreditation and global university ranking: issues before Indian higher education. In: Basu, S. (Ed.), *IDFC Infrastructure Report, 2012: Private Sector in Education* (). IDFC Foundation, New Delhi: Routledge.
205. Cheng, Y., Wang, Q. and Liu, N.C. (2014), *How World-Class Universities Affect Global Higher Education*, 1–10, Volume 30, Sense Publishers, Rotterdam, pp. 1–199.
206. Mohrman, K., Ma, W., and Baker, D. (2008), The research university in transition: the emerging global model, *Higher Education Policy*, 21(1): 5–27.
207. Altbach. P.G. (Ed.) (2011), *Leadership for World-Class Universities: Challenges for Developing Countries*. Routledge, London, pp. 1–251.
208. Altbach, P.G. (2009), Peripheries and centres: research universities in developing countries, *Asia Pacific Education Review*, 10: 15–27.
209. World Bank (2012), *Putting Higher Education to Work: Skills and Research for Growth in East Asia*, The World Bank, Washington, DC, pp. 1–246.
210. Altbach, P.G. and Wang, Q. (2012), Can China keep rising: world-class status for research excellence comes with a new set of challenges. Scientific American, October Issue, 46–47.
211. Salmi, J. (2009), *The Challenge of Establishing World-Class Universities*, The World Bank, Washington, DC, pp. 1–136.
212. Marginson, S. (2016), Dynamics of national and global competition in higher education, *Higher Education*, 52(1), 1–39.
213. King, R. (2011), *Universities Globally: Organizations, Regulation and Rankings*, Edward Elgar, Cheltenham, pp. 1–256.
214. Ranking Web of Universities, retrieved 24 February 2020 from http://www.webometrics. info/en/Methodology.
215. Academic Ranking of World Universities (ARWU), retrieved 23 May 2019 from http:// www.shanghairanking.com/index.html.
216. Times Higher Education (THE), retrieved 25 February 2020 from https://www. timeshighereducation.com/world-university-rankings/world-university-rankings-2020-methodology.
217. Academic Ranking of World Universities (ARWU), retrieved 23 May 2019 from http:// www.shanghairanking.com/subject-survey/survey-methodology-2018.html.
218. The City University of Hong Kong, Hong Kong (China), retrieved 26 May 2019 from https://libguides.library.cityu.edu.hk/researchimpact/university-ranking-lists.
219. SCImago Institutions Rankings (SIR), accessed 1 February 2020 from https://www. scimagoir.com/methodology.php.
220. QS World University Rankings, retrieved 25 January 2020 from http://www.iu.qs.com/ university-rankings/world-university-rankings/.
221. Bothwell, E. (2020), THE Emerging Economies University Rankings 2020: Hidden Gems Unearthed, retrieved 20 February 2020 from https://www.timeshighereducation.com/ opinion/emerging-economies-university-rankings-2020-hidden-gems-unearthed.
222. Bothwell, E. (2020), THE Emerging Economies University Rankings 2020: Neighbourhood Effects, retrieved 22 February 2020 from https://www.timeshighereducation.com/world-university-rankings/emerging-economies-university-rankings-2020-neighbourhood-effects.

223. FTSE Classification of Equity Markets (2019), Annual Announcement, 26 September, FTSE Russell, London.
224. Sustainable Development Goals (SDGs), retrieved 1 February 2020 from https://sustainabledevelopment.un.org/?menu=1300.
225. UN Sustainable Development Goals (SDGs), retrieved 28 October 2019 from https://sustainabledevelopment.un.org/.
226. UN Department of Economic and Social Affairs Disability, retrieved 1 February 2020 from https://www.un.org/development/desa/disabilities/envision2030.html.
227. Vertigo Ventures, retrieved 2 February 2020 from https://www.vertigoventures.com/.
228. Times Higher Education (THE), retrieved 17 December 2019 from https://www.timeshighereducation.com/world-university-rankings/impact-rankings-2019-methodology-partnership-for-goals.
229. Wang, Q. and Cheng, Y. (2014), Reflections on the effects of the 985 project in Mainland China. In *How World-Class Universities Affect Global Higher Education 1–10*, Volume 30, Rotterdam: Sense Publishers, pp. 1–199.
230. Yonezawa, A. and Chi-Hou, A.Y. (2014), Continuous challenges for world-class status among Universities in Taiwan and Japan as ageing societies. In *How World-Class Universities Affect Global Higher Education 1–10*, Volume 30, Rotterdam: Sense Publishers, pp. 1–199.
231. Suh, G.-S. and Park, S-J. (2014), The Korean government's policies and strategies to foster world-class universities. In *How World-Class Universities Affect Global Higher Education 1–10*, Volume 30, Rotterdam: Sense Publishers, pp. 1–199.
232. Zhu, J. (2014), Promoting research excellence: the excellence initiative in Germany. In *How World-Class Universities Affect Global Higher Education 1–10*, Volume 30, Rotterdam: Sense Publishers, pp. 1–199.
233. Filliatreau, G. (2014), Context and first observations on the "investment programme for the future" in France. In *How World-Class Universities Affect Global Higher Education 1–10*, Volume 30, Rotterdam: Sense Publishers, pp. 1–199.
234. Froumin, I. and Povalko, A. (2014), Top down push for excellence: lessons from Russia. In *How World-Class Universities Affect Global Higher Education 1–10*, Volume 30, Rotterdam: Sense Publishers, pp. 1–199.
235. Baker, S. and Thompson, A. (2020), Are Research Links with the Developing World Still a One-Way Street? Lecture Series at the University of Birmingham on 29 October 2019, THE World University Ranking, retrieved 24 February 2020 from https://www.timeshighereducation.com/features/are-research-links-developing-world-still-one-way-street.
236. Countries in the World by Population (2020), retrieved 24 February 2020 from https://www.worldometers.info/world-population/population-by-country/.
237. World Bank Data (2018), GDP per capita (Current US$), retrieved 24 February 2020 from https://data.worldbank.org/indicator/NY.GDP.PCAP.CD.
238. Elsevier SciVal, retrieved 24 February 2020 from https://www.elsevier.com/solutions/scival/releases/topic-prominence-in-science.
239. O'Malley, B. and Mitchell, N. (2019), First Global Impact Ranking of Universities Released, University World News, 5 April, retrieved 30 November 2019 from https://www.universityworldnews.com/post.php?story=20190404190925308.

Chapter 7

240. TEQSA (2017), Guidance Note: Academic Quality Assurance, version 2, pp. 1–6, retrieved 17 February 2020 from https://www.teqsa.gov.au/latest-news/publications/guidance-note-academic-quality-assurance.
241. Vlasceanu, L., Grunberg, L. and Parlea, D. (2007), *Quality Assurance and Accreditation: A Glossary of Basic Terms and Definitions*, UNESCO-CEPES, Bucharest, pp. 1–117.
242. Kinser, K. and Lane, J.E. (2017), An Overview of Authorization and Quality Assurance of Higher Education Institutions, Global Education Monitoring Report, UNESCO, pp. 1–27.

243. Chowdhury, H., Alam, F., Biswas, S.K., Islam, M.T. and Islam, A.K.M.S. (2013), Quality assurance and accreditation of engineering education in Bangladesh, *Procedia Engineering*, 56: 864–869.

244. Alam, F., Sarkar, R., La Brooy, R. and Chowdhury, H. (2016), Engineering education in 21st century, *AIP Conference Proceedings*, 1754 (1), 020002; https://doi.org/10.1063/1.4958344.

245. Alam, F. (Ed.) (2014), *Using Technology Tools to Innovate Assessment, Reporting, and Teaching Practices in Engineering Education*, IGI Global, New York.

246. Department of Education, Skills and Employment (2020), Upholding Quality - Quality Indicators for Learning and Teaching, Australian Government, retrieved 6 March 2020 from https://www.education.gov.au/upholding-quality-quality-indicators-learning-and-teaching.

247. Alam, F., Subic, A., Plumb, G., Shortis, M. and Chandra, R. (2012), An innovative offshore delivery of an undergraduate mechanical engineering program in developments. In Rasul, M. (Ed.), *Engineering Education Standards: Advanced Curriculum Innovations*, New York: IGI Global, pp. 233–245.

248. Kinser, K. (2014), Questioning quality assurance, new directions for higher education, *Critical Perspectives on Global Competition in Higher Education*, 168: 55–67.

249. Nordine, T. and Johnstone, S.M. (2015), Competency-based education: leadership challenges. *Change: The Magazine of Higher Learning*, 47(4): 61–66.

250. Lane, J.E. and Kinser, K. (2016), Internationalization, rankings, and national strategies: trade-offs, policy levers, and (un)intended outcomes, In Hazelkorn, E. (Ed.) *Global Rankings and the Geo-Politics of Higher Education: Understanding the Influence and Impact of Rankings on Higher Education, Policy and Society*. London: Routledge.

Printed in the United States
By Bookmasters